Torq...

After the End of

the World

by

Mark Wadie

Introduction

Hopefully you are reading this after reading my first book: 'Torquay ... to the End of the World'.

I am sat at a table in an empty house on the west coast of Wales. When I say empty I mean it is empty of humans! I have a couple of months to be by myself and focus on the task at hand.

I am grateful to David and Maryanne who own the house. I have never met them, but they are relatives of Simon and Jenny, who are good friends. So Thank You guys for getting me sorted with this secret retreat bolthole.

My writing window looks north west out into the Irish sea. There is a sandy beach below me and the tide is going out. My nearest shop is over a mile away, along a cliff footpath. The views are great. It is Autumn 2018.

There is more I could say about my situation here but suffice to say: it's perfect and Thank You God.

....

People have enjoyed reading, Torquay ... to the End of the World and many have pushed me to write this second book as soon as possible. With the offer of this house I could not delay.

So as I *grab shell,* I hope you *grab shell* too.

Let's see where this thing goes.

Over to you God!

....

Special note; to those who don't know, or have forgotten (I wrote about it in the *final word* section of my last book) I chose the titles of both books very carefully. They ascribe a geographical connotation, **but** that is only a shallow interpretation.

The deeper reason for choosing the titles is much closer to my heart and is explained in the following verses;

1 John 2:15-17 New Living Translation (NLT)

Do Not Love This World

15 Do not love this world nor the things it offers you, for when you love the world, you do not have the love of the Father in you. **16** For the world offers only a craving for physical pleasure, a craving for everything we see, and pride in our achievements and possessions. These are not from the Father, but are from this world. **17** And this world is fading away, along with everything that people crave. But anyone who does what pleases God will live forever.

....

John 15:19 New Living Translation (NLT)

Jesus said;

19 The world would love you as one of its own if you belonged to it, but you are no longer part of the world. I chose you to come out of the world.

1985

(Late September)

The entrance gate of this unknown territory, Lee Abbey, was now just a few feet away. I had to walk through a gate to enter the estate. It was there to keep the wild goats that roamed in the 'valley of rocks' behind me, from entering this Lee Abbey land in front of me.

I crossed over. **I was in**.

Sheep grazed in the fields to my left and right. This pasture land, unlike the uncultivated land of bracken and rock I had just passed through, sloped down to my right, eventually dropping towards the Bristol Channel, which was only 200 meters to the north of me. Beyond the Channel I could see the coast of South Wales in the distance. It was a beautiful location I was walking in but my mind was elsewhere. I was very soon going to be in the company of Christian monks and nuns.

Would they have empathy and understanding with what I had been through in Turkey? I believed there had been a battle for my soul out in Turkey. Would that be a palatable language for this new family I wanted to be part of? Would they accept me?

As I walked along the toll road through this estate and towards the Abbey, these were the thoughts that assaulted me. And boy, did they assault me. I was scared. I did not want this new discovery of God being real to be hijacked. It was too special. It was a treasure I had found and it was more precious to me than anything on earth.

He was the Rock I wanted to build my life upon. There was nothing else left for me but Him.

But I was new out of the womb in this revelation. And I felt vulnerable, unsteady on my feet. I needed help from Christians who hopefully knew their way around this sort of life.

I had not eaten any food since I was in Izmir 3 days ago. I had made a pledge to God that I would not eat anything until I was safe in the company of Christians who offered me food with loving eyes.

I was not going to ask for it. It was going to have to be a God thing.

But even food was not on my mind right now.

Love and understanding is what I craved the most.

The road started to slope down and there was a sign off to the right which welcomed me to 'Lee Abbey.' I walked down the incline towards the impressive building complex. I now started to see people. But I was concerned. They were not wearing monk and nun habits. What was going on? It was an Abbey. They should be looking like monks and nuns, but none of them were. Doubts started running around inside of me.

I was getting it all wrong. Why were things not as I expected.

These people just looked like ordinary people.

They are not going to understand me, the battle I've been through and am still in.

I reached the front courtyard and the entrance doors where there appeared to be a reception area. When I reached the desk a lady introduced herself as Mary Lou. She was an American with a sincere smile. I think she saw I was troubled and that I was a new face on the scene.

I had so much to say, but didn't know where to start.

I told her I had been walking through Turkey with a donkey and God had made Himself real to me.

I told her that I knew of Lee Abbey because a biker friend of mine from Torquay called Karen had become a Christian a year or so before and had disappeared to place called Lee Abbey, to be a nun I presumed.

She replied, 'Yes, Karen has been with the community since last year, but she just got married in Lynton last Saturday to another guy from Lee Abbey called Dave. The community attended the wedding and it was a great day, but she doesn't live here anymore.'

This was a shock. I needed Karen to introduce me to this new group of Christians and make sense of things for me. Now she wasn't here. What next? Circumstances were not lining up as I had expected and hoped they would.

But Mary Lou seemed compassionate and could see I needed help.

I had travelled quite a way to get here.

She said she would get someone to come and chat with me. She showed me a seat to sit on and I waited.

After a few minutes she walked back in with a tall thin guy about 10 years older than me called David Runcorn who, as it turned out, was ordained in the Church of England. He was part of the Lee Abbey residential community.

David was a very gentle guy who, in hindsight, was the perfect person to have dealt with me at this very intense and troubling time.

He sat with me and listened. I can't remember how long we were together but as I talked to him, there was a tap on my right shoulder and when I turned round, it was Mary Lou.

She looked right in my eyes with a lovely smile and said to me, 'Would you like me to get you some toast and marmalade?'

I nearly started crying. I said, 'Thank you, you don't know what that gesture means to me and how special it is.'

God had answered my prayer. I was going to eat!

....

It was apparent that I was in the right place and I asked to stay for a few days, even if it meant sleeping in a field there. And I was serious about sleeping in a field. The important thing to me was that I remained near this Christian community.

Like a fish needs water - I needed Christians at this delicate juncture in my journey.

It was arranged that I could sleep for a few nights in a vacant caravan they had tucked away on the land. I was introduced to Hoppy and Tim who were about my age. They were assigned to look after me and let me know when meals were being served.

I had so many questions, and they slowly tried to make sense of this new life I was venturing on. Tim was the son of John and Gay Perry who were the wardens of Lee Abbey at that time. John was also ordained in the Church of England.

Lee Abbey, I found out, is home to a Christian community that host retreats, holidays and conferences for individuals and groups.

It is set on a 280 acre estate on the North Devon coast and guests from all different walks of life go there for a week or a weekend to hopefully be refreshed in their walk with God. Most are Christians but some aren't.

The place is called Lee Abbey but has never actually been an Abbey!

It is an impressive building though, which looks out over Lee bay and is surrounded by stunning scenery. It was a good place for me to be.

The Seventy or so people that make up the Christian community and who actually live there come from all over the world. They have decided to live and work at Lee Abbey for anything between a few months, to a few years. They keep the place running for the guests that come each week.

Hoppy and Tim worked on the estate garden team. Other teams included; farm, kitchen, office, house, maintenance, dining room and pastoral.

Hoppy and Tim used to pop up to my caravan a couple times a day to see how I was doing. They had their work cut out dealing with this new guy on the block with all his questions and uncertainties but they did well. They loved me, made sense of certain things and prayed for me.

They were God's ambassadors.

Slowly I started to meet other members of the community. They were all so friendly and interested in who I was and how I got to be there. I met John, the warden, and his wife Gay, who both made me feel very welcome. I met Bob, the estate manager, who was like an old gentle farmer guy, but strong in his Love for God. He spent some time with me, listening to some of my story and also telling me some of his. I met various members of the community, many around my age. There was Faith, Chris, Suzanne, Trixi, Lyn, Margareta, Susie and many others who I have forgotten the names of now.

I felt so cared for. These people were really for me. They were all committed Christians and they were all part of my new family. I also met many of the guests who were staying at Lee Abbey while I was there. The Abbey accommodated well over a hundred guests at any one time.

After about 3 or 4 days of staying in the caravan, my time at Lee Abbey came to an end. I would have stayed for months but it was thought best that I return to Torquay and get involved with a Church in my hometown. John and Gay knew of a good chap called Peter who was the vicar of an Anglican Church in a posh part of Torquay. So at least I had a contact when I got home. He would be expecting me.

It was sad saying goodbye to these new friends I had made. Many of them promised to write to me, which they did, and their letters and cards were a real encouragement for many months to come.

Gay drove me to Barnstaple in her car and, among other things, recommended I listen to Christian music tapes as an encouragement to my faith. It so happened that there was a Christian book and music shop in Barnstaple called 'Doves', so I was on a mission to get a load of Christian cassette tapes. I found music artists like Adrian Snell, Amy Grant, Philip Bailey, Martyn Joseph and even Cliff Richard. At the time, they were the *in* names for Christian youth. The choice was limited but I was hungry for anything Christian and listening to those tapes over the next weeks and months really encouraged me in this new walk I was on with God.

I caught the train to Exeter and then on to Torquay. I must admit I felt very vulnerable on the trip back and also when I reached my destination. I was on my own now. How would faith hold up? I felt safe at Lee Abbey with loads of like-minded Christians but now I felt like a fish out of water again.

I moved into the spare room at my Mum and Dad's house in Goshen Road, Chelston. I think Mum was pleased to have me back safely in Torquay again.

I later found out that Goshen is mentioned in the Bible. It was the area of Egypt that the Israelites lived in when they were in captivity to the Egyptians. It is mentioned in Genesis and also in Exodus.

Robert my brother who was now seventeen, was also living there. I had a small box room as my bedroom which was not much bigger than the single bed! But I was happy. I didn't want for anything more.

On my first morning back in Torquay I decided to shave my beard and moustache off. I was now a clean shaven man. It sort of felt the right thing to do at the time. Making a clear statement that I had changed. Getting rid of the old life. It was all very black and white to me back then. All or nothing seemed to be the code I was living by.

I seemed to be afraid that I would somehow slip back into my old life, so I overcompensated, to guard against it. I felt I needed to hang onto God for dear life. I wasn't secure enough in my knowledge of Him and His ability to *hang onto me*.

So it was all quite intense. There was the giddy excitement of this new-found love affair but also deep-lying anxiety.

Within a few days of getting back I saw Jerry from my old bike club *Mephistopheles*. I was down by the harbour walking about and he passed by on his Suzuki lowrider. I yelled out to him. He saw me and parked up his bike, and we both went up to the open air Hoopers cafe that overlooked the harbour. He noticed my new clean shaven look, which I guess must have seemed a bit strange. He hadn't known I was back from my travels and within a few minutes I told him I was now a Christian.

There was a silence, and then he came out with something that was profound. I have never forgotten what he said, and never will.

He said, 'The thing that stops people becoming Christians is pride.'

I was amazed. I looked into his eyes and said, 'You're right Jerry.'

What he meant was people don't want to hand over control of their lives to God. They want to run the show. People don't want to be dependant. They want to be **independent**.

Over the next few weeks and months I would visit Jerry in his flat or he would come to my house and we would talk about God. To be honest, I would usually do the talking!

I was like a zealous Bible bashing Tigger in those days; bouncing all over my old friends and expecting them to see the **light**, just because I had.

I could not understand why other people wouldn't just get it. I was so full on. My poor old biker friends didn't really want me on their back. Of course I understand it now.

We live and learn!

Within days of getting back from Lee Abbey I discovered the 'Open Scroll' Christian bookshop in Palace Avenue in Paignton. It was a regular hang out for me. I started meeting local Christians from many different churches in the bay. I also bought my first black leather Bible (NIV version) there. It was a newish translation and was a lot easier for me to understand than the traditional old King James version, with its *Thees and Thous.*

I bought some coloured wax highlight crayons and marked the verses in my Bible that seemed especially significant for me. That way, it was easier to find the verses again when I needed them.

Another mission of mine was to get rid of all my anti-Christian paraphernalia: books, posters, jewellery and music. I didn't have loads, but I certainly had some.

My vinyl collection was, in my eyes, not conducive to my new Christian faith. So I took it into town and got what money I could from local second hand record shops.

It was now late October and I noticed that a big bonfire was getting prepared in a nearby park for bonfire night, which was only a few days away.

I gathered the books, posters and my old *Mephistopheles* bike gang arm patches into a carrier bag ready for the day of destruction. Also in the bag I put a solid silver necklace pendant that I had had made for my 21st birthday from my parents. On it was the *Mephistopheles* bike club emblem.

I was not now a messenger for the devil. I was a messenger of God.

Bonfire night came and I walked down to the park, which was opposite the Haywain Pub. When the bonfire was a blazing furnace I chucked the bag of goodies (baddies!) right into the heart of it.

You may be wondering what happened to going to Church; well that was all going on too. I had started attending the Anglican Church that John and Gay had suggested and had met Peter the vicar and his family. They made me feel part of Church and introduced me to a guy a bit older than me called Simon. Simon met up with me one night a week and he slowly led me through bits of the Bible and attempted to answer any questions I had written down during the week. He was a civil engineer and at one point he went away for a month to Turkey with his job. He was in charge of renewing and widening part of the main road from Istanbul to Ankara. If I remember rightly, his stretch of road was around Bolu, which was where I first cried out to God when walking on that same road.

*How flaming crazy is that! So flaming that it's almost too hot to handle. In fact, it's **way too** hot to handle.*

Anyway, Simon was good to have around and a great help to my early faith. There was also Charlie and Dawn and their young family. They had become Christians in London a few years earlier. They were down-to-earth people and we had quite a lot in

13

common. They were in their early thirties and I used to go to their weekly homegroup/Bible study, which they held in their home. We used to laugh a lot. Sometimes 'til we cried. We had the same sort of humour.

Then there was Dave and Gill and their young family. They also were a great encouragement. I remember once in the early days at the Church when I was feeling very lonely after a Sunday service. They unexpectedly approached me and invited me to their house for lunch. I spent the whole afternoon at their house. It really helped me feel I belonged. I always remember that day as being special; a real Godsend.

As well as going to the Anglican Church, I was also attending the big Baptist Church in the town centre. Upton Vale Baptist Church was run by an ordained minister called David Coffey. He was quite a famous chap. People often travelled from afar to hear him preach. He was also a kind and gentle man who encouraged me in my faith on more than one occasion.

This new life I had found seemed to be inspiring me to volunteer for things. I found myself enjoying weekly shifts in a variety of voluntary jobs, such as;

... Being part of a team that led disabled children on horses round a field in Cockington once a week.

... Taking elderly and disabled people out in a Social Services bus. I drove them to swimming lessons, cafes and even up on the moors.

... Volunteering once or twice a week to work in the Tea Cottage cafe that was joined to the Upton Vale Baptist Church. The proceeds went to a project in Cameroon, Africa.

... A lady called Mollie in a wheelchair put out a plea at Church one Sunday that she needed someone to push her around a couple of times a week, so that she could get out of her flat. Well

I had plenty of time on my hands. So Mollie and me became a unit for a few months.

I found myself doing things that I would never even have thought of before.

My brother Robert became intrigued with this new life I had found and for a time gave his heart to God. There was a short season where me and him used to go out late at night looking for homeless people to give some food to, and to talk with them about God. We were quite innocent and naive at the time but our hearts were in the right place. We prayed that God would lead us to people. I remember one old chap who wanted us to take him back to our house. But of course we couldn't because we were living in Mum and Dad's house and it was late. I remember feeling guilty and that I had failed God. But with hindsight I think it was the right thing to do.

....

Moving amongst the Torquay Christian scene had some surprises up it's sleeve. I remember when I walked into a Pentecostal church next to the Torquay Museum one Sunday. A guy handed me a hymn book at the door and as he looked at me he said, 'Mark, what are you doing here?' It was a guy called Kev, who was my age and was in another bike gang in Torquay called TMC. We were sort of rival bike clubs.

I said, 'Kev, what are *you* doing here?'

He hadn't heard I was a Christian and I didn't know he had given his life to God either.

It was a right buzz. An old biker mate; who had also become a Christian.

There was another time when I walked into Upton Vale Baptist Church and a guy turned round and looked at me and shouted, 'Mephistopheles, what are you doing here?'

It was a guy a few years older than me that I hadn't seen for a couple of years. His name was Neil, and he used to work in a Motor Insurance shop near the Coach Station in Torquay. He was a Bible thumping born again Christian, who used to preach at me when I went in the shop to renew my motorbike insurance each year.

I used to go in with long hair, dirty clothes and wearing my devil patch on my arm. He used to have a field day with me. We used to do it in good humour but Neil was always serious about pointing out the future destiny of my life if I kept living the way I was.

Now I was one of his crew!

We had a great laugh in that Church reception area that day. I told him how God had made Himself real to me in Turkey. He was well chuffed.

And these sort of occurrences kept popping up quite regularly. It was fun.

But it wasn't all a bed of roses. There were many days when I would be lonely, confused and even depressed.

But somehow God kept me walking with Him.

I remember the first few months just reading solidly Matthew, Mark, Luke, John and Acts. These are the first five books in the New Testament. I would read Matthew, then Acts, Mark, then Acts again, Luke, then Acts again, John, then Acts again.

I loved learning these new stories about the life of Jesus and it was surprising that I actually seemed to remember some of it from when I was younger.

But there many bits I didn't understand, so I would write the verses out and keep the piece of paper in my pocket for when I would meet up with a more mature Christian, like Simon.

Another good friend I found who had also found God while travelling through Europe was Tony. He and his wife and their young daughter Elina used to go to the Baptist Church. Those two, and especially Tony, were so important to me in that new season of my life.

He was half Maltese and with me being half Greek Cypriot, that made an exuberant mixture. We got on well. He had been a Christian for a few years and was a few years older than me too, so was able to have empathy with some of the struggles I had.

One of the struggles was the whole area of singleness and sexual frustrations.

I had decided that if I ever went out with someone now I was a Christian, it would be the person I would one day marry. There seemed no sense in just having a girlfriend for the sake of it. I didn't want to be distracted from my commitment to God with a casual relationship.

Of course, she would have to be a Christian. That was obvious to me. We would both need the same focus in life, or else we would pull each other in opposite directions.

So there was going to be no intimate relations with a woman unless God clearly led me to someone. And even then it would not be that intimate, until after we were married.

I wanted to find my feet on my own as a Christian before any relationship started. But it still wasn't easy. I was a man. (I still am actually!)

There was an evening in December when a couple I knew from the biker crew took me to a fashion show in their car about 30 miles away. They also brought along a girl who was very attractive. She was now single. I used to like her before I went travelling but she was going out with someone then.

I think the evening was a bit of a line up actually. We all sat in a row at the show and I was next to the girl and it was not easy for

17

me. There was a definite electricity between me and her and she was making herself very friendly towards me, touching me on the arm and laughing at various points during the evening's proceedings.

Before this change in my life, I would have melted to the excitement of a new relationship. There was a big part of me that wanted her but underneath that longing was a knowing that this was not the best way forward for my life. It would have derailed my new discovery in life.

It was a very anxious evening, where I was praying fervently that I would resist the temptation to go with my desires. I was turned on by this close proximity to her and the battle was on a knife edge.

Somehow, with God's help, I didn't respond to the advances that seemed to be there. It was a deliberate act of my will to not respond and was evidence to myself that my resolve was for God and Him alone.

I knew from past searching that there was nothing else that was going to satisfy.

Christmas came around and this year it took on a whole new meaning. The Anglican Church I belonged to had a dedicated liturgy that focused on the events leading up to the birth of Christ, so I was experiencing the occasion in a much more spiritual way than I had known before. This year, it was a real thing going on. It was relevant to my life, personally.

....

Before I rush into the New Year I think I will leave you with some verses from Psalm 40. You may remember the famous band U2 sang some of these verses in their song '40.'

Psalm 40   New International Version (NIV)

1 I waited patiently for the Lord;

he turned to me and heard my cry.

2 He lifted me out of the slimy pit,

out of the mud and mire;

he set my feet on a rock

and gave me a firm place to stand.

3 He put a new song in my mouth,

a hymn of praise to our God.

Many will see and fear the Lord

and put their trust in him.

4 Blessed is the one

who trusts in the Lord,

who does not look to the proud,

to those who turn aside to false gods.

5 Many, Lord my God,

are the wonders you have done,

the things you planned for us.

None can compare with you;

were I to speak and tell of your deeds,

they would be too many to declare.

1986

It was a cold January, with plenty of frost, and there was one person I had got to know who was struggling in Torquay more than most. His name was Ernie. He was an old friend of Dawn's father. Dawn was my friend from Church who was married to Charlie and who's homegroup I was attending each week.

Ernie was in his seventies and living quite independently. So independently that he was a recluse. He lived in a small terraced house near Watcombe that had no central heating and as far as I could make out, no plumbed-in toilet. So things were grim.

Dawn was going in to keep an eye on him when she could but she was also a busy mother. So she had asked me to get involved. I used to go in two or three times a week and empty his metal bucket that was kept behind the armchair that he sat, slept and lived in every day. The bucket had everything that comes out of the bottom end of a body and consequently smelt rank. I used to carry it outside and dig a small hole at the end of the back garden and hence empty the contents within. Probably against the law but hey!

I also used to cut up any old wood I could find out back as well, so that Ernie had some fuel for his fire that he sat huddled over in the sitting room. He was a prime candidate for social services but he didn't want 'none of that', he was old school!

It was like a scene out of a Charles Dickens book. He obviously never bathed, or even washed I suspect and he was not too healthy either. He was basically waiting to die.

I used to chat with him about God but he wasn't too interested. So one day I noticed an old framed picture of Jesus in the hallway. It was probably one his deceased wife put up. Well it was still up; so I moved its position. To one a bit more prominent. I hung it up above the fireplace in Ernie's sitting room. Better there than the hallway I thought!

A few weeks later, Ernie was troubled. He told me that Jesus kept looking at him and he felt uncomfortable.

I didn't move it. You know it makes sense.

....

Another person I visited on a fairly regular basis was an old employer/friend of mine called Paul. He owned one of the motorbike shops in town called PGH motorcycles. I briefly worked as a mechanic for him in the workshop in 1982 before flying off to Australia. We had struck up a bit of a friendship back then but we had known each other before from the biking scene in Torquay.

Well, I took it upon myself to try and convince Paul and his two assistants Chris and Luke about God's existence. Hard work but occasionally one or other of them would ask sincere searching questions and for those brief times of honesty it was all worth it.

Not that any of them wanted to hand their life over to God like I had, but my visits stirred up questions in them.

And 10 years later, things did change for one of them. To the same extent that it had for me and hopefully I will reach that story later in this book!

On the subject of motorbikes; I ended up buying one around this time. A chap called Murray, who was also attending the Anglican Church I went to, prompted me to get some 2 wheeled transport. Up to that point I had been walking everywhere, which actually suited me fine but having a motorbike would help me go further afield if I needed to. Someone in the Church had, a couple of months before, given me a free bicycle that their mum had owned but had since died. Although it was a lady's bike I really enjoyed getting to places a bit quicker than walking speed. But motorised speed would bring me into another league of possibilities again.

Murray had in fact lived with the Lee Abbey community before coming to Torquay and had married someone who also had been with the community.

He was now working for the Church. I told him that maybe if I found an old moped or something I would buy it. I didn't want anything bigger than that. I sort of didn't want bikes to become a priority in my life again. God was my priority. All very super spiritual! But joking aside; it was true.

However, he convinced me of the sense of getting something a bit bigger so that if I wanted to travel further than locally, a slightly bigger bike would fit the bill.

I ended up buying a 1974 Honda 250cc Motorsport trail bike. I bought it from an old biker acquaintance from Brixham called Skunk. It had been his father's bike and he was selling it for him. It was sound and well looked after. I paid £195, which was within my unemployed budget.

And speaking of budget... things were to change on that scene too in the near future. Work was coming. Not what I would have chosen but come it did.

I will tell you about that soon.

....

In February, St Matthias (the Anglican Church I attended) were going to go for a Church weekend away. To Lee Abbey, in North Devon! Love it.

About 120 of us left Torquay on a Friday night and stayed there until Sunday afternoon. It was a great time away getting to know each other better in the wonderful surroundings of Lee Abbey. And of course I was able to meet up with many of the community members that I had met 5 months before. Some of whom had been writing letters to me and encouraging me in my faith. It was so good to be back there and this time with many of my new Christian friends from Torquay.

....

The other Church I attended in Torquay; Upton Vale Baptist Church, was also a family for me and I usually went there on Sunday evenings and occasionally even on a Sunday morning if the Anglican service looked too traditional. I had enrolled on a weekly course at the Baptist Church to prepare me for baptism.

Although I had been baptised as a baby, I still felt I wanted to go ahead with it. This time it would be a full immersion baptism and I would be intentionally choosing to do it, unlike when I was a baby and my parents were choosing to do it. I honour their decision to have had me sealed for God as it were but now felt I wanted to publicly make my own statement of faith.

I saw that even Jesus himself did it as an adult, as did his followers, so why not me?

I was also part of a group in this Church called 20+, which was basically for anyone in their twenties. It was a fun group that often did things together after Church on Sunday evening and met in the week sometimes too. I remember we all went abseiling once, off some rocks on the coast near Slapton one Saturday. A qualified instructor from the Church came with us and showed us what to do.

In this 20+ group there was a couple of girls called Sharon and Eileen. I was sitting in the back of their car one evening and we were off to visit some Church event in Paignton and they said, 'Mark, have you been baptised in the Holy Spirit?'

It was not a term I had heard before but I supposed that I had experienced this when I was in the English consulate office in Izmir, when I was flooded with peace.

Then they said, 'Well it's a bit different to that and usually you can speak in tongues afterwards but not everyone does.'

(Tongues is one of the gifts of the Holy Spirit that is written about in various places in the New Testament).

So this information made me feel suddenly inadequate. It was not a nice feeling. I was missing out on some spiritual experience. I went into a tailspin for a few days.

Eventually I told Tony my Maltese friend about why I was depressed. He arranged for me to go round to his and Lynn's house in the week.

When I got there, his brother John from Sussex was there. I hadn't met him before but he also was a Christian.

They ended up laying hands on me and praying that I would receive the baptism of the Holy Spirit and the gift of speaking in tongues.

I felt very vulnerable, especially when John told me to try and make some language come out of my mouth that wasn't English. I felt very self-conscious and couldn't seem to make any noise come out.

But I eventually managed to push through the embarrassment wall and as I did, floods of Holy Spirit flowed through me and a simple unknown muttering flowed from inside of me and out through my mouth.

And with that - I was bubbling with joy like a little child.

God was in the house!

I remember leaving late that evening to walk back to my parents' house, which was about a mile away and on the way back everything seemed beautiful. The sky, the trees, sounds, the smell. Everything seemed so much more alive with such vivid clarity.

Who needs drugs?!

It was an amazing evening and I Thank God for it. I wanted it to last forever. But although the experience tapered off over the following day or two, I believe that night was a deep sealing in the Spirit. It had to be; it was too total to have been anything else.

I had been baptised in the Holy Spirit. It's not something I talk about much these days but the gift of tongues is mine to use whenever I want. Sometimes I can speak nothing else to God. It is spirit to Spirit.

Easter Sunday (Evening)

1986

Full immersion baptism.

Pastor David Coffey baptised me and about a dozen other adults in front of a full Church of regular members of the congregation and many other friends and relatives of ours.

In my official Baptism card it reads;

Upon confession of faith in Jesus Christ as Saviour and Lord

Mark Wadie

Was Baptized in the Name of God the Father, God the Son, and God the Holy Spirit, on 30th March 1986 at Upton Vale Baptist Church.

The Bible verse that was given to me for my baptism was;

May God Himself, the God of peace, sanctify you through and through. May your whole spirit, soul and body be kept blameless at the coming of our Lord Jesus Christ.

1 Thessalonians 5 : 23

My parents, brother and a few of my old friends attended; not as many as I would have liked but I guess it was a strange thing for them to be invited to. They would have felt like a fish out of water there. Whereas I felt like one *in* water there!

Jerry from the Meps came, which was touching and he brought his new girlfriend, Greer, who was also part of the bike scene.

Someone told me later that Jerry had said to them, 'When Mark came up out of the water, he was like a new person, somehow spiritually clean.'

I'm glad Jerry and Greer were there.

....

My parents were still not really attending a Church but these brushes with my Church events slowly had an effect and within a year or two, they started going again.

My life was actually getting very busy concerning Church events. In the end I decided that I needed to commit to one Church fully and not be quite so scattered in my Church attendance.

I felt I wanted to commit to St Matthias, as that was the Church I had first been led to by the Lee Abbey crew. It was not that I didn't occasionally go to Upton Vale and mix with the people there, just less so.

During this time I had been offered a job by a guy called Richard (from Upton Vale). He was foreman of the body and spray workshop at the main Ford dealer in town called 'Reeds.' It was opposite the hospital.

I had only just said to a lady earlier that day, when she asked me what I did as a trade and what I was going to do for money, that I was a mechanic by trade but didn't want to do that, because I wanted to do God's work!

Ho Ho Ho!

God had other plans it seemed.

Richard told me that he needed someone in the body workshop to sort out water (rain) ingress leaks and to get vehicles ready for spraying. And he would really like a Christian in there, so that he wasn't the only one.

It was not something I would have chosen but the arrow seemed to be pointing that way.

Another one of my concerns was that a big biker guy called Mike that I had known for quite a few years worked in the body shop at 'Reeds'.

He knew I was a Christian now, 'cos I had told him a few months back and he was not impressed that I had gone 'all religious!'

At my official interview to see the place and what I would be doing, I was introduced to Mike. He would be the one to show me the ropes and to assist when I started work there.

Great! Into the Lion's den.

And to some extent that was what working there felt a bit like. Everyone swearing, blaspheming, not at all a 'Godly' atmosphere.

I was the fish out of water now.

It was a real test for my faith. How would it stand up, in *the world*??

I did that job for about six months and many incidents challenged how I would respond. Mike was seeing first hand how this *religious freak* was choosing to live. It wasn't easy and I can't say I really enjoyed going to work in that atmosphere but I also see the value of my time there.

It was creating some balance in my life. I couldn't hide from the world, even if I didn't want to be part of its ways. It was still out there.

If I was called to be salt in this world (which Jesus speaks of in Matthew chapter 5), I couldn't stay in a salt pot all my life.

....

That said......!

There are seasons for salt pot life. As I was to find out. And oh, how glad I was when my calling to it came out of the blue one day.

It was around early Summer and a group from St Matthias were visiting another Church in Mid Devon. We were all sat around in someone's sitting room there in the evening and Peter, our vicar, picked up a magazine that was on the table and started reading it. Then he said out loud, 'There's a job here for Mark Wadie I think!'

He proceeded to read out the job advertisement he had seen. It was for a position with the Lee Abbey community for a year, in the estate and garden team.

He really thought I should go for it. So I sent in an application. It was exciting. Could God really want me to live there. It was a dream job if He did.

Very soon I was up there for an interview with John Perry, the warden, and Bob, the estate manager, both of whom I had met and got to like the year before.

After the 3 day interview in which I worked on the estate with other community members, John suggested I go away and pray over the next week about whether I felt God was leading me to go and live there and join the community.

He said that he and others would pray also and hopefully all of us would come to the same answer.

So I went back to Torquay, on a mission to hear from God whether or not He wanted me to stay in Torquay or move up to Lee Abbey on the North Devon coast. I knew what I wanted!

But I wasn't the lead dancer in this life anymore. I had handed over my life to Him to be the lead dancer.

It wasn't about what I thought was best.

I needed to do what it says in the Bible;

5 Trust in the Lord with all your heart;

   do not depend on your own understanding.

6 Seek his will in all you do,

   and he will show you which path to take.

Proverbs 3:5-6 New Living Translation (NLT)

....

Well, I got to the end of the week and I had heard nothing from God.

He had led me very clearly to work at 'Reeds'. When I had prayed to Him about that in the Spring He had thrown some verses at me that made me know I should get a paid job at the garage.

They were;

11 Make it your ambition to lead a quiet life, to mind your own business and to work with your hands, just as we told you, **12** so that your daily life may win the respect of outsiders and so that you will not be dependent on anybody.

1 Thessalonians 4:11-12 New International Version (NIV)

....

So if He wanted me to *leave* 'Reeds' and go Lee Abbey, He was going to have to tell me *twice* as clearly.

It got to the point where I needed to tell Lee Abbey the next day what God was saying to me. So I sat on my own in the empty dining room of my parents terraced house and tried to hear from Him.

I started reading some of the Psalms in the Old Testament but nothing was coming clear to me. After about two hours of this, I gave up. I closed my eyes and said something like, 'God you have got to make this clear because I don't know what to do and I need to tell them tomorrow.' I somehow felt a Peace come over me and when I opened my eyes the room was quite dark. The only light was from my little digital clock, and it read **9:56.**

These numbers seemed to be jumping out at me and I felt they were a clue to my answer. So, as I had been reading the Psalms, I felt I should go to Psalm 9 verse 56.

But there was a problem! Psalm 9 did not go up to 56. It only has 20 verses in it!

So, feeling a bit despondent, I started reading the next Psalm. Psalm 10. It read like this;

2 In his arrogance the wicked man hunts down the weak,

who are caught in the schemes he devises.

3 He boasts about the cravings of his heart;

he blesses the greedy and reviles the Lord.

4 In his pride the wicked man does not seek him;

in all his thoughts there is no room for God.

5 His ways are always prosperous;

your laws are rejected by him;

he sneers at all his enemies.

6 He says to himself, 'Nothing will ever shake me.'

He swears, 'No one will ever do me harm.'

7 His mouth is full of lies and threats;

trouble and evil are under his tongue.

Psalm 10 New International Version (NIV)

....

Well, nothing really jumped out at me but it did remind me of some of the guys in the garage where I worked and their attitude to God.

But it was not enough to make me believe God was saying leave and go to the pleasant land of Lee Abbey.

Then out of nowhere another thought popped into my head. I felt I should go to the next book in the Bible and read Chapter 9 verses 5-6.

The next book is Proverbs.

I looked the verses up in Proverbs chapter 9. They read:

5 'Come, eat my food and drink the wine that I have mixed. 6 Leave the company of ignorant people and live. Follow the way of knowledge.'

Proverbs 9:5-6 Good News Translation (GNT)

I knew God was speaking loud and clear. He had a feast ready and waiting for me at Lee Abbey.

I Thanked Him. I was happy. I personally wanted to go Lee Abbey anyway. But I had needed His leading. His will.

....

Then I started to doubt. Oh dear.

I remembered that I had wanted God to tell me twice as clearly to leave 'Reeds' than the time He had told me go there (back in the early Spring).

I felt bad doubting God but I needed more confirmation. So I prayed that He would tell me again.

As soon as I finished that quick prayer, the thought came in my mind to go to the next book in the Bible and read chapter 9 verses 5-6.

The next book after Proverbs is Ecclesiastes, which I don't think I had read any of before in my short Christian life up to that point.

I found Ecclesiastes chapter 9 and read verses 5-6 but they didn't jump out at me with any real relevance.

I then said sorry to God for doubting Him and wanting more proof. It was then that I suddenly felt an urge to read the next verse; **verse 7.**

7 Go, eat your food with gladness, and drink your wine with a joyful heart, for it is now that God favours what you do.

....

I was flabbergasted. God was speaking good and loud. Amazing.

I felt Him right there in the room with me.

Talk about twice as clearly!

No problem for God.

And I was very very happy too.

It turned out that the Lee Abbey leadership also felt that it was very right that I join the community.

I was going to go to Lee Abbey. Hallelujah.

The Lee Abbey Years

Sep 1986 - Nov 1988

On September 3rd 1986 I rode my Honda 250 Motorsport from the south coast of Devon to the north coast of Devon, passing through Exmoor, which marked the entrance way to my new home.

Charlie and Dawn from St Matthias followed in their Ford estate car, carrying my belongings.

That day was so exciting for me. I was going to eat the food and drink the wine that God had mixed for my life. And I was indeed glad.

(*I have been reading a couple of my journals from that time at Lee Abbey over the last few days. I could really write a whole book on that period of my life and it still would not do justice to the fullness of experience I encountered while I was there. But realistically, in this book I am writing now, I need to glide over and dip down into the bits I feel I need to. Hopefully you will get a taste of the meal and it will enrich your palate too*).

When we arrived at Lee Abbey there was an excitement about the place because the TV cameras were filming Harry Secombe (from 1950's Goon Show fame) for an episode of Songs of Praise.

My first night there I went for a walk on my own and looked up into the night sky. It was pitch black around me. The sky was so clear - the stars like crystals. I felt close to God and happy to be in His plan. I was too excited to go straight to bed, so I went down to the main house and started to look through the books in the book shop.

A name jumped out at me that somehow I was sure I knew. It was David Runcorn. Of course! It was David who I first talked to when I turned up at Lee Abbey one year earlier. Here I was again; and this time it was my home!

The view from Lee Abbey, looking west over Lee Bay

David was still with the community and it seemed that he had written a small book called 'Silence.' I opened it up at a random page and started reading about a time he had spent living in a Kibbutz in Israel. He wrote about spending many wonderful night's walking in the surrounding hills looking into the clear sky, amazed at the whole mystery of God and in it all, knowing a peace that he was wrapped up in it all.

God knows how to get our attention. He certainly got mine that first night! I was deeply buzzing.

It wasn't long before I was in the full swing of Lee Abbey life.

Working in the gardens with, among others, my old friend from a year before, Hoppy. Tim was about the place too.

Richard was our immediate boss and he and his wife were very good at making our small team feel like a family, having drinks and fun round at their house from time to time. We used to do comic sketches for the 120 guests each week at meal times. Hoppy was in charge of drama in the community so he was well hot on entertainment. I remember one night in my first week Richard asked me to wrap myself in loads of cushions and bean bags and dress up as a Sumo wrestler. He did the same, and me and him did a comic Sumo wrestle in the middle of the large Octagonal lounge (known as the Octag) in front of about hundred or so guests and community members.

There were so many things happening every day. Some very serious and deep, some totally ridiculous and fun, some amazingly beautiful and some tear-jerkingly sad.

It was an experiential hothouse.

I met different people nearly everyday from all over the country and beyond with rich experiences of life. Guests came for many different reasons but one thing was for absolutely sure, they left different from when they arrived. It was that sort of place.

The community members that lived and worked there, like me, were so much fun to be around. We basically lived, worked, ate, prayed and hung out together. Obviously, not all at the same time but hopefully you get the idea. It was quite a unique experience for all of us.

And it wasn't all easy. People fell out with each other, got hurt, got rejected, got jealous, got bitter even. But as Christians we all had to take this stuff to God and sort it out in ourselves and with each other, 'cos you can't live that close to each other and hold resentments for too long.

Enjoying an evening's entertainment in the Octag

It was a bit like being in a pebble polisher container. Put together and rattling around against each other and getting your sharp bits knocked off. At the end of the journey, coming out smoother and more beautiful than when you went in!

When people first join community at Lee Abbey they make some promises to the whole community that they will seek to further their relationship with God and to each other. They are then given a green name badge. After 3 or 4 months there is an opportunity to develop and make some extra promises of commitment to the community, after which they are given a red name label, which signifies that you are a full and longer term member of the community.

The ethos of the promises is to hold one to account concerning attitudes to each other. Basically love & forgiveness being the order of the day.

Everyone is also given a copy of the book 'Life Together' by Dietrich Bonhoeffer. It was compulsory that we read it.

It is a challenging and meaty read. Not a long book but one you can't just skip through if you are sincere in digesting its truths.

The nice thing about the green and red name badges was that you could get arty and paint or draw labels for each other as and when you felt like gifting one to someone. So you could, after a few weeks, have a choice of what label to wear with your Christian name on because different community members would make one for you. I was given some really beautifully designed labels in my time at Lee Abbey. And on the back, the person giving the label would write some words of encouragement or affirmation for the recipient. Love gifts really.

And with us all wearing our chosen name badge, the guests would know our name and we would know theirs too, because they all wore a white round name label.

Christmas came around and the yearly Lee Abbey pantomime was rehearsed and rehearsed, so that we were sharp for when we performed it in front of the guests who came for the week-long Christmas houseparty.

Because a lot of the community members were from other countries, the rule was that we all stayed at Lee Abbey for Christmas. So it was all one big happy family in North Devon. It really gave us all a sense of belonging and of course we were all still needed there to serve the guests in the capacity of our various jobs and as hosts at mealtimes and recreation times.

I remember one meal-serving moment that was embarrassing. It was a week long silent retreat. Guests had obviously paid good money to come to this, so we needed to be respectful and serious to their time at

Lee Abbey. I had not been living there for long when this retreat came up on the programme and I was serving food at the head of our table of guests. Twelve people at each table. Two community members at each end and usually about four guests either side of the table. The dining room had about 150 people in there. And it was silent apart from the gentle noise of cutlery.

I think a lot of us new community members were quite nervous about having to stay quiet. I think there was also a sense of childish fun under it all too. It was such a new experience for us.

Anyway, I needed the salt pot and it was at the other end of the table, so I waited until I had eye contact with Simon, a community member who was a few years younger than me and was also on the gardening team. I indicated with my hand that I needed the salt pot and for him to pass it to my end of the table. He knew what I wanted and with a slight grin, he shook his head to say no.

With that and the nervous energy I had going on inside of me, I cracked up, even spitting some of my mouthful out onto the table, which made it even more full on. The whole room was silent apart from me weeping with barely controlled hysterical laughter. I covered my head with my hands but the more I tried to be serious the more funny it all was.

Looking back now, it was a beautiful experience that definitely, although temporarily, loosened up the atmosphere!

1987

January 14th

It was snowing and some of us spent a couple of hours sledging down the long field in front of the house that led to the Lee Abbey beach. It was a glorious time. Even a couple of surf boards were being used on the snow.

Today was the day I was to take my extra promises in front of the community and get my red label.

The day was turning into a very special day for a number of reasons. I had been reading a book that was quite special for me. It was about one of the Desert Fathers called Charles de Foucauld.

The Desert Fathers (along with Desert Mothers) were early Christian hermits, ascetics and monks who lived mainly in the Scetes **desert** of Egypt beginning around the third century AD.

The book was called 'Two dancers in the Desert', basically inferring that our walk with God in this life is like a dance with God. Coincidentally, as you've already read, I had thought of it in the same way, before I had even come across this book.

I ended up talking to David Runcorn about it during the day and began to share with him about the early struggles that I had had when I first got back to Torquay after becoming a Christian and how I often felt I was not doing enough for God.

David seemed to be nodding as I shared and the time was so special that I ended up resting my head on his chest and feeling quite broken. After a bit he said twice, so lovingly, these words, 'Mercy not Sacrifice.'

It was a very special moment that went deep in my soul.

So many deep things went on at Lee Abbey.

That evening was a communion service in the Octag. Wednesday evenings was a time when just the community (not the guests) came together for a special communion service together. It was always a special time for us each week and tonight was the night I was making my red label promises. After I said the promises, the community all said as one, 'We accept you into the community.' Then I was handed a couple of red labels from David Runcorn and Chris who was on the Estate team.

I wrote in my journal that *I was so happy and my face was so joyful.*

After the service, we went to our different homegroups. I was in John and Gay's homegroup with Alex (short for Alexandra), Suzanne, Arika (from Holland), Beth (from America), Chris, and Katherine (who had just joined and was soon to go out with Kent, who was on the Estate team). We all chatted and prayed together and it was a perfect end to a perfect day.

Soon after this time I started to find myself getting fond of Alex, who was in my homegroup and who worked on the Kitchen team.

We had chatted a few times and found we had a few things in common. She was about my age, she had asked Jesus into her life about 3 years earlier whilst in Germany. In her mid-teens she had travelled thousands of miles around Australia on the back of a Honda Goldwing motorbike, often through outback terrain where there were no tarmac roads.

But one of the most endearing things about her was that she was genuinely interested in me and even seemed to care about me.

We would often find ourselves laughing and hanging out together.

I think I had liked her soon after I arrived but there were so many nice girls around I decided to not get too friendly with anyone in particular. I didn't want to rush into a relationship when so much else was going on. So, as previously, I tempered my affections.

But, as the days and weeks went on in 1987 I seemed to be allowing my affections to be known to myself and even probably to Alex as well. I was getting the impression the feelings were mutual; but you can never be too sure!

One evening, we all had a disco in the Octag. I was quietly impressed that my Christian brothers and sisters could let their spirits go and enjoy a good dance session. I have always liked dancing, so it was encouraging to me that we all could enjoy this type of music together. Hoppy, Simon, Nigel from the media dept, Ian from the farm team, Claire from kitchen, Jo from the house team and of course Alex. These are the ones I seem to have mentioned in my journal who were having a dance empathy such as my own.

Soon after this event, the community had a 4-day retreat. There were no guests in the house that week, as it was a dedicated community retreat week with teaching from a local Catholic Priest called Peter.

I decided to fast from food for the retreat, which made me quite weak and slow physically but brought my spirit into a new level of intimacy with God.

On the last day of the retreat, one of the older ladies on the pastoral team of the community called Sheila said to me that she felt God was telling her that, *Mark is a marked man for God.*

She was not someone to say things for the sake of it, so I treasured it in my heart.

In February, Lee Abbey was sending a mission team to St Matthias Church in Torquay!

Mission teams were sent out to Churches around the country on a fairly regular basis at the request of any Church who wanted some fresh input into their congregation. Some trips were for a weekend only and some for two weeks. During my time at Lee Abbey I went on a few missions, one of which was for two weeks.

This one was for a weekend. One person from each team (kitchen, estate, house, office, etc) was chosen to go at any one time so as not to put too much strain on any one team. Also, a couple from the pastoral team would go along to lead the proceedings.

From the estate team they chose me, because I was affiliated with the town of Torquay, which made sense.

John Perry led the team which was a treat.

He asked me to prepare for being interviewed by him on the first evening there, in front of the Church congregation. So, I prayed that I would explain well what part Lee Abbey played in my life, because he was going to ask me that question.

In the interview I explained that:

Being at Lee Abbey was like being and growing in a family. The family of God. And in this family I was being accepted, loved and being given confidence.

Like with a child in a real family, who for 18 years or so is built up, so that when they come to leave and go out into the big wide world they will have courage, having roots in a foundation of confidence and love.

I was to go on another mission to Huddersfield the following month with a totally different team. I enjoyed missions but there was a lot of giving of oneself, which left you pretty tired by the end.

....

February was a soul-searching and emotion-churning month for me and to be honest I was in a mess. I didn't know what to do about Alex. This whole Christian relationship journey was proving to be an emotional maze that I didn't know how to navigate through on my own.

I arranged to see Alan Smith who was one of the ordained ministers at Lee Abbey.

After listening to all my worries and concerns, he suggested that I approach Alex and ask her if she wants a closer friendship.

I was scared but the next day I asked her and she seemed to take it in her stride. So the feeling had been mutual. I was overjoyed.

A few days later David Runcorn left the community. He had been there for a few years and now was his time to leave. He gave me a slip of paper with a few lines on from an old saying he had found. This is what it said:

Pilgrim;

When your ship,

Long-moored in harbour,

Gives you the illusion

Of being a house;

When your ship

Begins to put down roots

In the stagnant water by the quay;

Put out to sea!

Save your boat's journeying soul,

And your own pilgrim soul,

Cost what it may.

When people left the community, there was something called a leaving circle and the person leaving would walk around and get a hug from each member of community who had come to say goodbye. They were often quite emotional affairs. This one was no different.

I went up to the greenhouses on my own to do some gardening after David left. I was feeling quite bereft and vulnerable. He had been an important person in my new Christian life. He was the person that spent time with me when I turned up at this very same location in quite a desperate state eighteen months earlier.

In the late afternoon after work I felt moved to phone my mum. Mum had briefly got to know David over a phone call or two around that time eighteen months earlier.

I told mum that he had left community that morning. And then I started crying. I told her that God was doing a lot in me here at Lee Abbey and it was a lot to do with the areas of rejection, love and security. I'm not sure she fully understood what I was getting at but then again maybe she did.

Around this time, quite a few community members were moving on and new ones were arriving. It was unsettling because Lee Abbey is like a close knit family in some ways.

Also my closer relationship with Alex was causing many insecurities to rise up in me. My needs to be loved and feel safe were causing a storm inside me.

Not long after this occasion I found myself slipping into a terrible state. I was swearing and cursing inside, angry, depressed, confused and scared.

I needed help.

I remember walking into Thelma and Jenny's flat one day (they were a couple of community members who were in their thirties) and just collapsing on the sofa in floods of tears, with no explanation of why.

My journals from that period illuminate quite well what a mess I was in.

God was, it seems, intending Lee Abbey to be a safe hospital for me to get healed of some deep problems in my life.

It was coming to light that my emotional insecurity stemmed from the trauma I experienced as a baby. You may remember from my first book that I had been adopted soon after birth and the attachment that a baby needs from its birth mother was not put in place in my life. So I never allowed myself to rest in love. To even trust love.

Basically, deep down in my psyche I did not feel safe and never had. Hence the short term relationships that I had before I was Christian. They never made it past 5 months. Longer than that was too dangerous and intimate. If I entered into intimacy and trust, I could get rejected again. Hence I had been quite a loner most of my life in some ways, to keep myself safe from being hurt.

This was probably one of the reasons why I ended up in Turkey on my own with a donkey; so that I could be self-contained and get stronger in that area.

But if you read the first book, you will know that I started to crumble and eventually cried out to God in desperation.

....

There was to be a few months to wait yet before some surgery was done in this area but God was definitely on my case.

He's always on my case actually. If He wasn't, my natural instinct would be to hide and avoid the pain. And stay bound up!

Jesus spoke about the different agendas that He and the devil have for humans:

The thief comes only in order to steal and kill and destroy. I came that they may have *and* enjoy life and have it in abundance [to the full, till it overflows].

John 10:10 (Amplified version)

....

In March, I went away for a few days. Caroline, who worked in the kitchen, dropped me off at the Lee Abbey International Students Hostel in Kensington, London. A sister community to Lee Abbey in Devon. I stayed in this community for a week and among other things went to hear Bishop Desmond Tutu speak at Westminster Abbey. The place was packed and you could have heard a pin drop while he spoke. It was a very special evening where he spoke about the irony of separating people of different colours being aligned to that of hypothetically separating yourself from people with bigger or smaller noses. Obviously there was more to it than that, but I remember that analogy.

My time in London was not always enjoyable. I found the busyness and constant activity wearing and even intimidating. I was used to the slower pace of the countryside.

It was good to get back to my friends in North Devon and fit back into that lifestyle again.

....

One of my good friends at my time at Lee Abbey was Nigel. He worked with me in the garden team. Although my main job was to mow the lawns on the ride-on lawn mower (a job I loved doing), I was also occupied with many other gardening jobs with Nigel and the other guys on the team.

Before Nigel came to Lee Abbey he had been working at Bath train station at the ticket desk. He was a gentle spirit like myself and we would have such good talks. We would laugh until we cried sometimes and at other times we would cry, without the laughter.

There was a time that I turned up in his room after being hurt by somebody's words. My value in who I was as a person had taken a hit. It was nothing horrible but it had made me feel inadequate.

After some time of silence together with me feeling totally weary emotionally and mentally, he said to me quietly, 'Please don't change Mark, you're fine just the way you are.'

I just burst out crying and couldn't stop for quite a while. Nigel was prepared to stay with me for however long it took. After a few minutes, I felt at peace. Love had filled me.

This was life with community! Nigel was a special friend.

....

In April, a most amazing thing happened. I walked down to the Lee Abbey beach chalet to see some small girls I had been looking after during the week (I was on the kids programme that week).

When I knocked on the door the girls' mother wasn't there; she was down on the beach with the girls. I was told this by another lady who opened the door. I had never seen this lady before.

She proceeded to tell me that her name was Virginia and that she was a friend of the girls' mother. She then said, 'And you must be Mark!'

I said, 'How do you know that?'

Then she told me that she had prayed that I would come down this morning because she knew she must meet me.

I said, 'Why did you want to meet me?'

She then said, 'Because I know Elaine in London, who you used to go out with. She is working for me!'

I won't get into the whole story but basically, Elaine was the last person I went out with in Torquay before I went to Turkey.

She had recently turned up in Virginia's design studio and asked her for a job. Virginia was a Christian and God was obviously on Elaine's case.

Elaine had mentioned that she had had a boyfriend who walked round Turkey and found God. She also mentioned that he was apparently now at a place called Lee Abbey.

To which Virginia replied, 'Well that's funny because I am going to Lee Abbey next week.'

Me and Virginia were buzzing on this whole God-incidental adventure. We chatted about all sorts of things, getting to know each other's story and, after a couple of hours, finalising our time together with praying for Elaine. It was such an exciting day. I love stuff like that.

God is crazy... and being a Christian isn't boring!

....

Earlier in the year I had felt a strong urge from God to commit to Lee Abbey for a second year. This would mean not leaving in September '87 but extending to September '88. I had had a few hints that this was the right thing to do and the leaders were really pleased to hear of my decision too.

It felt good to know I was there for a longer stint. It made it feel more like home than it did already. I really felt like I belonged.

The community needed that type of commitment from some members, so that there was a sense of consistency and stability there.

....

Every month was eventful at Lee Abbey and I am giving such a brief overview of my life there.

But May was a significant month. Oh boy!

50

May 1st

My mum and dad came to Lee Abbey for a few nights. This was a special time for both of them I think. In fact I know, because mum wrote me a letter later in the month, which I may share in a bit.

May 15th

Alex was leaving the community on Monday 18th, so we went out on my Motorbike together for the day to Porlock and then onto Dunster, which is just past Minehead.

We ended up in a field on the edge of Dunster at a place called Butter Cross. It was there where a question had to be asked. A question I was afraid to ask but needed to be asked.

It was about our relationship and where it was going after she left the Lee Abbey community.

She was a trained nurse and was going to go out to India to help with Mother Teresa's charity in Calcutta.

I asked the question, 'Alex, have you got hope for our relationship?'

And she replied sensitively, 'No, I haven't.'

A killer blow.

I tried to talk about the way I was seeing things to Alex but I was weak. The killer blow had weakened me a lot. I was caving in, I was in swampland. My security had been washed overboard.

I was alone again.

After five minutes or so I said I needed to pray, 'cos I needed help.

So we prayed.

Well, I prayed!

It went something like this:

God I need your help. I don't want Alex to be a part of my life if it is not your will. I want your will. You know my future and I want to know your plan.

Please let me know what is in the future and let me know in the next 48 hours.

If you don't speak to me very clearly about Alex within that time; then I will let her go.

And right now God, I ask that you will give me a peace that will transcend my understanding, 'cos I am in a mess inside right now.

In Jesus's name, Amen.

The last bit of the prayer was connected to some verses that meant a lot to me in the book of Philippians:

Do not be anxious about anything, but in every situation, by prayer and petition, with thanksgiving, present your requests to God. And the peace of God, which transcends all understanding, will guard your hearts and your minds in Christ Jesus.

Philippians 4:6-7 New International Version (NIV)

Well, I came out of that short prayer with what I can only explain as a mini-spiritual epidural in my emotions. Not that I have ever had a real epidural!

But I was at peace. Even Alex said to me, 'You look peaceful!'

We didn't really speak too much after that. Alex was in her own thoughts, probably feeling bad she had hurt me. Not that she had meant to. She was just being honest about how she saw things.

And I was quietly just enjoying God's touch on my life.

We ended up going into a cafe in Dunster called 'Willow tea rooms'.

After ordering our drinks we just sat in silence, not even looking at each other. It would normally have been a very uncomfortable time but for God's Spirit on me.

I really felt God was in the room. There was like a pregnancy in the atmosphere; like something was going to happen. Like God was on the move somehow.

After a few minutes I felt an urge to study a glass framed manuscript that was hanging above a fireplace. It was to the side and behind where Alex was sitting.

The frame was about three feet wide and one and half feet high. The manuscript was pretty old and was quite faded. Some bits had darker ink and it was obviously a very old manuscript that took the form of a letter or document.

A few parts of the letter were in darker print but because it was all in an old English style of writing I could not read what any of it said.

But there seemed to be something leading me to strain and work out what the first three words were. They were bigger than the rest of the words in the letter and they were also in a darker ink, so I slowly deciphered what each letter was in the first three words.

And the first three words were: **This in future**

These were the exact words that I had used back in the field only 15 minutes earlier:

Please let me know what is in the future, and let me know in the next 48 hours.

This was ridiculous. The atmosphere was pregnant now alright!

Alex was still looking down at the table in her own thoughts. She had no idea what was going on between me and God.

After a few minutes of wondering where God was going to jump out at me next, I felt an urge to look back at the manuscript again.

There was another darker printed word a few lines down in the manuscript that, although smaller than those earlier words, still stood out on the page. But again, it was hard to decipher because it was in squiggly old English writing.

I felt I needed to work out what the word was. Slowly I worked out that it said: **t o g e t h e r**

This was getting crazy. If ever I didn't believe in God, there was no excuse now. I was blown away.

Alex was still in her own thoughts. Not a word had been spoken between us.

Then God seemed to be leading me to again look up at this framed manuscript.

There was one final group of words a few lines further down that were also in the darker bolder ink.

I knew I was being led to find out what they said. So slowly, letter by letter, I deciphered what the five words were.

They said: **t o h a v e a n d t o h o l d**

Well, with that, I got up and went to the washroom. Once there, I jumped around and went crazy because I couldn't just sit at the table and keep it all in.

I jumped and danced about and continued to say to God: **You're CRAZY!**

I went back into the cafe and Alex looked up at me and said, 'You look happy.'

I replied, 'Yeah, God is really helping me.'

Before we left I felt that God wanted me to take one last look at the framed manuscript. At the bottom of the page there was a big round red wax seal, the sort that the Victorians used to use when writing letters.

I believed God was saying to me that it was His will for my life and it had His royal red seal on it. It was going to happen.

....

After about five or ten minutes Alex and me left the cafe, got on my motorbike and made our way back to Lee Abbey. It was a great ride back.

Sunny on the outside... and sunny on the inside!

I didn't tell Alex what had happened. I just treasured it in my heart and gave Thanks to God. Loads.

Back at Lee Abbey, we went to her room and there, on her wardrobe, was a picture of a rainbow with the words **'God keeps His promises'** written underneath it.

....

That same day I had received a letter from my mum referring to their visit to Lee Abbey at the beginning of the month. It read:

I just wanted to let you know that Dad and I really enjoyed our weekend at Lee Abbey and felt refreshed and strengthened in every way by it. It was great to see all the generations enjoying themselves together.

I think it is the atmosphere at Lee Abbey more than anything which makes it so unique. I realise that a lot of people work very hard to achieve this, but there is something more as well - one gets a glimpse of how much more simple and pleasant life would be if everyone everywhere put God first.

Many Thanks for making the experience possible and for helping to rekindle my own faith and (I think) stirring Dad's a little. We are very glad you are our son.

Lots of love Mum and Dad x x

Mum was at this time working as a Sister (nurse) at a nursing home in Chelston, Torquay. She was much valued there by staff and residents alike. Dad was still working as a gardener at the Imperial Hotel.

I've just realised as I write this that me and him were doing the same job - gardening. It has never occurred to me before now!

....

Alex left the community on the Monday. Too sad.

....

I had also made two new friends around this time. Really good friends. I loved them. Clive and Katherine were from Cape Town in South Africa and were about the same age as me. They were free spirits & enjoyed travelling.

Clive worked with me on the garden team and Katherine was on the house team (getting rooms ready for guests - cleaning, laundry, changing bed linen).

Katherine was an artist and was also very prophetic too. She made me some lovely red name labels and a few drawings too. My favourite red label was one she made for me. It was of a thin long man, like myself lying down and at peace in a universe of stars. So at peace he was. Resting and very safe.

On the back she wrote. *You will rest in His everlasting arms of Love. It will happen.*

Clive just went after my friendship. He persisted even though I was pretty closed around this time due to hurts and confusion from the Alex relationship. I was guarding my heart. But he was sensitive to that and kept making it known that he wanted to be my friend.

I loved those two.

In a later book maybe I will tell you what happened to them both.

....

In May quite a few people were leaving the community. It was just one of those seasons. Bob and his wife Pat left - Bob was the Estate manager and one of the special people who encouraged me when I first turned up on the Lee Abbey doorstep in 1985.

Also Suzanne left. She too was around in those early days and had become a good friend. She gave me her kite when she left, which at the time was a very special gift.

New community members were joining but it was hard to make new friends when established friends had moved on.

....

The last really significant thing to happen in May was writing an important letter to Alex.

She had written to me about a week after she left saying that she was having her various injections before going to India, that she'd like to stay friends but only if it was OK with me and wouldn't muck me up.

Well, a couple of days later I found myself needing help again. I went to Charles and Mary who were another pastoral couple on community - Charles was ordained.

After pouring my heart out to them and even sharing about what had happened in the Dunster cafe about ten days earlier, they responded with some wisdom that I didn't particularly like. They said, 'At the end of the day Mark, the fact of the matter is - Alex's will is not for the relationship to be any more than just good friends.'

It was a hard truth but they were right. It hurt. But they were right.

I needed to write a letter to Alex. I needed to let her go.

This is what I wrote:

Dear Alex,

I've got to write. I've been praying with a couple of the pastoral team today. This won't be a long letter. I know what I've got to say to you.

Alex I can't be just good friends. If I write to you and stay in contact with you, it would be a pretence - I would be always living in a dream world of future hope.

So I want to cut all communication with you because if I don't, I won't be living in reality.

I will still pray for you when you come on my mind or I hear about you through others.

May God be with you Always.

Love in Christ

Mark

It was a hard letter I know. But it was what I needed to do. Because what if she met someone else, fell in love and got married?

I would have been in a right mess, 'cos I would have still been hanging on.

Like when someone lets a bird go free, I was handing her back to God. If God wanted me to be with Alex in the future, then he would have to do some kind of miracle, because I was keeping my hands off trying to manufacture something.

It was over to Him. I had got out of the way.

....

Told you a lot went on in May didn't I?!

June

Rode my motorbike to Derby to attend the wedding of Jon (one of the original Mephistopheles bike club members) to his fiancée, Jo.

It was good to see some of my old friends from the club up there.

After the wedding I made my way down to Norfolk to spend a few days at my Auntie Margaret and Uncle Paul's place. It was a fairly big family gathering because my Gran & Grandad (my Mum and Margaret's parents) were celebrating their diamond wedding anniversary.

I nearly put diamond 'weeding' there - that was funny! Good job I spotted it before it went to print.

My parents were there, my brother Robert and my cousins - it was a good few days.

Back at Lee Abbey we bought a brand new ride-on lawn mower. I was well chuffed. Made mowing the lawns so much more fun for me, plus I did them so much better - even cut out a permanent mini golf course layout on one of the lawns, which guests really enjoyed using.

July

Bishop Chiu Ban It, who was the first Asian Bishop of Singapore came to Lee Abbey to be the speaker for a week.

I was working in the gardens most days so didn't get to hear him but Audrey, one of the pastoral team who was leading the houseparty that week, told me that he had a special prophetic gifting.

She told me because I had been to see her quite a bit during my time at Lee Abbey concerning my mixed up emotions, and she felt that it would be good if I could have a time with the Bishop.

So she arranged a slot for me, when he was free.

I remember going into the small room where he was (it was just him and me in there) and he looked at me and said, 'You are adopted - yes?' I nodded my head.

He then said, 'You have a lot of fear don't you!' I nodded again.

Then he said, 'Sometimes, fear to the point of death?!'

I nodded again and started to cry.

Obviously something deep was going on.

He started to pray to God.

Then he said, 'There was an attempt to abort you - you were fighting for your very life in that womb.'

'But God was with you and He wanted you alive - that's why you are here now.'

I then repeated a prayer that the Bishop led me in - acknowledging, forgiving and thanking.

He then said, while we were still in prayer, 'There is no bitterness in you - it's amazing. You have a lot of love in you to give to people.'

Before I left he said;

' God was with you - you are accepted and special. Don't be afraid to let people in. You have been afraid to let people in, as your very safety has felt threatened, so deep.

You are secure in God. '

....

I just found out twenty mins ago that Bishop Chiu Ban It died two years ago. I happened to look his name up on the internet before I wrote that last bit - so that I would spell his name correctly.

Crazy.

Thank you for him Lord.

....

Elaine - my old girlfriend phoned me up out of the blue. She wants to come and stay at Lee Abbey next month.

And she is pregnant.

Crazy.

God you are up to something!

....

August

Elaine did come. She spent a few days in the caravan and we had a lot of good chats and laughs together. By the time she left Lee Abbey she had a lot of things to think about concerning God and her life. It was the start of a stirring in her soul. The baby is due in eleven weeks.

She would return the following year.

September

Old deep insecurities and restlessness rising up from somewhere deep in me.

Wrote in my journal;

I'm sick and restless and tired of God substitutes: music, food, fun, ego, activity. I WANT THE REAL THING. Help me spend more time with you Lord.

November

Went on a Lee Abbey mission to a Church in Wimborne for a few days, which John and Gay led. It was good to have a break from the normal routine and get out and see new places.

Back in the Spring I damaged my back while cutting some grass with a flymo. As I a consequence I needed to go to a chiropractor most weeks. My back still was causing problems and made working in the gardens a problem. This and other frustrations were getting me into a right state. I was depressed most days it seems. Alongside this I was often feeling angry, resentful, lustful, restless, bored, empty, guilty, confused and a load of other things that made me feel rubbish; causing me to internally swear and curse.

Not a good place really and it had been going on for a quite a while but was coming to a head this month.

I went and sought help from Fergus and Jackie (pastoral team) and got some prayer; ended up crying loads. Also I went and saw Audrey (pastoral team) and she asked if I could hang on for one more week, because the Warden of another Christian community in Yorkshire called Scargill House was coming to Lee Abbey for a week to lead a conference on healing.

His name was Ian and he specialised in Christian healing and Gestalt, which I had never heard of!

Well, he came and Audrey lined up a meeting with him and me.

After chatting and praying together, Ian felt I should come to Scargill House for a week in December and attend a healing week there that he was leading.

December

What a month!

It just so happened (as it often does with God!), that Alan Smith was driving up to the Lake District the day before the conference at Scargill was to start. He had a couple of other passengers in his car but there was still a spare place.

He dropped me off at Manchester train station around 2pm and I caught the train to Leeds. From there I caught another train to Skipton.

I had left Lee Abbey at about 8.30am that Sunday morning and the whole day my emotions were in turmoil. There seemed to be a very strong subconscious fear deep inside of me. My spirit somehow knew I was on my way to deep surgery. There was something inside of me that didn't want to go there.

I was almost in panic.

I wanted to get off the train and not go to Scargill. But alongside that urgency was the fear that if I didn't go on this healing week, I would cover up my pain and never be really free. I'm telling you, I was in a MESS.

I just kept praying that God would help me to keep going forward.

I reached Skipton around 5pm, and hoped to catch a bus from Skipton to Grassington at 5.30pm but the bus never arrived.

No bus service on Sundays!

Someone drove from Scargill House and picked me up, bless them.

I arrived at the house at 7pm.

The next day I got up and walked about the place. I found the chapel and got down on my knees and prayed that God would look after me. I felt like a very vulnerable little boy. I knew something deep was going to happen that week, and I was scared.

I decided to go for a walk on the moors surrounding Scargill and ended up hiking to the top of Great Whernside. I could see for miles. Far in the distance to the South West I could see smoking industrial chimney stacks. I presumed it was Burnley or Blackburn.

Around 7pm that evening other guests started turning up for the healing week. I was still extremely frightened. Irrational really. But in another way it wasn't when I look back.

After supper, Ian introduced himself and explained what Gestalt was. Don't know if I was really any the wiser after the talk but I did know God had led me here. God was the only surgeon that knew me inside out and certainly much much more than I knew myself.

I just had to Trust Him.

Still scared though.

The next day the sessions started. I was in a group of ten people. Ian was leading the group.

Now the next bit was slightly weird to start with but I acclimatised myself to it. We all sat on the floor in a circle and a big round wall of mattresses was placed around the outside of us!

It certainly made us more intimate. There was no hiding.

Each session was one and a half hours long and each session would totally concentrate on a different individual within our group. Ten people - Ten sessions.

Intense!

Someone decided to go first. Ian would ask them questions and the rest of us would quietly pray for that person, in tongues or with words.

So man, we have got some serious Spirit work going on.

Hope you don't mind my use of words and figurative way of saying things.

Sorry if you do.

I had never really seen raw human souls before that day. I saw the real person, no masks could survive in that arena. Vulnerability was all on show, each person needing healing deep down within.

God was gently and tenderly meeting each person's deep pain. At the end of each session there was a freer person. It was full on.

On the second day there was a guy about my age who was struggling with aggression. I won't say his name but it became apparent to Ian that the guy was not going to let God reach his wound by the conventional method of questions and body language enacting. His wound was too hidden.

So Ian led the guy to stand up, commit his spirit over to God for wherever God wanted to take him and then to let himself fall back and be caught by us, literally.

He did this and after we lowered him to the floor it was obvious that he was resting in the Holy Spirit.

He lay there totally quiet for a few minutes and we were all very aware of the Presence of God amongst us. It was very still.

We were all praying for the guy quietly.

Then all of a sudden, deep desperate wailing came from his mouth. His pain was causing me to weep also. It was such deep pain.

I won't tell you what it was all about but basically God had taken him back to age eight and to some deep trauma which the guy slowly explained to us while he was still resting in the Spirit of God.

Me and him corresponded with each other for a few years after that week and he told me that the whole area of aggression he had had totally went after that week at Scargill House.

On the last day, it came to my turn!

It transpired that I also needed to do the free fall method. I was putting up too many barriers with the conventional way.

Something in me was really scared to go where God wanted to take me it seemed.

I even didn't want to go through with the free fall method but the guy who I mentioned before crawled over to me from the

65

opposite side of the circle, grabbed hold of me, looked me in the eye and said, 'Mark you've got to! Come on, you can do it.'

Makes me cry just thinking about that moment.

I told everyone to quickly get ready to catch me before I got too scared and backed out.

I stood up, committed my spirit to wherever God wanted to take me and fell back into the arms of the people behind me.

They lay me on the floor gently and, like the other guy, I found myself somehow at rest in the Spirit of God.

Crazy isn't it? But true.

After a minute or two I rolled over and curled up in the foetal position. In my mind I knew where God was probably taking me. Ian instructed people to pack cushions around me.

I lay there in a surreal peace.

Then, when I was just relaxing there fully, some pointed fingers started jabbing at my ribcage and instantaneously shrieks came out from my mouth that were unheard by human ears ever before.

They were obviously the shrieks of a foetus fighting for its life. Certainly nothing I had ever heard before. They were death shrieks.

It didn't last for long but put me on high alert (something I had probably been on all my life).

I waited for more invasions into my secret place but they didn't come.

After a while I had to come out of there.

It's called birth!

I didn't want to come out. What the hell was out there?

I ended up in a cot, at which point Ian had unbeknown to me instructed an older woman in the group to enact being my birth mother and lean over me and tell me something.

(I was still lying down on the floor resting in the Spirit, with my eyes closed, waiting to see what happened next - *I know, it's weird* but true).

Anyway, when the lady came near me, I wouldn't let her speak. I just kept saying, 'Don't want to hear, don't want to hear.'

Somehow I knew she was going to tell me she couldn't keep me.

In the end I just started raising my voice and just saying, 'Go, Go, Go.'

Ian must have indicated for her to start walking away. But I could still hear her in the room. So I kept loudly saying, 'Go', until she eventually left the room.

It then went very quiet and I realised I was totally on my own as a baby in the cot.

I then said out loud, 'Okay - I don't need you. I don't need anyone. I'm going to make it on my own.'

And soon after that I came out of the Spirit and was engaged with the people in the room again.

At the debrief, I was asked by Ian if I would forgive my mother, which I did. I also prayed a few other things and they all prayed for me. The Holy Spirit came and touched me deeply.

Afterwards I felt very different. Very free.

Ian told us later that God had given him a picture of knitting needles, which had led him to poke me in the ribs as an enactment of what God was showing him.

I could say a lot more but in a nutshell that is what happened in my session.

Pretty crazy stuff. But Thank you God.

That sort of stuff stays buried. Without God, for me, it would still be there.

When I got back to Lee Abbey a couple of days later, people who knew me were saying how different I was. More settled. There was a confidence about me that wasn't there before.

Even a guest who had been to Lee Abbey a couple of other times during the past year said to me, 'I can really see a change in you. You are a lot more articulate. A louder and more confident speaker in public. You also are caring for the younger community members, whereas before you were the one that needed caring for.'

The guy that said that to me was a Christian probation officer. I was encouraged to hear such things.

Also, my good friends Clive and Katherine really noticed the change. They had seen that my face was not stressed. It was relaxed and at peace. No more furrowed brow.

Feeling so happy with a kestrel on my shoulder

In my journal I have written: *So many people are telling me I have changed.*

1988

January

Went to Lee Abbey London Students Hostel again. This time to do a week's work on the maintenance team there. It was good to get away and have a change of environment.

Ended up working with a guy called Charles Swainson, who used to work on the Estate team at Lee Abbey before I joined. He then went to work in Uganda for over a year and was now working at the Lee Abbey Hostel in London.

I had been told by a few people, including Alex, that me and him would get on. He was about 10 years older than me and had done a variety of different jobs in his life. What I liked about him was that he was very practical and liked working with his hands, also he was funny and very down to earth. We got on well. It is a friendship that remains to this day.

While in London I also got to see Elaine again. We went to the cinema and spent quite a few hours together. She hoped to come to Lee Abbey in Devon again that year.

Also I went to St Barnabas Church in Kensington. I was very impressed with everything about that Church; the welcome, the amount of young people in their twenties, the whole place was carpeted, it was warm, people turned round in their seats and talked with new people, the vicar was a good bible teacher and there was a peace about the place (must have been God).

The sermon was called, *Flee fornication*. So not even a hint of political correctness either! Go for it.

February

My good and very special friends Clive and Katherine went back to South Africa to live, which made me too sad.

A few days later Elaine turned up at Lee Abbey with her boyfriend and their newly born daughter. They were passing through and Elaine said that she wanted to come and stay for a few days in the summer.

Went to the wedding of Chris and Soobie (two community members that had got together at Lee Abbey) in Swansea. Bridget (another friend who had been on community and had now left) drove me there and we talked about relationships.

The subject of Alex came up. Bridget and Alex used to work on the kitchen team together.

When I got back from the wedding I found myself quite depressed and in a bit of a mess again. I went to see Audrey who made sense of things for me and after a time of prayer all the pent up emotions came out.

God was on my case again. When will it ever stop?!

I felt good after though.

Around this time I was asked to go on an exciting adventure as part of my job at Lee Abbey. It entailed taking the Lee Abbey Land Rover and:

- Picking up a caravan from Cullompton in East Devon and taking it all the way to Hull, over the Humber Suspension Bridge.

- Driving back to Cambridge, to pick up another caravan, and taking it all the way to Penzance.

En route I stayed at various peoples houses. It took me nearly a week in all and I travelled nearly 1000 miles.

When I eventually got back to Lee Abbey I was ill and needed to go onto antibiotics, the result being I was off work then for two weeks.

After all this I again got depressed and was feeling sorry for myself. I seemed to lack purpose, I was bored, I was not in a good way. Best if I don't labour the point!

March

I led a work party of Oxford University students on a fencing project on the estate. Had a great time, even though the weather was bad. Got back into the swing of things.

Made a new friend. A new community member called Johannes from Holland had joined the garden team. He is a sensitive chap and very tall and thin like me. He's even taller.

He has become a good friend. Thank you Lord.

April

I felt moved to phone my friend Tony (Maltese) in Torquay. I needed to get a lot of things off my chest. After a long chat, he said to me, 'Mark, I feel it may be time to start thinking about moving on from Lee Abbey. To start asking God for guidance for the future.'

It was good to speak to someone outside of the community, who saw things from a different angle. He talked about the importance of getting time and space on my own. He then prayed for me.

It was a really good phone call and gave me a new perspective on things.

I started to pray that God would begin revealing what was next for my life.

Later that month I went down to Torquay for five days. I spent a lot of the time catching up with old friends from the 'Meps' (bike club). Spent a few hours with Jon at a local pub in Paignton, with

71

Jerry at another pub down at Babbacombe and with Gordon and some of his workmates during lunch. The talks with Jon and Jerry were very honest and real and involved the deeper issues of Life. We were a lot more relaxed in each other's company than when I had first got back from Turkey.

Also had very honest conversations with Mum too, one of which Dad was in on as well.

Then I went to see Tony (Maltese) and Lynn, my good Christian mentor friends at the time. They asked me about how I was getting on at Lee Abbey and whether I had had any guidance from God about where He wants me next. Tony told me that rather than just wait for God to drop out of the sky with guidance directions, it was better to put out feelers, like writing letters to possible places and ministries that I have a heart for and see what comes back. Like knocking on a door to see if anyone answers.

He also used the analogy of a ship - in that, if the ship is not moving, the rudder will not have any influence on which way the ship will go. It is only when the ship is actually moving forward that the rudder can have influence on the direction the ship goes in.

It was a good analogy. I would start to knock on doors. I would do my bit - and leave the rest to God.

At the end of the evening we prayed together that God would lead me in who to write too.

After the time of prayer Lynn said, 'I think you should write to Alex and tell her how you feel about her!'

I told her that I was leaving it to God for anything in that area to move forward.

She then said, 'I feel that if you don't - you might lose her!'

Then Tony said, 'You know what Mark: it's the same principle as the ship.'

Oh crikey... I couldn't wriggle out of that.

That was quite a revelation and shifted something in me a bit. I decided to talk to Audrey when I got back to Lee Abbey and see what she thought of the idea.

As I rode back to Lee Abbey the next day, I was sort of excited by the idea but also afraid.

But it definitely appeared that God was wanting me to shift in my attitude.

I talked and prayed with Audrey when I get back and she felt it was a good idea and the way forward.

I wrote the letter - nothing heavy, just saying `Hi' and telling her about some of the events and happenings that had been going on at Lee Abbey.

I also said that I still cared for her and maybe we could meet up sometime and chat about what we have both been up to for the last year.

Then after praying about it again with Audrey - I posted it. Over to you God.

After a few days, I got a nice letter back. She would like to meet up.

I also got a letter from Elaine in London. She wanted to come and visit in August for a few days with her new baby daughter.

It's all happening!

Plus so many other things too, that I just can't write about, 'cos there is soooooooo much!

One thing I will tell you that was crazy. Soon after I got the letter from Alex, I had a dream about her in the night. When I woke up in the morning I still remembered it. Then I opened my curtains and right in front of me arching over the hills in the distant was a huge perfect rainbow. Filling the sky. *The rainbow in the Bible signifies God's promise.*

Come on!

May

Alex and me met up in Tiverton for most of the day. We had not seen each other or talked since she left the community in May of last year. She had been living with her parents since getting back from India and was doing agency nursing around East Devon.

It was a sunny day and it went really well. Thank you God.

June

I received an official letter from Lee Abbey management, informing me that Lee Abbey was hoping to start a new small community house in Aston, Birmingham. They would like me to pray about whether God is calling me to be part of the pioneer community there.

Went on an adventure with my Honda trail bike for ten days;

20th - Rode to Chester and stayed with relatives for the night.

21st - Rode up to Glasgow and stayed with a family who had recently left Lee Abbey community.

22nd - Rode up the West coast of Scotland and set my tent up on the beach near a little place called Applecross. Looked out across the sea to the Isle of Raasay. Seals swimming all over the place. Wilderness - love it.

23rd - Rode further north past Ullapool and put my tent up on the moors next to Loch Assynt, near Lochinver. It's getting more remote again. Privilege.

24th - Rode up through Sutherland around the coast until I reached Durness. Love it. Came across some guys who were ringing puffins on a steep cliff top. I got to stroke a puffin. Come on.

Travelled on around the north coast. So beautiful. To a small village called Tongue. Met a stranger in the only shop there. His name was Brian and he was a Christian and he knew Bob and Pat. Bob was the previous estate manager of Lee Abbey I mentioned earlier in the book.

I ended up staying for three nights with Brian and his wife Jenny in their little cottage near the base of Ben Loyal.

I had tried to camp in their garden to start with but the midges were too full on. It was my first proper experience of the midges in Scotland. From then on, I was invited to sleep in the sitting room of the cottage. Much better.

25th - Spent six hours on my own walking up to the top of Ben Loyal and sitting up there for a while. On the steep climb up from their cottage, I decided to commit my walk to the top to God. That in climbing to the peak, I was saying to God that I always wanted to be Loyal (it was called Ben Loyal, remember) to Alex. So it was like a prayer climb of commitment. There was no actual path on the side of the mountain I was climbing. I was just clambering up over rocks and steep moorland grass. On my way up I began to find light plane wreckage. I found out later it was probably from an RAF Handley Page Hampden bomber that crashed in bad weather there in 1943.

I reached the top. Enjoyed the amazing views all around me, including the Kyle of Tongue estuary to the north. Beautiful.

26th - Went to local Church with Brian and his family in the morning and again in the evening. Open time of prayer for quite a while. It was good.

27th - Left Tongue and rode bike south to Glasgow - via Inverness this time. Took me nearly the whole day. Stayed with the family of Anthea (another friend from LA community).

28th - Went and saw Ray Charles in concert at the Glasgow International Jazz Festival.

28th - Rode down to Leeds and stayed with relatives I hadn't seen for over ten years.

30th - Travelled the last 300 miles south, back to Lee Abbey.

In all, it was an 1800 mile trip. It refreshed my spirit and gave me a new lease of life. Good to get away and mix it up.

July

Alex turned up at Lee Abbey with another friend called Penny who used to be on the community with us. I didn't see so much of Alex but the times we chatted were good.

Started reading the Henri Nouwen book 'Reaching out'. Alex gave it to me a year ago. It is speaking to me deeply. *Not literally!*

Alex started her Midwifery Training in Taunton. She was living now with two Christian girls in Taunton.

August

I am on host team for a week with the guests. And, two of the guests are Elaine and her baby daughter.

Amazing week. Had so many deep talks with Elaine.

One day I led a day trip to the Island of Lundy. Me and two other community members (Gillian from South Africa and Michaela) took twenty guests to Ilfracombe and from there we all got on the boat and travelled 25 miles west to Lundy. Elaine and her daughter were with us too. Such a good day, sunny too. Loved it. So many good chats.

By the end of the week Elaine had been doing a lot of thinking. God had been on her case totally.

I won't give all the details, but she said her **Yes** to Him.

When she left, her last words to me were, 'I will pray for you and Alex.'

Such a beautiful week.

Three years earlier, me and Elaine were going out with each other in Torquay. I finished the relationship because I needed to find out what life was all about and as you know from the first book - that search ended me up in Turkey.

Got a letter from Alex asking me if I wanted to meet up this month outside Exeter Cathedral.

We met up in Exeter. It was a good time together. We are getting closer.

....

So many encouraging letters and words from guests. People getting touched deeply by God and some giving their lives to God for the first time this year. I must keep moving on through this book though, else I will get stuck in 1988.

....

September

Dad retired from his job at the Imperial Hotel.

Got given a red Lada (Russian) car by the local Catholic priest in Lynton. Not sure what I will do with it but took it anyway.

Got a letter from Dr Dick Stockley, who is a link missionary with St Matthias Church in Torquay. When I first started attending St Matthias three years earlier, he and his wife Rosie had been out in Uganda for a few years with CMS.

They were working in the tribal North East area called Karamoja. They had always needed a mechanic even when in late 1985 I first started going to St Matthias. I had felt at that time (1985) that God was calling me to drive there and help them but Peter the vicar of St Matthias told me I was a very new Christian and it was inappropriate to do such a thing.

Which looking back was good advice - but I didn't like it at the time!

It seemed now that Dick was very desperate and had written to me personally asking me to pray about whether God was calling me to come and live out in Uganda.

I showed the letter to John Perry (the warden) and he told me that it might be God's leading.

The funny thing was, this letter arrived the day before the introduction day up in Birmingham about the new Lee Abbey community that was due to start soon in Aston. John was taking me up there with him in his car. That was the way I thought God was leading me, until this letter from Dick Stockley turned up in my postbox.

I travelled up to Birmingham, but I could not ignore the letter from Uganda the day before.

It's all going on!

A few days after getting back from Birmingham, Hoppy's time to leave community had come around. He had been one of my first friends from that day I turned up at Lee Abbey from Turkey three years earlier.

Now we had spent two years together on the gardening team together and he was a special friend that had helped me a lot in my faith.

He was moving on to new pastures and I was very sad. When people left the community it was always sad letting go but when Hoppy left, it left me feeling quite bereft. I also got a lovely card from him, letting me know that I had meant a lot to him too.

....

Wondered whether God was calling me to drive the Lada to Uganda. He wasn't!

Got rid of it soon after.

....

Have found myself getting angry. Not feeling happy at all. Feeling so alone, vulnerable and wobbly emotionally. Feeling on the edge all the time.

Then one evening - I found out why.

I was in the Octag with Rob from the Farm team. I told him I wasn't happy and was finding it hard with community members leaving.

He then said, 'I'm finding it very difficult too. We all come to worship together six days a week, we live together, we eat together, we pray together and we do so much together. It's not surprising we are feeling churned up when people leave.'

I put my head on his shoulder and hugged him. Then I just burst into tears. I stayed crying there for quite a while - 'till I was finished. I didn't feel like an alien on my own anymore.

After that incident I saw for the first time in two years on community that I was *AFFECTED* by community life.

That I wasn't an island. I was affected by my brothers and sisters. Their love did reach me - because when they left - I hurt.

My spirit had been mourning but my mind only received the revelation that evening.

And understanding the reason why I had been feeling so rubbish for weeks really helped.

I could accept the feelings of bereavement. It still wasn't easy but at least I knew what was going on deep inside of me.

Another three good friends (Susan, Ian and Caroline) left the next day, so it was good timing to have had the touch from God the day before.

I AM NOT AN ISLAND. *Hallelujah*

....

John Perry announced to the community that Audrey was going to be moving to Aston in Birmingham in the not too distant future, to be the first leader of the new Lee Abbey community house there.

....

Near the end of September, I rode to pick up Alex on my motorbike from Taunton. The old mustard coloured Hillman Avenger she was driving about in had developed a serious problem - the gearbox had totally packed up. We went on the bike to a scrapyard in Somerset somewhere and found a second hand gearbox. We didn't have any other transport other than my bike to get it to Plymtree in East Devon where the car was. Alex and I knew it wasn't going to be easy before we set out to the scrapyard, so we went with some old blanket to wrap the gearbox up with. Alex had the large bellhousing end of the gearbox on her thigh and knee and the other end pointed forward and rested on my thigh and knee. I think we also tied it to us with some rope as well.

It was not an easy escapade but was quite bonding, a lot of fun and quite an achievement.

What people do for love!

....

Concerning hearing from God as to whether He was calling me to Africa - and the details if He was - He gave me a picture in my minds eye.

It was of a photo kiosk that you go to and put a few quid in and get four photos in a long strip fall into a little cage slot on the outside of the kiosk when they are processed.

The wait is supposed to be four minutes, then they drop into the slot for you to take away with you.

You are diligently watching the slot for them to appear. And when they don't appear as quick as you want, you end up looking around at other things. It often occurs that the photos drop in the slot when you *are not* at that particular moment watching for them to drop.

God seemed to be saying to me through the analogy, that when I stopped striving to get a sign from Him (concerning my next move) that the answer would come.

Basically - *Let go and trust.*

October

My last time on a mission team before I left Lee Abbey. It was a ten day mission to a Church in Wimborne, East Dorset. The Church had invited us to come help renew their walk with God. We did talks, dramas, comedy sketches, led Bible study groups, led times of worship and basically shared our lives with them. People were challenged to go deeper with their devotion to God. Many lives were touched and changed as we asked the Holy Spirit to come in our midst. Many people wanted prayer and encouragement and the result was often tears, usually ending in joy. It was a crazy time. I say crazy because of the amount of significant things that were going on in people - our team included!

November

This was the month that I was to leave Lee Abbey. Midway through the month, Alex came and spent a few days there. One evening we went to a pub together, which was about 10 miles away from Lee Abbey and off the beaten track. As we were chatting about things, Alex came out with something that I was not expecting. She said something like, 'You haven't got any reason to have hope for our relationship have you?' By that, I took her to mean that *she* still didn't have any reason.

It was at this point that I realised that I had to tell her about the hope that I did secretly have. I was going to have to show her my hidden ace card, which I was scared about doing because once it was brought out into the open it could get destroyed!

Oh well, it was all I had left. There was no other option. I had to answer the question honestly.

So I told her what had happened 18 months earlier when we were in the cafe together in Dunster.

Then she was quiet for a bit and responded positively to what I told her. It put a different spin on her perspective and she felt that she also needed to hear from God about it. In one sense I think she was a bit excited about this new development.

We had definitely turned a corner.

....

Back at Lee Abbey there were a lot of goodbyes to say.

John and Gay Perry were still there, but even they were due to leave early in the new year. They had been such an important part of my time there and to this day have been the best example of leadership that I have ever experienced. John had been warden of Lee Abbey for about twelve years. The next year he was to become the Bishop of Southampton.

A few days before I left, I gave my leaving speech in the Library to the whole community. It was an emotional affair and one that left me deeply touched by people's love for me. The love and closeness in that community was something very special and the years I spent there really grounded my faith, giving me such a firm foundation in so many ways.

I left on November 31st. A couple of people really cried when I was going round my leaving circle in the yard. The love shown to me by everyone there was an honour.

It was hard saying goodbye and leaving Lee Abbey.

But at the same time - it was exciting.

What next Lord?

Life After Lee Abbey

I rode the eighty miles on my bike to Torquay with so many special thoughts going on in my head. I was transitioning into a whole new lifestyle.

When I got back to my parents house in Torquay I was greeted with the news that my sister, Julie, had just had her first child. It was a girl and her name was Tegan.

I was now an Uncle.

The news was refreshing also because it took away the poignancy of my leaving Lee Abbey.

....

The final part of the year was mostly taken up with preparing myself for the possibility that I would be leaving England.

1989

The way was paved by Dr Dick Stockley and also the Church of Uganda (Karamoja Diocese) for me to travel to Uganda as soon as I could get my injections and air ticket.

It seemed that God was opening this door more than any other for me to go through.

January was taken up with getting the compulsory injections, one of which seemed to make me quite ill for a week or more. My Church was paying for the air ticket and things like overalls and other small gifts were being given to me in those final weeks before I left.

There was even an interview and photo put in the local Torbay newspaper. St Matthias was quite a large prominent Church in the town.

The place I was going to in Uganda was a small town called Kotido, which was in a North Eastern area of Uganda, called Karamoja.

It was a tribal area and in a remote position.

There was a small agricultural seed project there that had a basic garage workshop in which to maintain the transport and equipment attached to the seed project. Plus any other transport that passed through the area - I found out later!

Before I left England I remembered that my old biker friend Danny from *Mephistopheles*, was out in Uganda. He had also gone out to help a project that was connected to a hospital near Arua in North West Uganda. His sister was a Nurse and her husband was a Doctor. They were both Christians and had asked Danny to come out and help in the garage fixing transport that was connected with the Leprosy Mission project there.

He had been with them for over a year and was due to finish in March and come back to England.

I wrote and told him I was on my way out to Uganda. Hopefully we would meet up over there before he left.

....

In February I left England and flew to Nairobi in Kenya.

As the plane was descending to land I looked out across the bare African landscape below me. I was going to land in Africa. Now this was an exciting and totally new experience for me. I felt like a little boy in a big, big world.

A Ugandan called David Okello was at the airport to pick me up and he was going to drive me to Kampala in Uganda, which was over 400 miles away. It was going to take us a couple of weeks to get there because he had quite a few errands to do on the way.

We stayed at a guest house in Nairobi. All the new smells, sights and sounds were an elixir to my senses. The plants and birds I came across in the guest house garden were enough to thrill me for days.

The following day was a Sunday. We went to a huge Church in the City called 'Christ is the Answer'.

I walked into that building and I was swept into the buzz of anticipation of hundreds of people in the presence of God. The service hadn't started as such but there was a guy playing some beautiful music on a grand piano on the stage at the front. Then as I went and sat down in the balcony at the back of this huge building, singing started from behind the stage and then about 20 singers appeared in blue robes and slowly marched onto the stage singing some sweet song from heaven!

It was all just so exciting. Here I was in Africa and I landed in this place. There were hundreds of people in there.

The day continued to improve. Everything so new to me.

After a few days we started to travel west through Kenya towards Uganda and saw many Giraffes, Zebras and various types of Antelopes.

We stayed at different people's houses over the next week or so while David picked up various things that people needed in Kotido. He was going to drop me off at Entebbe airport, near Kampala, to save me the uncomfortable and sometimes dangerous road journey up to Karamoja. The roads in rural tropical Africa are usually made with murram, which is a clayey material, and easily deteriorates after heavy times of rain, creating large potholes all over the place.

From Entebbe I was going to be flown in a small 3 seater Cessna light aircraft 250 miles north west to Kotido.

The day I was to fly I was quite nervous. Getting in such a small plane and going up in the air was not what I was used too. The plane was owned by a Christian charity called MAF (Mission Aviation Fellowship). They save many people's lives in remote areas that cannot be reached quickly by road, also providing cut-off areas with much needed medical equipment, food and many other basic provisions.

My pilot was from Switzerland and his name was Emil. He did his best to make me feel less nervous as we roared up the runway and took off over the water expanse of Lake Victoria.

I forget how long the trip took. I was the only person in the plane apart from Emil. Good job he was in there - else I would have been even more nervous!

There wasn't much room for anyone else apart from us two anyway, because there was a load of provisions in amongst us.

Halfway through the journey we flew over Lake Kyoga. I do remember the vast expanse of wilderness below us and thinking that if we came down in that landscape we would be pretty much on our own. I did wonder if anyone would actually be able to find us.

Then, eventually, we approached our destination. Far in the distance a spot became visible and even when we got close it was not much more than a spot!

There was a cleared part of scrubland that had some huts nearby and that was about it.

As we came into land, in the middle of what seemed nowhere, I thought, Wow this is where I am going to be living!

The plane bumped along the hardened murram runway and steered towards the left where a crowd of black faces were eagerly waiting our approach. This was obviously quite an attraction for the local people.

I got out of the plane and stepped onto my new turf. It was a very hot sunny day, as most days in the future also proved to be. The air was dusty, humid and filled with newness for me.

I was amongst a sea of faces, all looking at me it seemed. Many of them were dressed in the traditional and colourful Karamojong attire. Sometimes that meant not much at all but often it meant brightly coloured beads, hats and blankets.

I looked around with searching eyes to try and spot Dick or Rosie. They should be easy to spot amongst all these dark faces. Then I saw Rosie. I was home.

It had taken over two weeks to actually get there from when I'd first arrived in Africa.

We walked from the small airstrip to the nearby compound that had a basic wire net fence around it. Then we walked to Dick and Rosie's house, which was the nearest thing to a recognisable homestead to my western eyes. There were also a number of round mud huts on the compound that were obviously homes to quite a few people.

I was introduced to a few of the residents of the compound including Philip who was the only other white person there, apart from Dick and Rosie. He was probably about my age and was the accountant for the project. He was from England and lived in one of the mud huts on the compound.

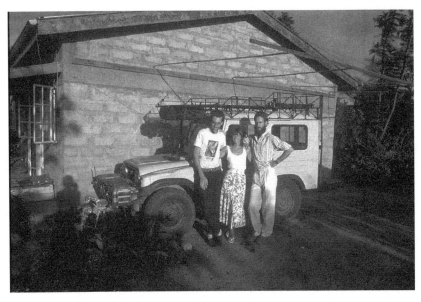

With Rosie and Dick outside their house. The Daihatsu jeep behind us features later in this chapter

They had decided to house me in the only other western style home on the compound, for which I was grateful.

It was like a basic chalet type affair with a tin roof. It didn't have a toilet but it did have a simple shower. The water was provided to us all by a small windmill water pump that pulled it up from under the ground. It was then stored in a large water tank that was up on a high metal frame and that was linked to a small water tank on my roof. The shower pipe came directly from the tank, as did my tap.

To go to the toilet, I had to walk up a path to a small 3ft by 3ft wide building with a long drop hole in it. This was used by a number of different residents on the compound.

The floor in my house was bare, as were the walls, but it did have a couple of chairs and a small table. There was no electricity. We each had a solar panel on our roof that charged a 12 volt car battery. One small bulb was connected to this battery that gave me light till about 9pm - at which point it died. Then it was candles.

But at the end of the day - I was living in luxury compared to most people living in that area.

I had gone to Uganda to be a mechanic but it soon became apparent that the workshop needed more than a mechanic - it needed a foreman and someone who could get the place running well.

So that role was given to me and that was a whole new ball game!

In at the deep end.

The workshop was very basic. It had a tin roof over the ramp and it had a few small tin shed-like affairs at the sides. One larger shed housed a machine that was used to crush and grind sorghum and millet seeds. This usually had anything from 3 to 20 people in there doing who knows what! It wasn't part of the workshop as such, but it was in the grounds of the workshop. Once I was called upon to fix the pressing machine.

There was also a tool shed that in some ways had got a fairly good system running. To prevent tools going *missing* in the day there was a chap who sat at the entrance and filed the names of any mechanics that borrowed a tool and what the actual tool was. He was a sensible and trustworthy chap and ended up being the only guy who seemed to be on my side and wanted things to change and improve.

There was another shed that was packed full of old parts and basically junk. It was a wasted space that was totally jammed with stuff. I planned to empty it and put a bench and vice in there, so that we had a clean place to work on engines. The only place mechanics were stripping engines when I got there was on the floor in the sand!

There were about a dozen employees in the garage. Most had overalls on but that didn't qualify them to be a mechanic, although it probably did in their eyes. The only name I can properly remember from back then is a chap called Fred. He seemed to be the guy who had the most mechanical knowledge and also seemed to have the most influence over the other guys. I don't think he was impressed with having this white guy turn up and being put in charge of them all.

I was in at the deep end alright.

It was very hard to keep tabs on everyone as they were often wandering about the compound or talking to people who would appear at the workshop gate entrance concerning some subject that was nothing to do with their job in the workshop. There were always loads of people through the day gathering around the gate, some even wandering in until I told them to get out. I think the new Mzungu (white man) garage foreman was the talk of the village. Someone who may upset the applecart. But the truth was to the contrary in my view; I was trying to bring some order and honesty to the applecart.

Which may not have been what was wanted by guys in the garage.

My first project was to get that junk shed emptied. There was a lot of stuff in there, some heavy too. I tried to get a chain crew organised to transfer it all to an abandoned lorry at the edge of the workshop land.

Most of the workshop employees

No one really wanted to do it and they worked as slowly as they could, showing no interest or commitment to the task. I could often only get about 3 or 4 people to stay on the job at any one time. Others went missing. People going missing was one of my biggest problems.

I was new at the job - finding my feet. I thought I knew where my feet were. But a few days into the job, my feet were hard to find!

After a few days the shed was empty and I got a bench set up with a vice. I think a few of them saw the sense in my effort.

In amongst this sort of activity there were vehicles to fix. The main priority was the fleet of Massey Ferguson tractors. These belonged to the Seed Project and were hired out to local farmers who were growing crops on their land (mainly sorghum). The tractors helped to cultivate more of the land for such purposes. Seed was sold to the farmers at a reasonable price and a return of produced seed was then brought back to the Project as part of the agreement.

The tractors were given by Western countries who wanted to aid the development of Africa.

I must say that, personally, I didn't see the wisdom in this type of aid. These tractors were brand new and also four wheel drive. They must have cost many thousands of pounds or dollars. They were given, I'm sure, with good intent - But ...!

There was no infrastructure or 'know how' to accommodate this type of technology in such an environment. A simpler and easier to handle next step of developmental assistance would have been more appropriate in my eyes.

When I arrived, there were tractors with an assortment of problems. Some were half taken apart and just lying about the place. These were nearly new and some had serious problems. I was to find out later that some engines had seized up due to not enough oil in them.

Crazy for a nearly new tractor to be laid up with such a serious problem as a seized engine!

Then the situation was exacerbated by parts being taken off it to replace broken parts from another tractor.

And do you know what?

The job was too big for me to deal with, because on top of all these needs I was stuck in the middle of nowhere and had no access to any parts. The only way to get the parts I needed was to write my needs on a list and whenever someone like David Okello was going to drive to Kampala - maybe I would get them in two or three or four weeks time.

Because what I haven't yet mentioned is that very soon after I got there, the MAF planes were grounded!

There was a lot of anti-government warfare going on at that time and there was much rebel activity up in Karamoja where I was.

It was too dangerous to fly there anymore. The rebels were threatening to shoot MAF planes down.

These MAF planes were a lifeline to the remote outposts such as Karamoja.

We had no phones in those days either. The only contact with other places was by radio and that didn't always work and could only be used by one woman in a small office on the compound.

So things were quite dire in all sorts of ways.

Other vehicles were always turning up needing repairs. We were the only real garage for many miles. Army soldiers would arrive and expect fairly immediate attention on their old green trucks. Often it was welding that was needed. While the work was getting done, loads of soldiers would be milling about amongst us. Then there would be people from the village who wanted some help with their bicycle or broken digging mattock. I remember one time a Land Rover arriving at the garage with hardly any brakes. It was the Bishop's transport and the driver was really struggling with the fact that the brakes were non-existent and the engine was not running right. I lifted the bonnet and saw that the servo pipe was not connected to the servo. It was easy to fix and he was well chuffed with the improvement to both the problems by fitting the pipe back on. This sort of fix was simple and satisfying but many mechanical problems around the place entailed a lot more complications.

I had cylinder heads that were stripped down and ready to put back on vehicles, but I could not do it until I had parts. Then there was the problem of where to store all these often precision parts, away from tampering hands and the ever-present dust and sand.

I'm afraid things got worse too.

For some reason my stomach was having problems nearly everyday. The reason for this materialised weeks later. But also the stress of my responsibility probably didn't help either.

I would often get no sleep at night and if I did it was only for an hour or so but some nights I literally got none!

There were large rats in the roof space of my bedroom that were always moving about. Not that this was really to blame but it's worth mentioning for shock appeal and did jolt me out of just dropping off to sleep sometimes.

No, the main reason was diarrhoea. It basically ended up just being water that would come out and this was a continual occurrence. I would lie down and have to get up again immediately to go back to the loo again. And of course the loo was down a path outside my property. And for a bit more shock effect, let me tell you about that loo.

Like I said it was in a tin building about 3 feet by 3 feet.

I would take my torch on the one minute trek to the tin hut. When I opened the door; hundreds of cockroaches would be crawling about the floor, walls and ceiling. They were there because they had come out of the hole that I was about to squat over. The hole was about six inches in diameter. Below that opening was a very deep hole that was about 4 ft in diameter. This is why that type of toilet is called a *long drop toilet!*

It would take many months, maybe years for that hole to fill up. At which point it would be covered up and a new hole would be dug somewhere else.

Well that was a breeding ground and restaurant for thousands of well fed cockroaches!

I would occasionally shine my torch down there and the walls were basically covered with them all scurrying about the place.

So before I would enter the tin hut I would hit the wall. This made the cockroaches that were out of the hole and on the walls and floor of the hut to run to the small six inch diameter hole and disappear back into their underground breeding hole.

Sorry folks for the details - but very true.

It would take a few bangs of my fist on the wall for most of them to go down the hole and some didn't even make it - they would just panic and stay on the walls.

In amongst this scenario please remember I had diarrhoea and was desperate to squat myself above the hole.

And all of this squatting, rather than sitting, was so wearing on my already weak and very tired body.

Then I would walk back to my house utterly exhausted in so many ways. I would get back into my bed still not feeling right in my stomach and then within seconds had to get up and do it all again. Honestly - I was in a right state. It even brought me to tears sometimes.

I would honestly not get a second of sleep sometimes and then the sun would rise and it was day again.

The illness was so volatile and sometimes invaded even the daylight hours. There was a time when a few of us were working on one of the tractors that was lying about outside the workshop fence. It was during the heat of the day and the sun was shining hard down on us. Then I felt my stomach was not well. I walked away from the group and tried speedily to reach the long drop loo near my house. I never made it. Say no more, apart from it's not how you want to operate on a daily basis!

My shower was the next point of call.

Another quick story on a different subject but concerning one of the tractors that was lying in the dirt and in a bad state of repair.

I was leading a small group of my mechanics to this particular tractor and just before I reached it a stone was thrown from behind me and just missed me. It smashed into the side of the tractor. I was cross and turned round to see who had thrown it. It was Fred. He then walked to the tractor and showed me a snake with it's head smashed.

I was only seconds away from coming into contact with that snake when it was alive. Fred had seen it and it was his precision shot that had killed it outright. Amazing aim. And it was a venomous one too.

Thanks Fred. Not that I suppose he will ever get to read this book. Not many people spoke English up in Karamoja. Why would they?

....

Dick's thatched hut surgery with the covered
waiting room to the right

While most of my time was trying to bring order in the workshop and fix vehicles, Dick Stockley was being a modern day hero fixing people's bodies. He had a small thatched hut on the compound, which was his surgery. There were often queues of people of all different ages outside that little lean-to. He was literally saving people's lives. People would walk for miles to get attention. Snake bites, bullet wounds, pregnancies gone wrong, broken limbs, malaria, tapeworms and other types of worm; like the guinea worm that would be found crawling around someone's body and emerge just under the skin somewhere. I saw one in a boy's leg once.

Dick was right there on the frontline. He and Rosie and their young family had already been in Africa for a few years. They were heroes alright.

....

The same can be said of my Uncle Paul and Auntie Margaret (my mums sister). They were out in Zambia for all of the 1960s. Paul was a doctor and Margaret, a nurse. They also had a young family and were in a very remote and primitive part of Northern Zambia doing similar stuff. Heroes again.

....

Dick would often have to deal with extremely bad bullet and machete wounds caused by rebel fighting or regular cattle rustling raids.

Most nights there was gunfire in the distance and sometimes nearby. And not just the odd shot, often there was an intense gun battle going on.

Dick would see first-hand the damage done to some people. Many of course died.

One night a grenade was thrown into our compound next to the workshop and office building. There was an old chap guarding the gate with a shotgun, but he was a token deterrent really.

On top of Dick's surgery duties he also used to go out into the small villages and run Primary Health Care sessions; I went with him once or twice. People would gather under a tree and he would teach them basic health care. A translator was often needed although Dick could also speak some Karamojong.

....

Back in the workshop I was continually challenged with the problem of getting my workforce to be around in the workplace. The problem would start in the morning when they would haphazardly drift into work with no punctuality whatsoever. Yeah I know - Africa time. But you try and get things done with that ethos being in place. And I was new at this job of herding cats!

It got to the point where I attempted to develop a clocking-in system to try and bring some discipline to the fore. When it was overheard that I would dock a percentage of the wages if it wasn't adhered too, another big problem was presented to me; most of the workers didn't come to work.

They went on strike I suppose you would call it.

I was left with about three guys. The rest stayed at home in protest. I expect there was a ringleader but I was definitely in a predicament. I'm sure word was out on the streets that the Mzungu has overstepped his mark.

It certainly reached the ears of the people in the compound.

I was in a sticky situation now.

I locked up the workshop and walked back to my house. What the heck do I do now? I was on the edge. My authority as foreman was being undermined as well as my underlying confidence in decision making.

I was even suspecting that I had totally failed God and was making a mess of everything.

Out in the middle of Africa on my own, I was scared, I felt a failure and the enemy of everyone.

I got down on my knees and cried out to God to make sense of all my troubles. I needed help. I was lost in confusion.

After a while and still feeling awful, I opened my Bible and right at the front on one of the blank pages were a load of Bible references I had written out a year or two ago.

My eyes were quickly brought to noticing a biro line that went vertical down through some of them and was in the shape of an arrow head at the bottom. It is still in my Bible to this day. I had never seen it before and wondered how it got there. It was pointing to where I had written the words Joshua 1 : 8 - 9.

I just knew God wanted me to look up those verses.

So I looked them up:

Joshua 1:8-9 New International Version (NIV)

8 Keep this Book of the Law always on your lips; meditate on it day and night, so that you may be careful to do everything written in it. Then you will be prosperous and successful. **9 Have I not commanded you? Be strong and courageous. Do not be afraid; do not be discouraged, for the Lord your God will be with you wherever you go.'**

Those words just penetrated me deeply as soon as I read them. God was speaking directly to me. He was on my side.

That was all I needed to know. A whole world could be against me, but if God was on my side - I was confident.

And that confidence came just at the right time because about 30 seconds after that there was a knock on the front door of my house.

It was Philip the accountant and one of the main bosses of the project. They had heard the news about the walk out, and had rushed over to my place to see what was going on.

I explained that the guys were not happy about being brought to account concerning their casual attitude of turning up at the garage whenever they wanted. I also explained to them that if the project wanted me to be the foreman then they needed to give me the freedom to run the place as I saw fit. If they didn't stand behind me and I lost this current battle in the workshop, then it was going to be a mess.

My authority would be undermined.

....

I told them it was up to them.

I didn't mind just being a normal mechanic, as was the deal when I first travelled out to Uganda. It was them that had asked me to be the foreman. It wasn't something I was expecting, or particularly wanting.

But if they still wanted me to be in charge, the only way I was going to carry on was if they supported me in trying to bring order and diligence in the workplace.

Well, they could see my point. I was rocking the boat in the workshop but unless someone did, then nothing was going to change.

They knew something needed to change to make the workshop operate more effectively and efficiently, so they endorsed my authority and we prayed for God's help to come into the present situation.

They then arranged for a meeting to be held the next day, which all the workshop staff would have to attend.

The next day there were about twenty people gathered in a circle and the project bosses explained that the mechanics needed to adhere to the rules of punctuality. It was an uncomfortable situation, but I was encouraged still by the word that God had spoken to me the day before:

Be strong and courageous. Do not be afraid; do not be discouraged, for the Lord your God will be with you wherever you go.

....

My stomach was still causing daily problems. It was one of the main reasons I was continually feeling weak, tired and vulnerable.

Then I found something that could have been the cause of my illness, and even the reason for another illness I had further down the line, that I will tell you about later.

Someone suggested that it might be a good idea to get up on the tin roof of my house and look in the water tank to see if it was clean inside, so I did.

The tank was fairly small really and when I took the flimsy lid off I found a lot of long green algae in there... and a fairly large half dead bat!

Yeah I know - not good eh?

Well, in one sense it was quite encouraging to find a probable reason for my persistent illness. This was the water I had been drinking from. It supplied my one and only tap.

Obviously I spent the next couple of hours emptying it out, cleaning it, and refilling it.

While I am telling you about life up on the tin roof of my house let me tell you of more pleasant things up there for me.

After this event, I got into the habit of going up on the roof to look around and enjoy my surroundings. It was like my contemplation lookout spot. In the evenings I would go and sit on top of the roof and enjoy the African panoramic landscape all around me. Some evenings there would be thunderstorms on the distant horizon all around me. It was amazing. I would try and count to ten after each flash of lightning and before I could even get to five, there would be another flash at the edge of the landscape surrounding me - it was a continual light and sound show. God's alternative to TV for me. Which I much prefer (I've chosen to not have TV since 1985).

And with those distant African storms, there was also that surreal characteristic atmosphere that brought onboard with it the sense of smell too. The smell of dust and rain blowing around in the wind was mixed in with the pregnant expectation that a storm was brewing.

Up there on that tin roof I saw some good sunsets too. Uganda sits on the Equator, so day turns to night pretty quick and there is no real twilight.

That said - the sky still showed off some good sunsets.

But of all the sunsets I have ever seen around the world in my life, the best ones were in North Devon at Lee Abbey looking out West over Lee Bay into the Bristol Channel. Those blue, pink and red masterpieces filled the whole (and I mean the **whole***) sky on a few occasions.*

....

Another one of my treats while living out in Uganda was receiving letters from family, from my Church in Torquay, from Lee Abbey community members and from old biker mates.

Of course my favourite ones were from Alex, who corresponded well, as I did also.

But there was one letter that had me shouting Hallelujah at the top of my voice around the compound.

It was from my old biker mate Danny who I mentioned earlier had been working as a mechanic in North West Uganda near Arua for over a year before I arrived in the Country. We had not had any opportunity to meet up in Kampala before he left to go back to England. We missed each other by a few days when I was there in early March.

Anyway, this letter from Dan turns up about 3 weeks after he wrote it, such was the state of getting any post out there in those days.

And this letter was a joy to my soul. In his time out in Uganda his life had changed. Quoting his letter - he wrote:

I came to realize that without Jesus, I am nothing. My soul was born out there, thanks to the patient love, understanding and encouragement of almost everybody, and so I offered my life to Christ. Many times in conversation with people at Kuluva I'd said that I would have to be given a sign before I could really believe that Jesus was alive.

There have been no signs, other than the Resurrection, but nevertheless, I believe and trust in Him. I must confess, sometimes I doubt that God should want to save the soul of such a habitually bad man as me, but I've made my promise to Jesus, and He's made His promise to me, and I believe and trust in Him. I owe every breath to Jesus, and devote every action to His Name, and I wonder how I ever got this far without knowing He was there.

My life hasn't changed dramatically - more fundamentally. There was one day at Kuluva that began for me before the sun was up. I was at the peak of a particularly busy time, and I couldn't sleep, my mind was in chaos! I watched Sunday slowly begin, and recorded everything as accurately as I could in my diary. It was then that I realized that although I was intensely aware of the beauty of Life, it was still a mystery to me - no matter how obvious was the wonder of whatever fell under my gaze, it was still a fuzzy image.

But, since I asked God to take the 'wheel', I'm beginning to feel a powerful connection to everything around me. The picture is getting clearer everyday. I believe that God has a purpose for me - I only wish I knew what it was!

One important virtue I was force fed in Africa was Patience, and I know that He will make that purpose known to me one way or another, sooner or later.

....

This letter from Dan so encouraged me. It arrived at quite a lonely time in my life, when things were far from easy, but getting this letter from my old friend who knew me in the old motorbike days just cheered my soul.

We were now Christian brothers. It don't get much better than that.

And on the subject of motorbikes, there was a project going on in the workshop that was giving me a lot of satisfaction.

In the small shed that I had cleared to make room for a workbench I had found amongst other things - two red Honda XL 185cc trail bikes. They were both in a state but I knew that I could make one fairly good one out of the two. I relished the task.

So, once I got the workshop area tidied up and arranged things in a better order, I started to strip down the engine on one of the two bikes. Parts of the other engine were missing and broken, but would provide me with some parts that I would need.

There was always other vehicle maintenance going on but I plodded on with the bike project as and when I had a spare moment.

Most of the guys in the workshop had improved with turning up for work on time. However, there was an undercurrent resistance to putting their heart and commitment into the day's activities, often reinforced by them going missing at times when I needed them. It wasn't an ideal situation as I'm sure you can envisage from the way I am writing.

By the month of May, the demands and the state of affairs in the workshop had really got to me. I felt very alone in there. The fact that there were tractors that needed fixing weighed heavily on me. It became apparent that I was not equipped with what I needed to even scratch the surface of the problem. The things I needed to do the job were **not available:** parts (which was a big hindrance), particular tools for certain jobs, enough clean working and storage places, and a workforce that was enthusiastic about getting things done.

Some of the tractors that had been laid up or were in various states of disablement had been in that state well before I arrived. The mountain of need in that area was too big for me to handle. It was very disheartening and I was struggling to the point of breakdown with the whole situation.

It came to a point one day in May when I just quietly walked out of the workshop and headed for Dick and Rosie's house. Dick was away in Kenya getting food and provisions. He had driven his two daughters to their residential school there. He had been away for over a week and it wasn't known when he would return to Karamoja, but Rosie was in.

I walked into their kitchen and said, 'Rosie, I need help, I can't take it anymore.'

I told her about how I was feeling and was close to tears. She could see I was desperate. There was nothing else to do apart from pray. In prayer I remember saying to God, *'God whatever it takes, get me out of this situation - I don't want to be here anymore. I don't want to work in that workshop or have this job any longer.'*

Desperate prayer I know! But that is where I was at.

And guess what?

That prayer got answered. And the start of the answer came within seconds of me finishing that prayer. Crazy as the consequences may seem.

As I finished that prayer, we heard someone running to the house.

It was one of the mechanics. The Church Diocese in Moroto had just radioed. They owned the two Honda's that I had been working on and had heard that I'd recently got one of them running.

I had literally got the Honda on the road the day before - word obviously had got out quick!

There was a Church leader who needed it in Moroto as soon as possible, so that he could visit people in the surrounding villages.

Well I definitely needed a break, so I decided that I would ride the bike to Moroto.

I went and got myself ready for the trip. Within an hour I was ready and on the bike. Moroto was 70 miles away through African bush terrain. The route went along potholed and dusty murram track.

I was a bit nervous because that road was also known for having bandits on that would sometimes ambush vehicles that travelled on it. There was nothing but remote scrubland along the whole distance of that route, so I didn't fancy breaking down or coming off the bike. But also I wanted to go as fast as possible to avoid any ambush situation.

The bike was running perfectly. I had done a good job on it, so that helped my confidence for the trip.

Quite a crowd gathered around the compound to watch me off. I had wrapped some cotton material around my face to stop me breathing in too much dust and I had my sunglasses on too. There was no helmet to wear - it was too hot anyway.

I was free. I was getting away on an adventure. It was just what I needed.

Little did I know that I was never to work in that workshop ever again!

That prayer was getting answered but not in the way I had expected.

I had prayed: *Whatever it takes God, get me out of this situation.*

God was taking me seriously. As you will see.

....

I set out into the dry and dusty unknown. Nervous, yet thrilled too.

As I sped along the track south I continued to keep watching out carefully in the distance for wild animals and also for any humans hiding in the bushes ready to ambush and rob me.

I watched the bike odometer to give me an indication of how many miles I had done and, more importantly, how many were left before I reached civilisation. The trip was going to take about 2 hours if everything went well.

And, Praise God, it did.

It was an exhilarating ride but I was relieved when I started to come across the few scattered huts that indicated the edge of Moroto.

I had been directed to find the home of the Burninghams, who were a missionary family from England. They had lived in Moroto for a few years and I was quite excited to meet some folk from my own country.

I found their house, parked the bike up in the garden and went in and met the Burninghams. They and their small children were a friendly crew and I was soon relaxing and lying out on their sofa. I was feeling pretty exhausted and as the afternoon turned into evening, I began to not feel well at all.

I was going to need to stay there because I had no way of getting back to Kotido. I would hopefully get a lift at some point with someone passing through Moroto on their way to Kotido.

It was not a route many people were travelling because of the tensions in Karamoja at that time. Alongside the danger of potential ambushes, there was also the ongoing concern of getting your vehicle stuck in the mud. The rainy season of May was helping many people fall victim to the famously bad murram roads. We would hear often of lorries getting stuck for literally days. The driver would be vulnerable out there on his own, especially if he was fully loaded with provisions of one sort or another - which he usually was.

It would cost him a lot of money to pay people to assist him.

My bike ride had been at times dusty but in other places wet and muddy!

It was easier for me on a bike to get through the tricky parts but even then, I had to slow the bike down to a walking pace to do it.

....

I was still lying on the sofa as it got dark - not feeling well at all. Then a surprise visitor arrived at the house. It was Dick. He popped in to see the Burninghams on his way back from Kenya. He had no idea I was there. His little old Daihatsu jeep was loaded high with provisions for the next few months. It was jam-packed and even had loads of stuff on the roof too! It was a very small 2 door jeep that had served Dick and his family well in their time out there.

I told Dick I had delivered a Honda motorbike to Moroto and that the timing of him passing through was amazingly perfect. He had been away for a week or two.

We set off to Kotido in complete darkness. He was tired from his long trip and I was feeling very vulnerable and sick. I forget what he said about me being ill but I think Dick's main concern was to get back to Kotido with all the gear onboard and not get stuck out in the middle of nowhere in the middle of the night.

And do you know what?

We got stuck!

The weight in the vehicle and the state of the road was too much for the little Daihatsu. We slid and sunk into the sucker-like grip of the wet murram. Dick turned off the engine and lights. It was totally quiet and black.

There we were. I think I had been dreading this scenario - feeling the way I was.

But Dick was a good person to be with in such a situation. He started to unload a lot of the heavy stuff from the vehicle. I was now feeling so bad I could not even properly help him, although I think I helped move some things to the drier part of the track. After about 15 minutes most of the stuff was off the jeep and in a pile further up the track. Dick was going to push and I was going to sit in and drive.

After some struggle the jeep moved forward a bit, then kept moving forward, and we were out.

Oh what a relief it was. I don't think I could have handled staying out there all night in the state I was in. My whole body felt ill. I needed to lie down.

Eventually we got back to Kotido and pulled up outside Dick's house late into the night. Rosie was still up. Philip also heard us arrive and came round to the house. The four of us told each other our news. But as time went on I got to feel so bad I just lay down on the kitchen floor.

The others were in the sitting room and I knew they were discussing the state I was in.

I think someone helped me get back to my house where I lay down in bed. But things weren't right and things were to get a lot worse.

I stayed in bed for days. Food was brought to me. I can't remember whether I ate any of it. At night I had a candle going in my room. I was definitely ill and very vulnerable.

Then, one evening, the pains in my stomach got so bad I thought I was dying. I tried to walk to Dick and Rosie's house to get help but I collapsed on the floor in my garden. The pain crippled me over. I just lay there writhing about.

Amazingly, Dick turned up. He found me on the floor, looked at me and said, 'What are you doing lying on the floor? You can't stay there. Come on - get up.'

I said, 'I can't, I'm in too much pain.'

But Dick is not an overly sympathetic person - **more pragmatic!**

Which I guess is what I needed at the time.

From that point on though it was obvious things were a little more serious than just a stomach upset.

If I remember rightly Dick started giving me antibiotics. I was also getting high temperatures.

I was just struggling through each day and wasn't even thinking about what was wrong with me but Dick obviously was - being a Doctor and all!

He was wanting to fly me to Kampala but, as already mentioned, the MAF planes had been grounded because of the rebel anti-government activity going on.

I forget how many days passed but one day Dick said to me that he needed to get me to a hospital and the only possible place was an Italian mission station twenty miles south west of Moroto called Matany.

He said that because of the rains it was not possible to get me there. They were praying that God would stop the rain, because things were quite desperate now. I still didn't know what was wrong with me and he didn't seem to offer the information to me.

The next day the rain stopped.

Dick came round to my house and said, 'Right we have got to go today, this is our only chance of making it.'

As I was getting in the vehicle to go I asked Dick, 'What is actually wrong with me?'

He said, 'You've got appendicitis.'

OH.

I look back and see the sense of not telling me days earlier. It would not have been in my interest to know. I would probably have panicked.

When we eventually reached Matany hospital, I was immediately taken to the operating room on a wheeled stretcher. I was told later that the appendicitis had developed into peritonitis and that I had 12 hours left to live.

I'm crying as I write this: God's love for me is so special. He's such a good Father.

As a kid, I had always feared getting appendicitis. I had heard about it from somewhere and was always asking my mum (who was a nurse) whenever I got a stomach ache if it was appendicitis.

As I was pushed through the corridor to the operating room, I was scared and asked God to be very close to me. Then seconds after - we passed a wooden plaque above a doorway and the words on it were about the goodness of God.

When we reached our destination I was quickly given an injection and told to count to ten. The general anaesthetic kicked in before I reached number ten.

....

I'm not sure how many hours later I woke up finding pipes coming out of me and into me. I felt weak, vulnerable and very confined to the spot.

I had a six-inch, sewn-up wound that went a couple of inches above my belly button and another hole in the side of my groin. The operation apparently needed a six inch incision to remove all the infection that was around inside my abdomen due to the ruptured appendix.

I was not allowed to drink any fluids for a couple of days and I remember struggling with that. The room I was in was hot. It was, at the time, quite a small basic hospital. There was no air conditioning or anything like that. There wasn't even glass in the windows. So the only coolness came through them and of course I was in a semi-desert region near the equator - so it was not cool anyway!

I was so thirsty and pleaded with the nurse to let me have some water. There was one occasion that a nurse gave me a very little amount in a glass. Enough to wet my lips and not much more.

I had a drip in my arm which was hydrating me but I wanted a drip in my mouth!

I also had a catheter pipe connected down below and there was another pipe inserted in the small hole in my groin area. This pipe was draining any excess fluids that were building up around my abdomen due to the infection that had been there.

I was to meet the Italian man that had performed the operation and it was nice to talk to someone from Europe. He was a gentle and caring guy and it was good to know he was around. The nurses were African and seemed to be mainly Catholic nuns.

I was in that room for a few days and they didn't pass without incident. I was lying there early on in my stay and my body started to shake and go very cold. Then it started to go stiff like I couldn't move. It was so scary and alien to anything I have ever felt before. I could just feel it coming on me within a period of about thirty seconds. I panicked and started yelling for help while I still had any voice - because it felt like it was going to take my life from me.

A nurse came rushing in and I said something was going wrong with my body. She was African and wasn't fluent in English but she quickly called for help and someone else came in and disconnected the IV drip pipe from my arm. My body started to recover within a minute or two.

They then replaced the IV plastic bag that was supplying me fluids and reconnected the drip to my arm.

The first bag had been faulty apparently and was contaminated with some infection.

That was a scary time I can tell you. I'm glad they knew what it was.

It happened again with another couple of bags. Not a nice experience.

After a few days, my pipes were slowly removed and I was taken to another room at the edge of the hospital. Nurses were not at hand now to look after me, so it was arranged by Dick and Rosie back in Kotido to send a teenage boy called Michael to the hospital to help me. He had been the gardener in my small vegetable patch on the compound.

He slept in an armchair in the hospital room I was in. Initially, I was still using a bedpan for going to the toilet but after a few days I was able slowly, with Michaels help, to get out of bed and go to the toilet.

He was a blessing. I was still very weak and had just started to eat proper food. Because of the few Italian staff that were on site, I was to get delicacies like feta cheese and bread most days.

But, although I was slowly getting stronger, I was not getting properly better. My temperature was not going down. Everyday a nurse would come and check my temperature but it remained high. The staff were concerned. I started to go downhill and get fevers. I would be very hot and at other times very cold. The nights were long and often uncomfortable.

Michael was around, which was reassuring. I wasn't in a condition where I wanted to be alone. It was good knowing he was there all the time.

Then one night, in the early hours, I started having hallucinations and got quite delirious. I was panicking about being in the hospital and desperate to get away from Africa because there was great danger around. I started to try and get dressed and told Michael that we needed to start walking to England.

I was really in a bad way. It was horrible.

It only happened the once but my temperature readings were always too high. My body wasn't beating the infection.

In the end it was decided that I could continue my recovery in Kotido. I could slowly move about on my feet now and to be honest I needed a change of environment. Matany hospital had served me well - it was time to move on.

Dick came and picked up Michael and me and drove us back to Kotido.

I was put in a small bedroom at Dick and Rosie's house. I was not well enough to move around or live in my house. I was still sick.

I was not even eating or drinking enough. I had no appetite and they were getting concerned about me, telling me I had to eat.

People from the local Church came to the house and wanted to pray for me. The prayer time was a noisy affair as was the way out there. About four or five people in my room raising their voices to God and the devil!

It wasn't really what I wanted - I was too weak and found the whole ordeal wearing. All I wanted to do was sleep - day and night.

One day I said to Rosie, 'Am I going to be alright Rosie - will I live?'

She replied with a worried look, 'I don't know Mark.'

....

During this time back in Kotido there was the odd occasion when I was more alert and I would ask God for His help and reassurance.

There were a couple of scripture verses that I kept coming back to and that gave me hope that I would make it back to England alive.

They were from the Psalms (I have highlighted the bits that spoke into my situation):

Psalm 121:7-8 New International Version (NIV)

7 The Lord will keep you from all harm -

He will watch over your life;

8 the Lord will watch over **your coming and going**

both now and forevermore.

....

Psalm 27:13-14 New International Version (NIV)

13 I am still confident of this:

I will see the goodness of the Lord

in the land of the living.

14 Wait for the Lord;

be strong and take heart

and **wait for the Lord.**

....

Those scripture passages were a lifeline for me. They were all I had to hang on to. They were like a little whisper from God. I had to hold onto His word by faith and it would settle me when I got really scared.

....

My health got to the point where I was hardly eating or drinking anything and Dick was not sure what was wrong with me. Then the vital clue came that he needed. My face and skin became jaundiced. The yellowing of my complexion indicated that my liver was having problems.

Now Dick knew what he had to do. He needed me out of Karamoja and in a hospital in Kampala. But that was not easy to do with all the travel problems in the area.

And this is what happened.

Well, to be honest, I don't really know the full details of what happened but it went something like this:

An urgent radio message was made to a government official somewhere in Uganda that there was a mzungu in Karamoja who was very ill and needed urgent medical attention in Kampala.

An agreement must have been made with rebel forces in the area that one MAF plane would be safely allowed to fly to Kotido to pick me up.

Sure enough, a small MAF plane was on its way from Kampala soon after. I was helped out of bed, got my shorts and tee-shirt on and grabbed a few belongings. I was very thin and weak looking and Dick told me weeks later that I did a great job in looking like someone who was in desperate need of medical attention!

As I walked slowly out onto the hot dusty airstrip runway there were about a hundred people gathered around to see the long lost mzungu who nearly died and still only looked half alive.

And for special effect had even coloured himself yellow!

I said goodbye to Dick, Rosie, Philip and a few others that knew me from the compound and beyond. Who knows when I would ever see some of these faces again. Maybe never.

The pilot of the plane was again Emil from Switzerland, so that was nice. We took off and headed South.

On the journey up in the air I started to struggle to get enough air in my lungs. I even started to panic inside myself and ended up asking Emil if he had any oxygen onboard. He didn't.

In the end I opened a side window slightly and just stuck my face in the blast of fast air rushing in.

What a state to get in!

....

I ended up being taken to Nsambya Hospital, which was the main Catholic hospital in the capital.

If I thought I had problems, compared to the people that were lying and sitting around in the grounds waiting to be attended to in the yard of that Hospital, I could see that I didn't.

It was an arena of suffering like I had never seen before. People with swollen limbs and disfigured faces. There were one or two people with elephantiasis, a condition I did not even know about until I walked into those hospital grounds.

I was led around all of them and was given preferential treatment, which made me feel very self-conscious and even

118

guilty. But also, I was extremely grateful too. I was out of my comfort zone in a multitude of ways, so being led to a place of safety in the bowels of the hospital building helped put my mind at rest a bit.

I was given a bed in a quiet part of the hospital and a doctor proceeded to do various tests on me. After blood tests and such like, it was firmly established that I had hepatitis. Fortunately it was hepatitis A.

I was in Nsambya Hospital for a week or so I think and they gave me whatever drugs were needed to address the situation. I also went onto a drip again at the start if I remember rightly.

Slowly, various people who I knew came and visited me. People from the City who had heard where I was.

I also started to receive letters from England. Word had got back there that I was ill. I was even sent newspaper cuttings. Newspapers with headlines such as; *'Mercy man in area of violence.' 'Church worker hit by illness.'*

When I was finally well enough to leave the hospital, Emil (the pilot from MAF) and his wife Margaret came and picked me up and very kindly took me back to their house in Kampala. I was to live with their family until I got better.

They were so kind to me. Emil was often out in the day with his flying job but Margaret was at home with their kids. They gave me a lovely little bedroom and at last I felt like I could relax and get well. My strength was very slowly returning. I was eating proper meals again, often at the table with the family. I used to go back to my bed afterwards but it was definitely an improvement.

I remember listening to the BBC World Service radio station most days. It was my lifeline to normality.

I forget all the exact timing details but there was word from Torquay that Alex was going to fly out to Uganda to see me near the end of July. Before I was ill, the plan was that Alex was going to fly out to Africa at the end of the year. But now everything had changed. It was thought by friends and family back in Torquay that I needed support and encouragement as soon as possible.

The day came that Alex arrived at Entebbe airport. It was so good to see each other and after a few days we both wanted to travel to Karamoja so that Alex could see where I had been living and working.

We managed to get a lift with David Okello who was passing through Kampala in the Toyota Land Cruiser. He was on his way north to Kotido.

It was a long arduous journey, and I still wasn't feeling properly well, but we eventually got there.

People were surprised to see me back but also pleased that I was looking better than when they last saw me.

I introduced Alex to people and showed her about the place as the days unfolded.

Alex with one of the local residents

Rosie was especially pleased to meet Alex and I think was very grateful to have a woman around that she could speak heart to heart with. It must have been lonely for Rosie being up there in that remote region of the country on her own as a white woman.

After a few days I realised that I still wasn't well. Alex had brought a thermometer out with her from England and was checking my temperature each day. It was not normal and I was not feeling right.

When we mentioned it to Dick, he was not too happy. He had not expected to see me back in Karamoja and felt it was irresponsible to have left Kampala.

He was probably right and Alex and I felt guilty about travelling up there.

David Okello was getting ready to travel south again soon in the Toyota, so it became obvious that we would go with him. There was no other way of getting back to Kampala.

I got the rest of my belongings from my house and spent the rest of the day walking around saying my final goodbye to people and taking a few photos.

The following day we left. The trip south became quite special to us both.

Alex had brought from England a cassette tape album called 'Watermark' by an artist called Enya. The Toyota Land Cruiser that David Okello was driving had a cassette player in the dash, so we put it on.

As it played the haunting melodies out of the speakers we were caught up in a magical experience.

We were travelling through this majestic barren African landscape in a big comfy vehicle listening to such tracks as 'Storms in Africa'. It was surreal and beautiful beyond measure.

We both knew and sensed this moment was a wonderful gift from God to us both.

Who needs flaming drugs!

....

We both spent the last few days of Alex's time in Uganda staying at an accountant's house in the suburbs of Kampala. I forget how I knew him but he was called Steven and he was from England.

My temperature was still not settling down and it was suggested by someone that I should go and have myself checked out in Nairobi Hospital in Kenya.

Steven was planning to go to Nairobi in his car with a few people in a few days time.

Alex flew back to England, by which time it was early August. It was sad to part again but we looked forward to when we would see each other back in the UK.

A few days later I got in Steven's car with a couple of other people and we headed east to Kenya.

We crossed the Kenyan border in the afternoon and proceeded south east towards the capital. But as the journey went on we started having alternator problems. The car came to a halt eventually and we had to get out and push the car. I was not feeling well again and this was the last thing I needed. The occupants of the car knew I was ill and didn't in any way expect me to push which was good. My six-inch abdominal scar was still not healed enough for pushing cars.

It was a strange coincidence because where we had broken down was just before the equator. The car was pushed over the equator and into the town that was just beyond it.

A garage took the alternator apart and spent too long fiddling about with it, but eventually we were on our way again a couple of hours later.

As the day started to dim, the car started to play up again. The alternator was still not fixed. Then, when it was dark, we came to a halt again. The car was dead and we were stuck on some road still quite a way from our destination.

In the end someone came and picked us up and took us to Karen, which is a district West of Nairobi.

We got there so late. It was gone midnight and I was really not well by now. But at least we were safe in some big house owned by I forget who!

The next day we were taken into Nairobi. I was taken to the hospital and was put in a bed. Tests were done to try and find out why I was still having high temperatures. After getting the results the doctor told me that they probably were going to have to open me up again because there were obviously still internal problems.

This really upset me. I felt so vulnerable already and could not handle being opened up again. They gave me some pills.

In the night I prayed desperately that I would not have to be operated on again.

The next day my temperature reduced and I was released but was told to get back to England as soon as I could.

I was so grateful. Thank you Lord.

The next few days were spent trying to get a plane back to England. My return ticket date was not supposed to be until February the following year. That was sorted out OK but initially, every flight from Nairobi seemed to be fully booked for some reason. A few days later, a seat eventually became available.

I was so desperate to leave Africa and get back to England.

....

I landed back in England on August 16th.

I had been out there for six months. It was the toughest time of my life but I often say to people that it was the most intimate time I have had with God. He was all I had out there. I didn't really have close friends or family. I felt very alone a lot of the time. But those times when I tried to cuddle up in the safety of God were actually very precious.

I think suffering brings an urgency to depend on God. Not everyone does of course, but I did, and I'm grateful for all His love and protection.

Psalm 121:7-8 New International Version (NIV)

7 The Lord will keep you from all harm -

He will watch over your life;

8 the Lord will watch over **your coming and going**

both now and forevermore.

....

Psalm 27:13-14 New International Version (NIV)

13 I am still confident of this:

I will see the goodness of the Lord

in the land of the living.

14 Wait for the Lord;

be strong and take heart

and **wait for the Lord.**

....

My dad picked me up from the airport and drove me to Norfolk. My parents were staying with my mum's sister Margaret and her husband Paul who lived in Aylsham. A room had been set aside for me to recover and rest in. It was so good to be back with people I knew and stay in a house I knew.

Paul being a doctor in Aylsham sorted out a time at the local surgery for me to have some blood tests as I was still not properly well. The blood sample was sent to Norwich where they specialised more with tropical diseases. A few days later we were told that there was a trace of brucella in the blood, so I went on a course of antibiotics that treated brucellosis. It is not a disease that is often found in developed countries. The disease is carried by animals such as cattle and if caught by humans can cause high fever and even depression.

It was good to have an antibiotic that was going to hit it on the head.

It was also good to be eating more familiar food. I was in luxury with all the lovely tastes of Western food that I had not had for six months. I was not to eat anything fatty though because my liver was going to have to recover from the hepatitis. Occasionally when I did eat anything fatty my body let me know it didn't want it!

It was also good to just rest and sleep in a lovely comfy bed. Margaret and Paul's house was in the quiet town of Aylsham and had a lawn, trees, pond and flower beds. Just what the doctor ordered. It was the perfect place to recuperate.

Mum and Dad showed me a recent article and photo from the newspaper back in Torquay. The headline was, 'STRING OF ILLNESS DRIVES MERCY MAN HOME.'

Yes, it really was all in capital letters!

Hollywood next!

After about a week we made our way back to Torquay and I stayed at my parents' house in Chelston. I was already feeling stronger than I had done for ages.

On September 2nd, Alex came and saw me in Torquay for the weekend. It was good to be back together again. We went out for a meal in a country pub nearby and I asked her if she would marry me. There was an unnecessary gap of time of about three seconds!... and she said, 'Yes.'

Praise the Lord.

She told me that God had sort of told her that I was going to ask her in the near future, so she had had time to be sure of her answer.

We phoned our parents from the payphone at the pub (no mobile phones back then) and they were really happy.

After a few days we set a date for May 5th the following year. We didn't want to leave it too long because being Christians we had always felt it wasn't right to sleep together until after we were married.

And of course being in love and wanting to be close to each other brings with it the temptation to let those standards fall by the wayside.

Two weeks after we got engaged my mum told us that she had just found out that she had got cancer. She was going to have to have a hysterectomy as soon as possible.

She told us that our engagement had given her some hope at that very difficult time in her life. She was looking forward to our wedding.

In early October my friend Charlie (who was married to Dawn) from St Matthias Church offered me a job. He had his own carpentry business and was working on his own but now needed an assistant.

So I started working for Charlie. We used to drive in his van to various locations around South Devon doing a variety of jobs. We did first and second fixing at building sites (building stud walls and then fitting skirting boards and door trims after the plastering). We also did a variety of other big and small jobs that would vary from building a loft conversion to fixing a gate. Every day was different. Charlie did the complicated work and I would assist in whatever way he needed - often that would mean driving around in the van getting wood or other merchandise from local building suppliers.

We used to have a good laugh most of the time and I think Charlie was pleased to have somebody around to spend the day with.

Alex was still living in Taunton with some Christian housemates and was due to finish her midwifery training early in the new year.

Christmas came around and it was nearly the end of the eighties. At the start of the eighties I was still doing my mechanic apprenticeship up on Dartmoor. I was in the Mephistopheles bike gang. I had long oily and dirty hair and clothes to match. My main focus of attention was my Triumph Daytona motorbike. Since those days a lot had happened in my life. The eighties had been life transforming for me. The nineties were about to start. I was going to reach the age of thirty. I was going to get married. I was going to enter a whole new era in my life and God was going to guide me.

Jeremiah 29:11-13 New International Version (NIV)

11 For I know the plans I have for you,' declares the Lord, 'plans to prosper you and not to harm you, plans to give you hope and a future.

12 Then you will call on me and come and pray to me, and I will listen to you.

13 You will seek me and find me when you seek me with all your heart.

1990

In January, the BBC came to St Matthias to film an edition of 'Songs of Praise'. The Church was packed. Where were all those people at usual services?!

Better not get on my soapbox!

Anyway, when the evening was finished, me and a friend of mine called David from Upton Vale Baptist Church went back to his house to pray about some stuff. It ended up being such a special time of prayer with God's presence so evident to the both of us. We just kept staying in that atmosphere of attentiveness. We actually ended up staying in prayer right through the night till the next morning, when the sun rose!

It was such an intimate time with God.

Writing this now it reminds me of a verse in the Psalms;

Psalm 46:10 New Living Translation (NLT)

'Be still, and know that I am God!

I will be honoured by every nation.

I will be honoured throughout the world.'

And that is what we were experiencing that night. We were being **still,** and we were knowing God was God.

We were hearing from Him. Not audibly but very deeply and clearly in our spirit.

David heard God say this about me;

Mark, you are a warm and gentle breeze moving amongst different people. Not set in one place.

It is something I wrote in my Bible all those years ago and have never forgotten.

I also heard God speak that night concerning both my parents, my sister Julie and her daughter, and my brother Robert.

It was good to start the new year with such a memorable time in God's presence.

In February Alex heard that she had been accepted for a job she had applied for.

She was to start on April 2nd, a month before we were to get married. She was going to be a midwife at... wait for it... Torbay Hospital in Torquay!

This was exciting news. We now knew where we were going to both live after we got married.

Soon after this news I moved out of my parents house and into the loft space of a flat in Ellacombe, which was near the town centre. A guy called Adrian lived in the flat but he offered me the empty roof space if I wanted it. It was only going to be temporary but it enabled me to move out from my parents house and give them space and time on their own.

The loft had no windows and I got up there by ladder. There wasn't even any furniture but it had everything I needed. I slept on a mattress on the floor.

In March, after Alex's midwifery training in Taunton had come to an end, we both went and had a week's holiday in Port Isaac on the North coast of Cornwall. We were going to stay in an empty house belonging to the the leaders of my Church in Torquay. The family kindly offered it to us for the week.

Most of the week I chose to fast from food and only drank water. I needed to really seek God for the way forward concerning work.

Alex also joined in the fast as we also needed to know where we were both going to live after we were married.

I went for a walk one day on my own along the coast and thought about what I would really like to do for a job. The work with Charlie was fine but I needed something more fulfilling and exciting.

A couple of months earlier I had contacted the Automobile Association to see if there were any vacancies as a patrolman but they were not recruiting people at that time.

I had always fancied the job ever since my apprenticeship in the garage on Dartmoor. There was an AA patrolman called Chris who would pop in from time to time and I used to think to myself - that's a good job.

The job had always felt beyond my reach, even back then, because it was a job where you were **on your own** out there on the roadside. I had often felt under-confident in that area of my mechanical ability. The job obviously required an overall knowledge of many types of vehicles and diagnostic skills would be vital.

As I walked along the coast I found myself having a real desire for the job. The more I thought about it the more I wanted to do nothing else but be an AA patrolman. I loved the idea of going to different places every day, meeting different people and fixing all sorts of mechanical breakdowns. I was worried about whether I was a good enough mechanic to handle it out there on the road on my own but I came to the conclusion that I needed to trust God.

So I made up my mind that the only job I wanted to do in this next period of my life as a married man, was to be an AA man!

I asked God to create an opening for the job, because I had hit a wall when I had contacted them earlier. God could get me in. And

God could help me do the job well. It was a bit scary, but somehow I felt it was the way forward.

As I was fasting as well, it would give some extra clout to my prayers!

I told Alex what I had been thinking and we started to ask God to open the door for where we should live in Torquay and also for me to get a job with the AA.

About a week later;

Now get ready for this!

I was in my flat (where I lived in the loft) having a shower after working all day with Charlie. When I came down to the kitchen, Adrian who lived there told me that a guy from the AA had just phoned to speak to me. I thought he was kidding me but he insisted he wasn't.

So I phoned the number back and a man called Ted answered the phone. He told me he had found my number from an enquiry I had made to the AA a couple of months earlier and then asked me if I was still interested in a job - because a vacancy for a patrolman had just come up in South Devon area.

I told him I was and he then asked if I could come to the Exeter headquarters for an interview in the week.

....

So I went to the interview and they asked me about my time in Africa, and also about my faith. My faith had come up in conversation when they asked me why I had gone to Africa.

Ted and his area supervisor were both nice guys and we seemed to get on well. A couple of days later Ted phoned me up to tell me that the AA would like to offer me the job as an AA patrolman to start on April 2nd.

AMAZING!!

On April 2nd I would be sent to the Nottingham AA training college for two weeks and then come back to Torquay to work alongside another patrolman for a week. I could then take two weeks off to get married and go on our honeymoon.

AMAZING!!

Then when I got back from that I would have a few days with one of the patrolmen again before I was given a van of my own.

AMEN.

So God answered my prayer alright. **I was so excited.**

....

Alex and I were to both start our new jobs on April 2nd - one month before our wedding day of May 5th. Love it!

....

By the end of March, Alex left Taunton and drove her mustard-coloured Hillman Avenger saloon car down to Torquay. She was due to start her new job at Torbay Hospital a week later. A couple at St Matthias, called Phil and Jan, offered to let her stay in their house for a couple of weeks. Jan was also a midwife at the hospital.

That mustard Hillman Avenger died a few days after, so Alex was without a car. But a chap from St Matthias who worked in a car showroom told us about an immaculate white Hillman Avenger estate car that had just been brought into the showroom in part exchange for a new car.

The garage wanted to move it on quickly and offered it to us for a couple of hundred pounds. Although it was nearly twenty years old it had had only one owner and it was very well looked after.

We bought it.

....

On the same day that Alex started her job as a midwife I travelled up to Nottingham to do my AA training. It went well for both of us and while I was away Alex moved to another house in Torquay that was owned by a lady called Vanessa from our Church. It was good timing because Vanessa was able to help Alex with some problems she was having in her new responsibility as a midwife. It really was a Godsend because Alex really needed the support and prayer that Vanessa was able to give her at that crucial time in her new job.

I got back from the training and had learnt some good diagnostic skills in my time there. I passed the exams that I needed to pass and although still a bit nervous, I returned to Torquay much more confident in my mechanical ability.

I went on the road with one of the older patrolmen in the area and going to breakdowns with him gave me a clear picture of what the job was going to entail.

....

Next step: MARRIAGE!

....

Alex and I had been attending a marriage preparation course led by a couple called Alan and Donna. We used to drive to the vicarage in Plymtree (near Cullompton) where Alan was the vicar. Plymtree was where Alex's parents lived, so we were going to get married in the Parish Church there.

It was good to have some guidance before we got married but the tyres hit the road after the marriage day, as we were to find out - as many other people who get married discover too!

I won't bore you with all the details of the wedding 'cos I guess you have been to loads yourself and in many ways they are often all similar.

But I'll say a few things to set some kind of scene for ours.

I think about 150 people came. Alex comes from quite a big family. She has four older siblings, Elaine, Lorna, Hugh and Loll. So these names will briefly pop up in the next few pages.

Alex had three bridesmaids: Jenny (who is Lorna's daughter), and Sophie and Megan (who are Loll's daughters). They were all quite young at the time, and beautiful of course.

I had chosen my Dad to be my best man because I felt he knew me better than any other male human on the planet. Mum was thrilled to be in good health and able to help with some of the wedding arrangements. I had six ushers, most of whom are mentioned earlier in the book for one reason or another: Tony (Maltese), Danny (Biker), Charlie (Carpenter), Nigel (Lee Abbey), David (late night prayer mate) and a guy called John (teacher) who I haven't mentioned yet.

Alex's parents Bernard and Isabella were well known in the village of Plymtree so they and Loll (who also lived there with her husband Peter and family) did a lot to get things organised at that end. One of the main points of focus was the reception that was to be held in the local village hall.

Anyway, the day arrived and it was a very hot sunny May 5th. People have commented over the years how glorious the day was.

The old Church was jammed, some people had to stand if I remember rightly. Alex looked lovely in a vintage style fabric off-white dress. I'm not good with this type of lingo but it wasn't all ultra overdone and glossy modern.

Both of us read out verses from the bible that meant a lot to us;

Alex read:

John 15:1-5 New International Version (NIV)

Jesus said,

'I am the true vine, and my Father is the gardener.

He cuts off every branch in me that bears no fruit, while every branch that does bear fruit he prunes so that it will be even more fruitful.

You are already clean because of the word I have spoken to you.

Remain in me, as I also remain in you. No branch can bear fruit by itself; it must remain in the vine. Neither can you bear fruit unless you remain in me.

'I am the vine; you are the branches. If you remain in me and I in you, you will bear much fruit; apart from me you can do nothing.'

....

And I read:

Psalm 18 : 1-6, 16-19 New International Version (NIV)

1 I love you, Lord, my strength.

2 The Lord is my rock, my fortress and my deliverer;

my God is my rock, in whom I take refuge,

my shield and the strength of my salvation, my stronghold.

3 I called to the Lord, who is worthy of praise,

and I have been saved from my enemies.

4 The cords of death entangled me;

the torrents of destruction overwhelmed me.

5 The cords of the grave coiled around me;

the snares of death confronted me.

6 In my distress I called to the Lord;

I cried to my God for help.

From his temple he heard my voice;

my cry came before him, into his ears.

16 He reached down from on high and took hold of me;

he drew me out of deep waters.

17 He rescued me from my powerful enemy,

from my foes, who were too strong for me.

18 They confronted me in the day of my disaster,

but the Lord was my support.

19 He brought me out into a spacious place;

he rescued me because he delighted in me.

....

Alan the Vicar then spoke, then the final hymn was sung as we walked out husband and wife, church bells, confetti, photos, sunshine, laughter, then Alex and I disappeared over the horizon in Hugh's old 1955 black Ford Popular car.

We actually only went just over the hill to Plymtree village hall for the reception but you get the idea!

The hall floor was totally covered with chairs and neatly-laid tables with much wonderful decoration about the place.

Food was eaten, speeches given and during it all, many friends and family members of both Alex and I got to meet each other, most for the first time.

By the end of the afternoon I was totally exhausted mentally; so much more social interaction than I was used to and being part of the focus of people's attention for the day just wiped me out.

We needed to get to Wales for our first night of the honeymoon, so slowly we said our goodbye to everyone.

Then we really did disappear over the horizon. This time in our white Hillman Avenger estate car. It was nice to be alone and chat about all the events and conversations we had had during the day.

We arrived at the bed and breakfast place just before it got dark at the end of a very eventful and special day in our lives.

The next morning we set off to our real honeymoon destination which was Ireland. We made our way to Anglesey, an island on the north west coast of Wales. From there we caught the car ferry from Holyhead to Dublin.

Alex's sister Elaine was a nun in a convent in County Wicklow, south of Dublin, so it had been arranged that we could spend a couple of nights in a guest lodge there. Elaine and the other nuns were very pleased to have us both staying as guests and it was a good welcome to the country of Ireland.

We then set off west alongside the Wicklow Mountains and drove from there through the remote and beautiful interior of the land. The roads were in a bad state with plenty of potholes and cracks but it was all part of the experience for us.

These roads in Ireland have since been totally overhauled and bear no resemblance to when we travelled on them back in 1990.

We headed to the west coast region of Connemara in County Galway and stayed in various places on route. Then we headed south via Galway to the famous Cliffs of Moher that rise to 700 feet above the Atlantic Ocean. They look out to the Islands of Aran which are a few miles out to sea to the north west. This is where the famous Aran jumper or pullover got its name from.

From there we continued south along the west coast of Ireland, eventually reaching the Dingle Peninsula with its sandy beaches, craggy cliffs and rolling hills.

....

I might mention at this point that our honeymoon, although idyllic in many ways, was certainly not so in other ways.

We had discovered early on that our expectations of each other were not actually materialising. We had both apparently brought our own emotional baggage into the marriage and this honeymoon had highlighted the wounds from our past in quite an abrupt manner. It was a rude awakening. In some ways it was scary. Our rose-tinted spectacles were dramatically broken.

Sorry to spoil the picture of a perfect Christian marriage. Oh well, it was going to come out *sooner or later*. You might as well find out *sooner* - like we did!

Good thing was and is - we had God on our side.

It was still scary though.

....

Right... let's get back to the trip. That's a lot easier to deal with!

From the Dingle Peninsula we drove to the Killarney National park area and stayed around Lough Leane for a few days. Then continued to the south coast working our way round Ireland via Cork and Waterford, back eventually to Dublin.

We spent some time in Dublin and got to see Elaine again. After nearly two weeks away we got on the ferry back to Wales and from there drove the 300 miles back to Torquay.

....

When we were driving back through Devon, a Bible verse came in my thoughts concerning our accommodation. It was an interesting verse and seemed to convey a mentality of holding things loosely concerning future accommodation ideas:

Matthew 8:19-20 New International Version (NIV)

19 Then a teacher of the law came to him and said, 'Teacher, I will follow you wherever you go.'

20 Jesus replied, **'Foxes have dens and birds have nests, but the Son of Man has no place to lay his head.'**

Maybe it was going to be a long-term future mentality, we weren't sure but we both seemed to feel God was saying something to us.

....

You will be pleased to know that we had somewhere to live when we got back to Torquay. Not perfect for a newly married couple I know. But somewhere to lay our head.

It was of course the loft space that I had been sleeping in for a few months beforehand. OK it had no windows - but at least there was a ladder to get up there with!

Luxury!

Very soon after we got back we were straight into our new jobs again. The first few days back I was with another patrolman again until the van I was going to be given was ready. I was grateful for those days because they allowed me to acclimatise to my new working environment again.

Then came the day when I was taken up to the Sowton Depot near Exeter to be given my van and tools. I already had my AA uniform (very posh for a character such as myself - *but horses for courses*).

My first van was a Ford Escort. I spent some time getting my paperwork and tools organised and then it was back to Torquay to start the following day.

The next morning Alex and me prayed over the van and asked for God's protection and help for the day ahead. We asked Him to lead me to the right places, the right people, at exactly the right times.

I actually prayed that prayer at the start of every working day.

So then came the moment that I was given my first job. The details of where the next job would be were given to me via two way radio. The radio operator up in Bristol would read the details out over the radio set and I would write them down as quickly as I could on a piece of paper. I could speak to them via a small radio handset microphone affair.

I didn't find all the radio lingo easy if I'm honest but I always managed to get the details of the job eventually.

My first ever job was a car broken down in Dawlish Warren. It was in a holiday camp and had an overheating problem. I forget what type of car it was but I do remember being so pleased with myself when I diagnosed what the problem was.

I was rolling!

Onto the next job, then the next, travelling all over the place, meeting all sorts of different characters, mending all sorts of different vehicles. It was so exciting. I was an AA man!

After about a week of living in the loft, Alex and I went to see a flat in a large house in Torquay. The couple who owned it had moved to the area fairly recently. They wanted Christians to live in the flats there.

It was perfect for us and a few days later we put our minimal stuff in the car and drove the two miles to our new abode (with windows!).

There were a few flats in this big old house and another lovely couple called Justin and Liz had also just moved in. They also had recently got married.

Our flat was up a big wide staircase and the living room in the flat was a delight because it had a big bay window and had a panoramic view of Torquay harbour, the hills surrounding Torquay and the sea.

The house was on top of a hill, so the view was extra special and had me getting my binoculars out many a time.

Also there was a shared garden, which had a small lawn with flower beds and bushes. The property had its own drive and car park, which meant my AA van was hidden from the road and safe from thieves.

Plus it was in Chelston just 400 metres up the hill from where my parents lived in Goshen Rd. Don't worry - they weren't the interfering type of parents that keep popping round. But it was good to have them nearby, especially as Mum had been diagnosed with cancer the previous year.

When I was in Africa, my parents had started to go to St Matthias Church where I attended. They could see that the Church had helped me and was supporting me out in Uganda, so they felt they also wanted to be a part of it.

While I was away they joined Charlie and Dawn's homegroup and started to make friends, which I was really happy about because they had been quite isolated in many ways, especially now they were both recently retired and not mixing with people at work.

My brother Robert who had been living with them was about to move up to North Devon and join the... wait for it... Lee Abbey community!

This was such good news because things hadn't really been going well in his life up to that point.

....

July 9th - My **30th** birthday (bit of a land**Mark**)

....

Alex and I enjoyed our new home that summer and I was enjoying being out on the road with my job exploring corners of South Devon I had never seen before. Alex was delivering babies on the maternity ward and we were both finding our feet in our new careers. Both of us were also fully involved with life at St Matthias.

Around September my mum wrote an article in the St Matthias church magazine. Here is what she wrote:

Some Reflections On A Special Anniversary

Then Jesus said, 'Did I not tell you that if you believed, you would see the Glory of God.' (John 11 verse 40)

These are significant words for me as I contemplate the last twelve memorable months.

One year ago, I was told that I had cancer. Not a date to celebrate you may think. Certainly that first day I would have agreed. Thoughts and feelings fell over each other in chaotic confusion;

shock, anxiety, sadness for the family, and depression. I even mentally planned my funeral.

Finally I prayed.

*The following morning I sought inspiration from the day's verses in Daily Light (A daily devotional book for the year). There at the top of the page were the words, '**I am He that comforteth you.**' (Isaiah 55 :12)*

Amazing! A page of helpful and comforting Bible readings ending with the lovely quotation, 'God shall wipe away all tears from their eyes, and there shall be no more death, neither sorrow, nor crying, neither shall there be any more pain.' (Revelation 21 : 4)

At this moment I knew deep down that whatever the outcome, all would be well. God was with me.

Fellowship took on a different meaning. I remember with gratitude the love, compassion and support of my family and so many friends at St Matthias, many of whom only knew me as 'Mark's mum'.

Prayers and practical help; patience in listening to me when I needed to talk; encouragement from those who had already been through similar experiences; time given generously in the midst of busy lives.

Here indeed was the Spirit of God at work.

Then just at the right moment came an uplifting day at Brunel Manor, where we were reading and studying about the story of David and Goliath, and 'Giants' in general. The day ended with special prayers for healing and to strengthen me against my personal 'ogre'.

Perhaps this explains why, two days later as I went down to hospital theatre, I found myself mentally singing 'He who would valiant be'. (I didn't quite have the courage to sing it aloud!)

But the deepest spiritual experience of all happened, as often it does, at the worst time.

Before surgery was undertaken, I had to undergo intensive radiation treatment. This necessitated being connected to a large machine, isolated and virtually immobile for seventeen hours. After ten hours I began to get very restless and uncomfortable. It was midnight and the night seemed endless. I tried praying, remembering hymns, poetry (these usually work well at the dentist!) and finally fell to contemplating the lives of people of courage.

Suddenly in my mind's eye, came a picture of Jesus on the cross. But this time it was different. It seemed that I could actually feel the pain of those long hours of torment; I could sense the public isolation, the hostility of the crowd, the thirst that could not be satisfied. Such intense, unbearable suffering - and not on his own account, but for others... for me.

And here I was complaining about a few hours private discomfort, lying in a comfortable bed, with kind nurses watching over me and iced drinks for my refreshment. I wept, for Him, and for myself, and fell asleep.

When I awoke it was dawn and the nurses were preparing to release me from my healing instrument of torture.

As I staggered down the corridor to take a bath, the words from Psalm 30 came to me: 'Weeping may endure for a night, joy cometh in the morning.'

There have been other dark days, but much joy has certainly come to me this summer - a return to good health, Mark and Alex's wedding, Robert's joining the Lee Abbey community.

Above all, as I look back over the past months, it is the glimpses of the joy and glory of God's love that shines through.

The pain has receded into the shadows.

'O Lord my God, I will give Thanks unto Thee for ever.' (Psalm 30)

Amen.

....

Praise God. I think those words from my mum are special.

I hope they will also be special for some people who read this book.

....

To lighten the air a bit I will tell you of a little bit of good news I was having at work. You remember I was telling you about the AA van two way radio and how I got my jobs given to me through it. It was always a struggle for me to fully understand everything that was being said over the radio message, but there was rumours when I started the job that things would change later in the year and a new system was being introduced as part of our equipment.

Around October time that new equipment was given to us. And I loved it!

Each van was detailed with a 'Mobile Data Terminal'. It was basically a small digital screen that gave us: name of member, type of vehicle and colour, details of the vehicles location, and the problem that the member was having with the vehicle.

Of course nowadays this sort of technology is everywhere. But when I was doing that job, it was new.

I can't tell you how much this improved my enjoyment of the job. I was giving Thanks to God on a regular basis - I really was.

....

In November there were clouds gathering at home. They were obviously around before that but they came right over me in November.

Alex wanted us to go to 'Relate' marriage counselling. Relate is a charity that helps people with relationship problems.

There was no way I was going to go. Even bringing up the subject felt like rejection to me. Made me feel a total failure.

Alex needed more emotional connection from me. She needed more of me from me. I was not being a good, loving husband.

When I was in Africa before we were engaged, Alex prayed and asked God whether I was the man He wanted her to marry. She needed to know from God. Well what God said back to her was, 'You can marry Mark if you are going to love him and stick with him.'

Alex knew that I had my issues from being adopted and understood what God was implying. She obviously chose her yes but it was turning out differently than she had hoped. I was not giving her what she needed.

I can understand this better now than I could back then. We had only been married for six months at that point.

She was desperate and booked in to go to Relate on her own. Relate told her it was better if the husband came along too but she went for a few sessions on her own anyway.

There was a lot going on in our lives with one thing and another. It had been a full on year with a lot of changes for both of us. I think Alex's job was bringing up insecurities in her that had been hidden for years, namely confidence, and she needed my emotional contact and support.

I wasn't being horrible or anything but I was not meeting Alex's expectations or needs.

I could go on but maybe it makes sense to some of you and to others it doesn't.

Life went on - even though I found this observation of my life scary.

We were both struggling in our own different ways.

Please don't turn off from this here writer - due to my failings. We all have our story.

We didn't really tell people about that Relate episode - so you're quite privileged actually!

As is often the case, the passing of time brings with it a modicum of healing, and the same was true in our relationship. Life went on and with God's help things started to settle down.

1991

This winter was cold. There had been snow and it was cold but it was going to get colder.

But aside from the weather, here's a bit of good news that we found out near the end of January:

Alex was pregnant!

Obviously we were happy, as were our family and friends. Goes without saying really. Thank you Lord.

....

February was a very cold month and that impacted my job on the road. I am pretty sure it was February when a crazy week unfolded for me and many other AA patrolmen on duty at the time.

There were so many breakdowns. Obviously a lot of flat batteries or batteries that couldn't cope with the added load being put on them, but there was another dilemma out there that was causing more serious problems. It was becoming a regular occurrence to be attending vehicles that didn't have any antifreeze in the water system. The customers could not start their car and called the AA. I would get to the job, lift the bonnet and there before me was a sight I had never seen in my life before and I have spoken to older mechanics over the years who had never seen what I saw either.

For many of you, you will not know what an engine *core plug* is.

They are round discs of metal that are placed in various holes in the sides of engine blocks. The holes are there from when the engine block was cast and made in the factory.

The cooling water that moves around inside of the engine block is also sealed in by these core plugs.

But they serve for another purpose too.

If for any reason that water turns to ice, then the core plugs will pop out with the expansion of the ice... rather than the engine block cracking with the expansion.

So there I was. I had lifted the bonnet and the sight before me was of about six or more tubes of ice protruding from the sides of the engine. Each tube of ice was about 2 inches diameter and about 10 inches long, and at the very end of each one was a 2 inch diameter core plug.

It was such a crazy sight. And I was turning up at different people's houses and this was what I was confronted with. They couldn't start their car. The only thing that could be done was to tow them to a garage where heaters were on and leave them there for a couple of days until the ice had thawed out. Then the core plugs needed to be replaced to seal the holes in the side of the engine again.

Garages had loads of cars just thawing out in this way. To start the engine ahead of time would have damaged the engine totally.

So antifreeze is important.

The snow and ice that winter brought no end of problems that kept us patrolmen much in demand.

That cold winter was also felt by Alex and I in our new flat. The place only had a small gas heater in the sitting room at the front of the flat. Our bedroom at the back was always pretty cold. To give you an idea of how cold, we woke one morning to find a glass of water on the bedside table had turned to ice.

We invested in an electric double blanket. It was one that you could leave on when you were in bed. We used to love getting into that bed in the winter after buying that blanket. It was the warmest place in the flat!

In the early spring Alex had her 16 week scan and we saw the baby moving. It was in the days when telling the sex of the child was not as accurate as these days. We chose not to be told anyway. We wanted to find out on the day of the birth.

In May it was our first wedding anniversary. Both Alex and I worked early and late shifts, never through the night, but sometimes our shift patterns were such that we didn't see each other for big chunks of time. This didn't happen regularly but was part and parcel of our first year together.

Such circumstances didn't happen much after May that year because in June, Alex went onto maternity leave.

....

In the early hours of Sunday 8th September Alex awoke with pains. It was the first signs of labour. By midday the pains were sufficient for her to know that she needed to get to the hospital. I drove her there, being the nice husband that I am!

Hazel, the sister on the maternity ward (and Alex's boss), was really kind to Alex and looked after her and was her midwife.

About three hours later at 3.21pm our first child was born. It was a girl, and she weighed just under 7 pounds.

....

Alex was given her own private room afterwards, which was one of the privileges of being a midwife. It was a kind gesture and allowed Alex to rest well and be looked after for a few nights.

When we drove away from the hospital and looked up at the windows of the maternity ward, we both realised that '**we**' were responsible for this little baby and it was totally up to us from now on to look after her!

When we got back to our flat, we prayed to God, to give Him Thanks. It was at that point I burst out crying. God had made us family and somehow, to me, it felt a fuller life - maybe because I was adopted, and had never known blood family before.

After a day or two we named our daughter Esme and we also felt we wanted to give her the middle name of Rose too, because she was given some little baby slippers in the hospital with small roses on.

Esme Rose Wadie.

It was good to have Esme in our life.

Now we were three.

....

Later on in September I was given another present, which also thrilled me in a different way. This other present was yellow (and not because it was jaundiced!) and it weighed more than 7 pounds.

It was a new J reg, Austin Maestro AA van.

It was a real treat. I transferred my tools and parts from the old van to the new one, and I was off.

Everything was so plush. Thank you.

One important improvement was that it had a more powerful engine, so it towed vehicles better, and with all the hills around Torquay and South Devon - that was a big bonus!

Man - life was getting good.

On the road overlooking the River Dart

....

In November our new family went to Norfolk and had a short holiday with my relatives there. My grandparents were able to see their 'great granddaughter', which I think was a treat for them.

Also on the drive back we popped in to see my great auntie Gladys, who was Esme's 'great great aunt'. You can't get much greater than that! *Unless you really want to show off!*

Later in November St Matthias had a vision day. Many members of the Church got together and spent the day talking and praying about the way forward for the Church.

I had forgotten about this until Alex recently dug her journal out from that year and found she had written inside that I had shared these thoughts with the group:

I see St Matthias as a ship tied up to the harbour. Instead, we should be going out to sea, blown by the wind of the Holy Spirit - but no one is putting up the sails.

It is more like a pleasure boat.

....

It probably didn't go down too well with most people, but a man's gotta do what a man's gotta do. Some people there thought of me as like a John the Baptist. Making a noise and disturbing the status quo.

I didn't do it just for the sake of it. I was just hungry for more *life*.

....

In early December, Esme really giggled for the first time. Come on!

1992

I was sent to a breakdown in mid-January in the car park of Oldway Mansions in Paignton. Soon after fixing the car and seeing the owner of the car drive off, I noticed a couple walking through the car park and one of them seemed to be carrying a Bible, so I started chatting with them. They were with a Christian organisation called YWAM (Youth With a Mission), which I had heard lots about, over the years. I had always liked the idea of working with YWAM. I mentioned this to them and obviously, seeing that I was an AA man, they told me that YWAM was always looking for mechanics.

I told Alex when I got home later that day about meeting the couple. Both Alex and I knew that as an organisation YWAM were passionate about God and fulfilling His call on their lives, but we both felt that it was mainly for people in their teens and twenties.

The couple I met were called Mike and Teresa, and we were to bump into them again in the future.

In that same month my mum said to us that she would be willing to look after Esme if Alex went back to work part time.

So the following month Alex did indeed go back to work for two days a week. Sometimes my shift pattern allowed me to look after Esme when Alex was at work, but of course that didn't always happen so it was nice that my mum and dad could walk up to our place and spend some time with Esme.

Another good development was that we had moved to a ground floor flat at the house, which was bigger and also had its own private back garden with a lawn. It was a lovely garden with flower beds and even an apple tree in the middle of it for shade in the summer.

The flat itself was also ideal because it had a very small room next to the sitting room that we eventually put Esme's cot in. We had lost our view of the bay, but by being on the ground floor I could park my AA van right outside our kitchen and occasionally spend time getting things organised in the back of it when there was not a breakdown to go on.

All in all, we were grateful for a more convenient set up.

The large sitting room also facilitated a weekly prayer and bible study group that Alex and I led. It was one of the designated house groups that St Matthias offered people in our Church. There were about a dozen of us all together and we ended up making some close friends in that group - supporting each other in many ways.

As the year went on Alex and I went to various Christian conferences such as 'Spring Harvest', which we went to as a housegroup, and had so much fun together. Another big event that Alex and I attended was a music festival called 'Cross Rhythms'. It started off in Exeter that year, but moved up to a big farm near Okehampton in the following years. It was run over a long weekend in July each year and was run by a crew in Plymouth that had their own radio station called 'Cross Rhythms radio'.

It really was a breath of fresh air for Alex and I spiritually and it often ended up being the highlight of the year. Hundreds of people from all over the country would camp for 3 nights and listen to some amazing contemporary new Christian bands, plus some teaching and talks in other marquees around the site.

I remember that first time we went to 'Cross Rhythms' near Exeter and pushing Esme around in her pushchair to various gigs.

My favourite gig was Sal Solo, who was originally the lead singer of the 80s new romantic band 'Classix Nouveaux'.

I just let myself go in abandoned dance when he played some of the tracks from his new album at the time, 'Look at Christ', especially one track called Spirit.

Like I said, the festival ended up moving to a big farm near Okehampton. The farm was also a drug rehabilitation centre run by a Christian Charity. The event got bigger every year and artists from all over the world came and performed. It was a buzz, and also great for meeting so many like-minded Christians from around the globe.

Alex and I would often travel to different events and gatherings as we heard about exciting things going on elsewhere. We in no way confined ourselves to just events going on in our Church.

In fact, on a subject slightly related to that, we both agreed not to baptise Esme as a baby in the Church of England. We both felt that we didn't want to slot her into a denominational mould. If she ever wanted to commit her life to God when she grew up - then she could choose to get baptised herself.

But within the Church of England there was a service where we could *dedicate* Esme to God and give Thanks to God for her.

And that's what we did. We gave Thanks to God for His wonderful gift to us.

Also that year we went away to Port Isaac again for a few days. It had been two years since we were last there. On that visit we had fasted and asked God to lead us to the right jobs and accommodation.

We were well aware this time around that it was again a time to give Thanks to Him. He had answered our prayers amazingly.

....

Later in the year we went away again to a bothy in Wales, where we also felt drawn to fast for a few days.

We gave Esme food!

We wanted to commit our future to Him and really seek Him for all that He wanted to do in our lives. We didn't want to just settle for status quo Christianity.

1993

The New Year started off with a bit of drama. Esme had started walking by now but was still wobbly on her feet. After Church on the first Sunday of the month she was wandering about at the front and fell over and hit her forehead on the base of a wooden church pedestal. There was blood flowing out above her eyebrow and she was in a right state. I ran and picked her up and was also in a bit of a state. I rushed into the church centre where there were a couple of doctors having coffee after the service. They told me to take Esme to the hospital. Alex was working that day on the maternity ward - so I was on my own!

Someone gave me a lift there while I tried to comfort Esme and hold a cloth over her wound.

When I got to there, Alex came to the A and E wing of the hospital.

Esme had to go under general anaesthetic and had a few stitches to restore her beauty!

At the time it shook me up.

On the subject of Esme, I remember taking her out on country walks with the pushchair on days when I was off and Alex was at work. There was one occasion when walking on a footpath near Brixham, I felt an overwhelming sense of contentment and purpose as I pushed her along. I was a father and part of my purpose in life was to look after little Esme. It felt good. Life felt good.

The start of the new year also was an exciting time for the house group that met at our home every Tuesday evening. We had each decided to fast from food during the day, and have a meal together when we met in the evening.

All of us wanted more in our spiritual lives. We were hungry for more of God.

Jesus said:

10 The thief comes only to steal and kill and destroy; I have come that they may have life, and **have it to the full**.

John 10:10 New International Version (NIV)

We wanted more of the fullness that Jesus promised. And it was our way of saying to God that we didn't want to settle for just *tick over* Christianity.

Around March time, Alex was feeling frustrated with 'work' (midwifery). She was wanting 'more', spiritually.

I was also wanting 'more.'

I suspect that the fasting was waking us up and 'tuning us in' to our spiritual condition.

....

A couple from South Africa who had recently moved into a flat where we lived encouraged us about not moving on until the right time. They said that our recent marriage and family was like a new wooden boat. God would keep us in the harbour for a time - so that the *gentle* lapping of the water against our side would cause the wood to swell and seal all the joints in the hull.

Then God would lead us out of the harbour into the sea.

....

My job as a patrolman was still good, but things were changing. There had been cuts. More demands seemed to be circulating. Ted, my immediate boss (Patrol Inspector), had been moved on and was now just a patrolman like me, but over in East Devon. I really liked Ted as a boss and was sad not to have him around anymore. He was one of the people who had interviewed me and shown confidence in me two years earlier.

There were still good times out on the road though and my proficiency at the job was now high. The AA had had a few letters of commendation sent in from customers who were very pleased with my service.

I will briefly tell you about one such occasion. I was in Paignton attending to a breakdown on an Alfa Romeo car. It was a bit of a *classic* car actually and the owner had owned it for quite a number of years. It was obviously his pride and joy.

It was, for some reason, not starting (I forget why now), but after a short time I got it started. He was happy. But I wasn't totally satisfied.

I said, 'Wait a minute, it's not running on all four cylinders.'

He said, 'It sounds normal to me.'

I said, 'No, let me do some checks to find out which cylinder is not firing properly.'

I located which cylinder was the problem and, after some more checks, I replaced the HT lead (a lead which goes to the spark plug) on that cylinder with a new one I had in the back of my van.

When I started the engine up, I could tell the difference straight away.

I told him to take it for a blast up the nearby hill and come back and tell me what he thought.

As he accelerated up the hill I could hear it accelerating beautifully all the way up. I was happy.

He came back smiling lots.

He said, 'That's the best it has ever gone since I have owned it. I always suspected it should have run better than it has, but the various garages I have taken it to have not been able to improve its power. Now it is amazing.'

He was so happy. And so was I. So satisfying.

Anyway it so happened that he owned a commercial vineyard and wanted to send me some bottles of wine to say thank you. He also wrote to the AA commending my work.

There were also a lot of funny incidents as well. Here is one for you:

I was called to Totnes railway station. Someone had locked their keys in their car. I got to the vehicle in the car park and waited for the owner to turn up. After about ten minutes I decided to just proceed with the job while I was waiting. I could see the keys on the passenger seat. I then got my tools for unlocking locked cars. After a few minutes I unlocked it and opened the door.

I left the keys on the passenger seat, but now of course the car was unlocked.

I had just sat back in my van and the owner (a chap in his mid-twenties) arrived in the car park. He walked straight over to my van and apologised for keeping me waiting. I told him it was no problem.

I then walked towards his car, that was parked about twenty meters away. As he followed me he was saying how stupid he felt about locking his keys in his car.

And I said with a straight face, 'Don't worry, with this type of car I know an easy way to unlock it.'

I then walked up to the back of his car, bent down and hit the back bumper with the side of my fist three times.

I still kept a deadpan face, **knowing** that he was looking at me seriously and strangely.

I didn't look at him, but just said, 'It doesn't always work, but sometimes it does.'

I then walked round to the driver door and opened it.

He was aghast and said, 'How on earth did you do that?'

I said, 'It's good isn't it, but it doesn't always work!'

He then spluttered out, 'But...???'

Then I burst out laughing and told him the real story.

We both had a good laugh about it.

That tickled me for the rest of the day.

....

In early springtime, Alex and I came across Simon, who was the guy from St Matthias that I had met up with once a week in my first year as a Christian. I mentioned earlier in the book that he had done Bible studies with me (when I was new to it all).

Well he had got married to someone called Jill and moved away from Torquay. So it was good that Alex and I bumped into them when they were having a brief visit back to the bay.

As we talked, they told us that they were out in Turkey, working with an organisation called Youth With a Mission (YWAM)!

They were both a bit older than us and we said that we thought YWAM was for young people. But they told us that the organisation also wanted more mature people too. So that was an interesting fact to find out.

....

In the late springtime one Tuesday evening we had been speaking together in our house group about insecurity in our lives. I shared about often feeling emotionally empty and restless - that there seemed to be an aching loneliness deep inside of me.

At the end of the evening after all praying together, Vanessa (one of the house group members) said to me, 'Mark, I feel that one of the keys to your healing will be to search for your birth parents.'

Vanessa was a good friend of Alex and I, and we both trusted her discernment. The search for my birth parents ended up being a path I would soon start to tread.

I found out that in 1975 the law was changed - allowing people to obtain their original birth certificate and other records from around the time of birth.

After finding out about this change in the law I arranged to see a Devon county council adoption counsellor so that I could obtain a copy of my original birth certificate. The meeting went well and the lady told me that she would put in the application.

....

In late June we happened to notice that a ship owned by YWAM called the 'Anastasis' was going to be in Avonmouth Docks for a week. It was an opportunity for people to come on board the ship and see the work that YWAM was doing around the world.

We felt we needed to go up to the docks near Bristol and see if God was trying to get our attention.

On Saturday July 10th (the day after my birthday), Alex and I drove up to the open day.

The 159 metre long ship was originally an Italian cruise liner. It had been built in Malta in 1953.

In 1978, 'Youth with a mission' had bought it and converted it into a 40 bed hospital Mercy Ship, with: 3 operating rooms, a dental clinic, a laboratory, an X -ray unit and three cargo holds.

Originally called the *Victoria* - it was renamed the *Anastasis*.

It had accommodation for 420 crew. The crew were all Christians and were from all around the world, and the ship was continually travelling the globe and stopping in ports to minister free care to all sorts of people who would otherwise go without. There were many other strands to its ministry too.

As we were queueing up we bumped into Mike and Teresa, the couple I had met the previous year when I was working on a car breakdown in Paignton when they had been working with YWAM in Torquay. It was good to see them again and we remembered the chat we had had when I was with my AA van. They were visiting some of their friends who were on the ship.

We eventually got on board and started to meet some of the crew and talk to them about the work of YWAM.

We were told that to be part of YWAM people had to first attend a six month *discipleship training school (DTS)*. But they confirmed what Simon and Jill told us earlier in the year - that YWAM was also interested in older people (and even families) joining them.

They also told us that the DTS they ran on the ship was not suitable for families with small children because there were no creche facilities for that length of time. But we could send off to the YWAM headquarters in Harpenden for application forms if we were ever interested in attending a *discipleship training school.*

It was a very educational and exciting day for us both and we went away with much to think about.

We were going to spend the night at Alex's parents' in Plymtree and go back to Torquay on the Sunday afternoon. As we drove south along the M5 we chatted about the Christian life and different ways people choose to live it. We both wanted a more vital and alive faith in our lives. We felt that it might only be possible when we were really dependant on God, and that having comfy reliable careers could be minimising our dependence on Him.

The day on the Anastasis had really stirred us up in asking some big questions about our life and where it was going.

When we reached Plymtree, we put Esme to bed and I started reading a book I had started a few weeks before - I only had three chapters left to read but hadn't picked it up for a while.

The book was written by a lady called Melody Green and was called 'No Compromise'. It was a biography about the life of her husband Keith Green. Keith Green was a musician who died in a plane crash when he was 28. In his early twenties he had become a Christian after being involved with drugs and eastern mysticism.

He was a famous name in the Christian music scene in the late seventies and early eighties. He died in 1982.

As I was reading the final chapters of the book, Melody wrote of a time when she and Keith had gone to Europe and met Christians who were working with 'Youth With a Mission.' Then they were asked to go to the launch of a mercy ship called the 'Anastasis' in the Mediterranean Sea.

When they got there and started meeting some of the crew, they met a couple who had previously been very successful in the business world in America. But they had chosen to sacrifice that success and were now living in a very small cabin on board this new mercy ship.

Melody was writing about how that example of dependence on God had really impressed Keith and her.

As I was reading this I was gobsmacked that the words in this book corresponded so amazingly with the events of the day.

I excitedly showed Alex. Even our conversation on the M5 tied into what Melody had written. God was on our case.

The next morning Alex's dad Bernard encouraged us to go to the local Plymtree Church (where we had been married). Bernard had spent some of his life in the Merchant Navy as a Captain, so he had a love of the sea, and this particular Sunday was apparently 'Sea Sunday'. He was a bit involved with the service and asked us both if we could read out some Bible verses from the front.

There was a visiting preacher who stood up to give the sermon. He lived in Bath and was a chaplain to the armed forces there. I made an assumption that the sermon was going to be boring I'm afraid! Boy was I wrong on that one. I later repented of my judgemental attitude. He stood up and spoke about Peter, James and John, in the Bible. How they were fishermen and how they left their nets and everything they knew, to follow Jesus. Then he said, 'I don't know whether any of you are aware, but in Avonmouth docks right at this moment there is a ship called the Anastasis'. He then went on to tell people about what it does. Alex and I just looked at each other!

At the end of his sermon he came out with; '**I challenge you** - is God calling any of you to leave **your** nets, and follow Him? To leave your jobs or your own resources and trust Him?'

Well as you can see - it was all quite full on that weekend. No escape!

The following week we wrote off to the YWAM base in Harpenden for some, *discipleship training school* application forms.

A few days later they arrived in the post. They were long forms and wanted lots of information about us, which was ok, but they also wanted current references from our present employers.

Both of us didn't want our employers to know that we were thinking of moving on. We wanted to just explore the possibility - without upsetting the *apple cart*. So we decided to not go ahead and fill out the forms. Instead we put them in a drawer and filed them away, until a later date - maybe.

Around this time my grandad died (my mum's dad, who lived in Norfolk). He had definitely been my favourite grandad - being the one, when I was young, that used to take me out on trips in his Ford Anglia. We used to go fishing together and, like I mentioned in my first book, go and see Leicester City play at Filbert Street.

I sent some flowers to the funeral with the words: *In gratitude for exciting adventures with you, before I was old enough to discover my own. Love love love Mark.*

At the end of July I was privileged to be chosen to attend a conference in Nottingham for a week. It was called 'Springboard' and it was run by Revd Dr Michael Green who was a big name in the Church of England around the eighties. The evangelist J.John was one of the main speakers there too. The event was not a big affair, probably about forty participants, and about half a dozen famous speakers came and spoke with us during the week. I made some good connections with various people, and it really was an honour to be amongst a group of like-minded evangelists.

We were all asked to share something during the week and I felt drawn to share a poem I had written about different people's attitudes to Jesus;

For Those Who Have Ears.

Don't mention Jesus - I'm having too much fun.

Don't mention Jesus - I wanna stay number one.

Don't mention Jesus - It makes me wanna hide.

Don't mention Jesus - It stirs me up inside.

Don't mention Jesus - Yeah him and that cross.

Don't mention Jesus - How dare you say I'm lost!

Don't mention Jesus - It seems to halt my flow.

Don't mention Jesus - Then he might quickly go.

Don't mention Jesus - I've already been told.

Don't mention Jesus - What do you mean, my heart is cold?

Don't mention Jesus - Just leave me alone.

Don't mention Jesus - I wanna keep my throne.

Don't mention Jesus - Let me live a sham.

Don't mention Jesus - I'm happy as I am.

Don't need to mention Jesus - I go to church twice a week.

Don't need to mention Jesus - Why on earth let the truth leak?

Don't need to mention Jesus - Let's be nice and proper.

Don't need to mention Jesus - It's such a gossip stopper.

Don't need to mention Jesus - Let's not make a fuss.

Don't need to mention Jesus - And so say all of us.

Don't need to mention Jesus - I'm busy doing good.

Don't need to mention Jesus - What do you mean, it's just a hood?

Don't need to mention Jesus - I've put my £3 in the plate.

Don't need to mention Jesus - My tithe will have to wait.

Don't need to mention Jesus - Well, it's not very cool.

Don't need to mention Jesus - Besides, our church is fairly full.

Don't need to mention Jesus - No, that doesn't involve me.

Don't need to mention Jesus - Cos, my vicar smiles at me.

I will mention Jesus - He is the King of kings.

I will mention Jesus - My heart jumps and sings.

I will mention Jesus - I will not stop the fight.

I will mention Jesus - He turned my darkness into light.

I will mention Jesus - He came to set the captives free.

I will mention Jesus - He's here for you and me.

I will mention Jesus - He is the Father's Word.

I will mention Jesus - His name is to be heard.

I will mention Jesus - Oh, I was so lost!

I will mention Jesus - He paid the sacrificial cost.

I will mention Jesus - He's my Rock, and that's for sure.

I will mention Jesus - He's alive for evermore.

I will mention Jesus - With God's help I'll finish this race.

I will mention Jesus - Cos I'm gonna see him face to face.

....

In August my sister Julie flew out from Australia with her daughter Tegan (nearly 5 years old) to see us all. She had not been back to England for over ten years. While she was over here I told her that I loved her and we both ended up crying, which was a special time. I drove her up to Lee Abbey to see Robert, who was on the estate team. It was Robert's second time on the community. He had been there for a year and a half, then gone to horticultural college in East Devon for a year, and was now back again on the community.

The three siblings

Julie, although pleased to see us, didn't want any *God Stuff!* She was happy as she was, thank you very much.

We didn't see lots of her as it turned out because she wanted to hang out with old biker mates most of the time. It was the last time she was to see Mum alive.

In September, Alex and I went once a week to a minister called Roger near Salcombe and got some counselling. We both had some soul ties to break, from past intimate relationships we had had before we were Christians. Alex had some ministry concerning an abortion she had in that period of her life also. So it was all deep stuff. I had more ministry concerning my abandonment issues but at the end Roger said that it was going to be an ongoing slow and painful process of healing for me.

Also in September, the Devon county council adoption counsellor contacted me. She had received a copy of my original birth certificate. We made an appointment and I went to see her soon after. In her office she handed me the birth certificate.

There right in front of me was the name of my birth mother, and even her occupation and address back in July 1960.

I was born in the Queen Charlotte Hospital in Hammersmith.

Like I told you in my first book - she named me Colin. But of course my adopted parents renamed me Mark.

I won't divulge the full name of my birth mum to you because it is a bit of a tricky situation as you will find out, as the book progresses.

It was the start of a crazy journey.

The next step was for the adoption counsellor to locate the adoption agency that held my records. It was going take to few months before I would actually cast my eyes upon **them**!

Autumn came and went and we entered into the chillier temperatures of November.

It was then that we found out that Alex was pregnant again.

It was also in that month that a sense of pregnancy came upon us concerning a need for change. A lovely chap called Roy from St Matthias wanted to meet up with us to tell us some news. Roy and his wife Molly were a lot older than us, but they were good friends and were very alive in their faith and walk with God.

Roy wanted us to know first before other people knew, that he and Molly were going to leave St Matthias. They had become upset with the ethos and views of some the important people there. There had been a radio interview about an up-and-coming General Synod Meeting in London, and they had heard some things in the interview that made them feel the church was trying to reflect society too much. Which they felt it shouldn't. We both understood their concern - even agreed.

They were going to attend another church that they felt was not ashamed to speak out about what it stood for.

We were sad that our good friend Roy was leaving, but it shook us up, and like I mentioned earlier: a sense of pregnancy came upon us concerning a need for change.

On a Friday evening a few days later I went to a Pentecostal church in Newton Abbot where they were running a youth disco. My old friend Tony (Maltese) had taken his daughter to the event, so I had gone along to see him and some other friends of mine.

After the disco had finished he called me to one side and said, 'I want to say this carefully Mark, but I am concerned for you both. I feel it's time for you and Alex to move on, because I fear your spiritual health is at risk. To go where life is and where your light won't be snuffed out.'

He obviously spent longer talking to me about issues around the subject, but he was concerned about where we were at in life. By that he was meaning our church affiliation, which I understood but I was also hearing it from God in respect of *moving on* into something that was going to be totally new and different in our lives as Christians.

Two days later on the Sunday morning, Alex and I drove to that same Pentecostal church for their Sunday service. Earlier in the week our friends Kevin and Miranda who attended that church had invited us for Sunday lunch. So we thought, let's go to their church, seeing as we are going over there for lunch.

The pastor of the church was called Barry, and he spoke about Moses and Joshua. About how Moses was only able to take the people so far but Joshua took the people all the way (into the Promised Land). Which seemed quite relevant somehow to what we were feeling.

Then he started talking about something that really spoke deeply to us.

He began telling us about an incident in World War 2 where thousands of British soldiers were on the beaches of Dunkirk in northern France.

They were surrounded by German troops and had lost all their morale, their spirit to fight, their sense of hope, and were basically in a pitiful state.

They were stranded and stuck. They needed to be rescued. That was their only hope.

As Barry spoke about the state these soldiers were in, it resonated with how we felt spiritually in our lives.

We felt stranded in a lifeless situation. It's like our spirits were being denied the oxygen they needed to thrive and live as God intended.

We needed to be rescued.

That morning we cried out for God to lead us into life.

Afterwards when we were having lunch with Kevin and Miranda, we both spoke to them about the things that we believed God was starting to say to us. Kevin felt led to give me a book he had been reading by a guy called Philip Keller, called 'Predators in Our Pulpits'.

Over the following couple of days I read it, and many things were brought to my attention. Near the end of the book it spoke on the theme of sacrificing our career - to move on. Much like the disciples did when they moved on from everything they held dear, to follow Jesus.

The following day was Monday, and in the the evening after our respective shifts at work, we felt led to start pushing doors. (I am speaking figuratively!)

We decided to write letters to some Christian organisations that we felt were possible ways forward in our spiritual life. We prayed that God would open the right door.

We wrote letters to: Rev Roy Weaver and Decade Ministries, A Christian community in Guernsey, The Church Army and finally to a Bible College in Bristol.

After we had written those four letters, I went to the post box down the road and posted them.

Right. Done it. Over to you God.

When I got back to the flat, Alex said to me, 'I feel we still haven't done everything. We need to fill out those, 'Youth With a Mission' (YWAM) forms.

They were still in the drawer where we had put them four months earlier because it had stated that references from our present employers were needed!

So we laid them out on the table and started to fill them out. We only got to writing Alex's name at the top of one of them, when, all of a sudden, we could hear Esme being sick in her cot!

We stopped what we were doing and rushed into her little room. There was obviously something wrong with her. We brought her out of her cot and she was sick again. And again. Then Alex felt we should take her to the hospital because she remembered that Esme had fallen off a chair earlier in the day and bumped her head. She was concerned that Esme was maybe showing signs of concussion.

We went to the hospital and it was busy. While we were waiting, Alex and I talked about the strange occurrence of starting to fill out the YWAM forms, then this happening almost straight away.

At midnight we were still there and I needed to get back home because I had an early shift the next morning. The hospital did some checks and were not too concerned, but wanted Alex and Esme to stay there overnight, just to be on the safe side.

The next morning I got up early and spent some time praying to God before I started work.

I prayed something like, 'God, do you want us to carry on with those YWAM forms? Because if you don't - we can do without the hassle of filling them out.'

I also prayed, 'So if you don't give us another clue specifically about YWAM, we won't continue with the application.'

Over to you God.

Alex came back from the hospital later in the morning, after I had left for work. She had gone straight to bed because she had not got much sleep at the hospital in the night.

I came back home around lunchtime and was eating my sandwiches in the van outside our flat. I didn't want to go in the flat in case I disturbed Alex and Esme who were sleeping.

As I was out in the van, I was also chatting with one of the tenants in the big house.

Meanwhile, unbeknown to me - the phone in our flat was ringing.

As I was talking to the other tenant, Alex came out of the flat and started knocking on my passenger window. She then said, 'Mark, someone is on the phone and he wants to talk to you.'

I got out of my van to go into the flat and I said to Alex, 'Who is it?'

She replied, 'I dunno... he says he's from YWAM.'

I said, 'That's crazy - I don't know anyone from YWAM but it's strange because I prayed this morning that God would give me a clue if He wanted us to proceed with the YWAM application.'

I got to the phone and said, 'Hi, who's that?'

He said, 'It's Mike. We met in Paignton once with my wife Teresa and we also met you again a few months ago in Avonmouth when the *Anastasis* ship was docked there.'

He then proceeded to tell me that they were back living in Torquay and starting a family and needed to buy a car and was hoping that I could help him look at one he had found.

I had forgotten I had given him our phone number.

I confirmed that I could, but also told him that he had phoned at a very interesting time and asked if he and Teresa could come round for supper at our place the following evening.

It turned out that they were free and indeed came round the next evening.

As we were all eating and chatting together we explained what had been happening in our lives since we had last seen them. We told them that we had sent off for the YWAM application forms from the headquarters in Harpenden, but when we received them back in July we were put off because they required references from our present employers.

Then we told them how we had pulled them out of the drawer a couple of nights earlier, but had not been able to fill them out because Esme had been sick.

I then explained that I had prayed the next morning that if God wanted us to continue the application, could He please give us a clue concerning YWAM.

I then finished the story by obviously telling them the significance of Mike's phone call only a few hours after my prayer.

We showed them the forms we had been sent and they looked at them and immediately said, 'Oh, these aren't the forms you need. These are for the Harpenden base, which is more focused on relief and development work.'

They explained that the usual forms for the other bases are a lot less complicated and present employer references are not required.

Well that was some good news, and made us grateful we hadn't spent time and effort filling them out unnecessarily.

Then they suggested three other YWAM bases in the UK that ran a six month *discipleship training school (DTS).* They were;

1. Holmsted Manor in West Sussex.

2. Overtoun House near Glasgow.

3. Kings Lodge near Nuneaton, Warwickshire.

As we wrote the three places down, they both remembered that Kings

Lodge did a special DTS for people who were in their mid-thirties and above and that it also catered for families with children.

It was called a 'Crossroads DTS', for people who were at a *crossroads* in their life.

Having Mike and Teresa come round and explain more about YWAM that night really gave the momentum we both needed.

They suggested we phone a couple called Steve and Liz who used to lead YWAM discipleship training schools. They would give us any advice we needed, especially which base would be suitable for families who want to do a DTS.

After Mike and Teresa left, we chucked those original forms in the bin!

The next day we phoned Steve and Liz, but they were going away for a few weeks and could not meet us until December 2nd.

When I told Alex, she said, 'We can't wait that long - we need to keep this moving.'

As she left the flat to go to work I told her that I would phone the three YWAM bases that Mike and Teresa had told us about.

I phoned the first two and could get no answer or just an answerphone. Then I phoned Kings Lodge, in Warwickshire. A lady answered, and I proceeded to tell her that my wife and I were wanting to know more about the DTS that they ran there. We talked for a few minutes, and eventually she said, 'OK, I will send you application forms. What is your name and address?'

I said, 'My name is Mark Wadie.'

Then she shrieked, 'I knew it was!'

I said, 'Who are you?'

She said, 'It's Kathryn, who lived with Alex for 2 years in Taunton when she was doing her midwifery training, just before you got married. I was at your wedding!'

Then I knew exactly who it was. We were both buzzing. Kathryn, it transpired, was now working for YWAM at Kings Lodge.

After a few seconds I said, 'Kathryn - this is exciting!'

She replied, 'It is exciting - I **knew** God had more for you and Alex.'

We chatted for a while longer and Kathryn mentioned that, as yet they did not have anyone to run a creche for the next years Crossroads DTS. I said, 'Well, that's going to be a problem for

Alex and I then, because we will obviously need Esme to be taken care of while we are in the classes.'

Kathryn pointed out that if God wanted us to do a DTS at Kings Lodge, then He would sort everything out. Which of course made sense!

She told me that she would talk to the base leaders there and tell them about us, and see what happened.

When Alex got back from work that day, I told her about Kathryn, working at Kings Lodge. We were both excited by how God seemed to be revealing the way forward.

I might mention here that the letters that we had written to the other four organisations didn't seem to have brought about any real developments that really made us want to pursue them any further.

A few days after my chat with Kathryn, an official letter arrived from the King's Lodge. It informed us that there was a choice of two *'Crossroads discipleship training schools'* the following year (1994).

One started on January 13th, and the other on September 22nd. They also mentioned that they still had no one to run children's cover for families with small children.

At this point I thought I should phone the other two YWAM bases in Sussex and Scotland to enquire about their Crossroad DTS. My enquiries resulted in finding out that they had no facilities for families.

Well that was nice and clear!

After a few days, Alex and I began to feel quite disheartened. We still hadn't been sent any application forms from Kings Lodge and they had no child cover as yet for Esme anyway.

Things had seemed to have got hazy and come to a halt. We didn't really know how to proceed. We needed help.

I decided to start fasting. We needed to get more guidance from God as to what to do.

The next day I was sitting in our flat on a day off, and I got to thinking of the two different DTS dates that Kings Lodge had informed us about. It occurred to me that the September 22nd date might not be good for us anyway because our next baby was due in June - so it wouldn't really be easy for Alex to study in class and be having a three month old baby to look after at the same time.

With this thought in my mind, I shouted out to Alex to have a chat with her. She told me she was just about to hang some washing out on the line, and would be there in a few minutes.

While she was in the garden I said to God, 'Lord it would be good if you could make things clearer.' Then I thought to myself, it would be good to get a `God-incidental' phone call - like when Mike (from YWAM) phoned out of the blue. Then I thought - it would be *really good* if the phone just rang and it was Kathryn.

And after about thirty seconds the phone rang! And it was Kathryn!!!

I told her that I was just thinking, it would be so good if Kathryn phoned, and that we had been quite disheartened and did not know what to do.

She then gave me the reason of why she was phoning.

She had just come out of a prayer meeting with the leaders of Kings Lodge, and they had been praying about the DTS that was due to start on January 13th. Only seven people so far had signed up for that school and they needed at least a few more to make it viable.

Then they had prayed about us, and they had felt that the school starting in September would not be suitable, because our new baby would only be a few months old and that would not be conducive to Alex studying in class.

I said, 'That's crazy, because I was having that very thought going on in my mind, just before you phoned! But that means January and that's only a month away, plus, there is no one there to look after children.'

She told me that they were going to write to someone they had thought of, to see if she would be willing to come to Kings Lodge and look after children during classes. I also mentioned that we had not been sent any application forms. She told me that she would make sure to get some in the post as soon as possible.

The next day the forms arrived. We stayed up until midnight filling in the forms and sticking little photos of ourselves on the space provided. We also wrote down the names of some friends that would give a reference.

The forms were not as complicated as the ones that we had been sent before from the other YWAM base, which was good, and they didn't require references from our present employers.

Things were getting easier - the haze was clearing and the momentum had started up again.

It was November 26th and we were aware that if God was leading us to go in January, that we needed things to happen quickly because we both had to give a month's notice to our employers. That would mean by December 6th, because we also needed a week off before the school started so that we could empty our flat out, get ourselves organised and pack the car with the remainder of our possessions.

We posted the forms off the next morning and made sure that our referees would send a reference off as soon as they heard from Kings Lodge. Also on that very same day I bumped into our

Doctor in the street with his wife. I warned him that he would soon get a letter, asking for a reference for us both, and asked him to please reply quickly. They were both Christians and Rachel the wife had once been with YWAM. When I told them we had applied to YWAM, she said, 'Oh David, do make sure you get that reference sent off quickly.'

Little things like this were happening all the time. The ball was really shifting along!

But not everyone was fully behind us when we told them. My dad said, 'Well if you ask me - you're a bloody fool.' He thought that it was stupid to give up our careers and security. Mum also told me later that he was upset that he wasn't going to see Esme as much if we went away. He had let his heart get soft to her and now we were taking her off.

Also, Alex's mum was not happy about it all. She felt it was not good because my mum still had cancer and was struggling. Also the fact that we were about to have another child soon did not put her on the side of what we were doing.

And when we told our vicar that we had applied to YWAM near Nuneaton, he was not happy either. He wanted to meet with us to discuss it. Kings Lodge would be needing a reference from him, so for him to not be behind us was a bit concerning.

A day or so after these discouragements we read something that really encouraged us. During the year we had both been reading a *'Through the Bible in a year'* study book - which entailed reading the whole Bible through completely in one year, and attached to it were study notes. Well at the end of November we had reached Daniel, in the Old Testament.

The study notes for the chapters we were reading said this: **Like Daniel, we need to avoid letting others influence our response to God's call or urgings in our life.**

Well, reading that really strengthened us to have confidence in how we felt God was leading us.

The curate in our church at that time was called Philip. He and his wife were good friends to Alex and I, and have even kept in contact to this day. Philip had encouraged us to meet with Peter our vicar and listen to his concerns, and also share with him how we had both felt led over the last few months.

On Wednesday December 1st, we met up with Peter. At the start of the meeting he informed us that he had a meeting the following day, so the earliest he could write a reference and send it off to Kings Lodge was on the Friday.

This was concerning because on the Monday (Dec 6th) we needed to give our employers one month's notice - if we were going to leave our jobs on January 6th.

But anyway, it was out of our hands!

As the meeting progressed Peter told us the doubts he had about us leaving our jobs, our accommodation, and my mum. As he was talking he suddenly remembered how God had told him to quickly leave his secure job and go forward for ordination. This had obviously happened many years ago, but the thought dropped in his mind as he was speaking. After he had finished telling us why he was not happy about what we were doing, he said, 'OK, I've finished - now you tell me what you have to say.'

After we told him how we had felt led over the last few months, the three of us concluded with praying to God.

As we were in prayer Peter said, 'I keep getting the words from that song: Lord the light of your love is shining.'

After we had finished praying and we were on our way out, Peter told us he felt he should cancel the meeting that he'd arranged for the next day (Thursday). Instead he would write our references out and get them sent off to Kings Lodge - rather than wait till Friday.

Bless him. It ended up being a precious time together.

Later in the day we went back to our flat because Philip, the curate, wanted to meet up with us and find out about what had been happening over the previous weeks.

While we were chatting with Philip the phone rang. It was a lady called Dorothy from Kings Lodge - they had all our references apart from the one from our vicar.

I told her that, *hot off the press*, was the news that he would be sending it to them tomorrow!

The following day was Thursday December 2nd. It was the day that we had arranged to meet Steve and Liz, the couple who had led discipleship training schools before they moved to Torquay.

We felt that we didn't really need to talk to them now, because we had found out a lot since we spoke to them on the phone a few weeks before - but we kept the appointment anyway.

And it was a blessing that we did. They told us that when they first joined YWAM and had to go on a DTS, Liz was pregnant with their second child. The birth was due right at the end of the five month long school.

It was exactly the same situation that Alex and I were in. If we ended up going to Kings Lodge and starting the school on the 13th January - the birth of our second child was going to occur just as the five month DTS finished, in mid-June.

They also told us not to worry if people thought we were nuts leaving our jobs and security, to go to a missionary training college that was going to be costing us money. Because people thought they were cranks also!

The next day was Friday 3rd December and I was on a late shift that started at 3pm.

In the morning Dorothy from the Kings Lodge phoned to tell me that they had received our vicar's reference. She wanted to chat about a few things, one of which was our vicar's concern that we were leaving our place of security and stability.

I responded with, 'Well, when does anyone start this stepping out in faith? The longer someone leaves it, the more inclined they are to become anchored in their *own* security.'

She asked me other questions, and at the end, told me she would phone in the evening to let us know their decision.

During my late shift later that day, I was sent to a lady who was locked out of her car in Newton Abbot. In conversation she told me about her son who had some problems, and other tough things going on in her life. As I listened and offered sympathy and understanding, she said something to me that spoke into my life. It was yet another clue that God was leading me on, into something new.

She said, 'You're too nice to be an AA man.'

She was meaning that there was more to my character and giftings than just fixing cars.

Somehow I just knew at that point - Alex and I were soon going to be on the move.

After getting the car door open, the lady went on her way. It was now time for my lunch break, so I drove to a friend who lived in Newton Abbot, to eat my sandwiches. While I was there I phoned Alex, because it was about 8pm and I guessed that she would have had a phone call from Kings Lodge. Sure enough - she had. She said tearfully, 'Mark, we've been accepted.'

It was a special moment, and also very exciting.

Life was going to change!

At the weekend we started to tell our friends, and on Monday (6th December), we gave our employers a month's notice.

My AA Inspector told me that he would have liked me to stay, but knowing that I was sure in my decision, said, 'Mark, I think you've found what you've been looking for!'

....

Earlier in the book, I mentioned that I had six ushers at our wedding - one of whom was a teacher called John.

John used teach at the Torquay College, but was also drummer at Upton Vale Baptist Church. He had now left his job as a teacher and gone off with YWAM to be the drummer in the outreach band on board - wait for it...... the 'Anastasis' ship.

The band, alongside drama and dance performers, would set up their presentations at locations around the world whenever the ship harboured.

I wanted to somehow let John know that we were also going to join YWAM. (Remember, that this is before internet and mobile phones were the norm). I had heard that he was dating a girl called Sue, who apparently was lodging with some people we knew in Torquay. If we could meet Sue, then she would know how to get in contact with John. So Alex and I went round to the house where she was staying and managed to meet up with her.

It turned out that Sue also was about to leave Torquay. She was going to do a 'discipleship training school' with YWAM that started in January! *But she was doing hers at the Harpenden base.*

We had a right blast of stories to share with each other. And it was a blast!

We told her about how God had been leading us through the year to leave our jobs and apply to YWAM. We reached the part where a few weeks before we had gone to the Newton Abbot Pentecostal church. We explained how we had felt stuck in our lives and needed God to say something. Then we told her that the sermon was about the British soldiers in World War 2 being stuck on Dunkirk beach and needing to be rescued. We explained how it had really spoke to us and that our prayer afterwards was that God would rescue us, and give us hope.

At that point she stopped us and said, 'Do you know where John proposed to me recently ?'

'No,' we said.

She then said, 'He proposed to me on Dunkirk beach!'

Amazed, we then asked her why they had even been on Dunkirk beach in the first place.

Sue replied, 'Because the 'Anastasis' docked there and John invited me to visit for a couple of days seeing that it was near to England. Then he proposed to me on Dunkirk beach!'

....

Alex and I were taken aback by all the corresponding imagery in these stories.

I hope you can see how these stories collide into a skillful masterpiece from God.

And to finish it off - Anastasis is a Greek word. In English it refers to;

1. *A recovery from a debilitating condition.*

2. *Rebirth.*

3. *Resurrection.*

COME ON!

....

Nearing the time we were to leave, my mum told me that she had written a list of *fors and againsts*, concerning our decision to leave. She said she had looked at all the reasons *against* leaving but they had paled into insignificance compared to the reasons *for*.

....

To the mentality and logic of many, what we were doing may have seemed foolish. A bit like Peter getting out of the safety of his boat and trying to walk on water!

He only did it though because Jesus called him out of the boat. So he stepped out of it, in faith.

What he did was a lot braver than what we were doing but to us also, we were stepping out in faith.

....

Mum also told me that the Doctor had warned her she probably only had about two years left to live. She proceeded to tell me the hymns and Bible reading she would like at her funeral.

I wrote them down at the front of my Bible, so that I wouldn't forget.

1994

We had both been in our jobs for nearly four years and they came to an end in the first week of the new year. We now had one week in which to get ourselves organised before driving up to Nuneaton on January 13th.

....

Please excuse me if I talk in pictures for a bit, which is what I like doing!

Alex and I felt that leaving Torquay and going off to YWAM was like us leaving the safety of the harbour and travelling to a big ship a few miles out to sea.

Let's call that big ship figuratively: YWAM.

Once onboard, we were going to complete a discipleship training school. That ship was not going to travel anywhere as such, but would be floating out there in the ocean.

Then after five months of that school, we hoped and believed that God would reveal his mainland of calling to us (where to go next).

Basically we needed to *move out* into step one, and only after that was completed would step two be made known to us.

....

After saying our goodbyes to people we knew and handing the keys to our flat back to the landlord, we started up our laden Hillman Avenger and set off into the new adventure ahead of us.

Esme who was now two years old, sitting in the child seat behind us and our other child sitting in Alex's womb.

As we drove north, Alex and I felt so good that we had actually done it, and left Torquay. We had stepped out. We were so excited about what God was going to do in our lives.

This excitement on the arrival at Kings Lodge was doused with water a bit when we met a couple of the main leaders and after a few seconds of introduction were greeted with the words, 'Well first things first - let's sort the fees out.'

It was obviously something that needed to be done but it was a shame it was asked of us, minutes after we arrived. The excitement of our adventure was brought down to earth very quickly, and to be honest left a bad taste in my mouth.

We wrote out a cheque for a few thousand pounds and were shown to our room. As the day rolled on we slowly started to meet the other students that were arriving. There were people from Australia, Canada, Egypt, Czech Republic, France, Wales and England.

In all there were roughly twenty students, which included about four children. There were about a dozen staff that were helping lead the school. They came from Scotland, Canada, South Korea, Denmark, USA and England.

Kings Lodge was a large historic building, built in 1886. It was set in a few acres of countryside and had been taken over by YWAM in 1984.

Alex and I were allocated a good sized bedroom that was in the roof and had a dorma type window that looked south west over a large lawn, the A5 main road, some fields beyond and the horizon beyond that. The room was easily big enough for us to set up a cot for Esme. This was our new home.

We had the weekend to all settle in and get to know our way round the place. The lecture phase was to start on the Monday, when a speaker from USA was going to come and speak to us about missionary work around the world.

After a couple of weeks we were getting into the swing of being students. Most of us had not been in a classroom setting for many years and it was it not natural to take in so much information every day. We had to write and journal what we learnt in each session and I found it quite demanding. It would leave me tired at the end of the day. It was a similar experience for others in the class too but they could rest more easily than Alex and I because they didn't have a small child to look after. There were two women in the class that had children, but theirs were nearer secondary school age and more independent.

One Sunday morning in early February, a few of us drove to a big church in Bedworth, about six miles away. At the end of the service, people were invited to the front to be prayed for. The talk had resonated with me and I went to the front of the church to get someone to pray for me.

A guy came and introduced himself to me and, after asking my name and where I was from, started to pray for me.

After a few minutes he said this:

God is saying that you are like an apple tree. His fruit is being prepared in you. The blossom on your life will slowly be blown off this year, as the wind of His Spirit comes across your life. It will hurt a bit - but not much. He is pleased with your maturing and you are favoured. His peace is on you. Be patient and wait.

It didn't make sense at the time, especially the bit about blossom getting blown off, and I didn't like the sound of it hurting either.

But as you will see, it's what ended up happening.

....

Within the first month of the Crossroads DTS, I was getting quite confused with some of the teaching and ministry at Kings Lodge.

There had been a particular speaker one week who was teaching about the 'Father Heart' of God. I had asked to meet with the speaker one afternoon to get some ministry/counselling. I was feeling that because of my adoption and the sense of abandonment that came with it, I tended to hold back from receiving love.

Well, I saw this guy and explained to him what I felt. But he had picked up in the class that I was not being responsible with my relationship with God. He had quite a hard go at me and because I was feeling vulnerable and not sure of myself, I swallowed everything he said. It ended up really rocking my boat and made me feel unsure of who I was.

But also it could be said that some blossom was getting blown off me.

Well, there was certainly a lot more of that to come as the year went on.

....

In March, I was called to the Kings Lodge reception desk. There was a phone call for me from Torquay social services. The adoption counsellor had located the adoption agency that held my records and now had them in Torquay. She was prepared to fax them to me and also send the original documents in the post. She informed me that within the paperwork was also a handwritten letter from my birth mum!

The faxed paperwork came through to the office at Kings Lodge and was given to me that same day.

BUT, when I had it all in my hands, I was not able to look at any of it!

Emotionally, I needed to find a very secluded space. Safe and totally on my own.

Do you know where I looked at that stuff?

Late in the evening when most people were in bed, I went to a large wardrobe that was used for dressing up clothes. It was in a quiet part of the building and in a room that wasn't frequently used. I went to the back of that wardrobe box room, hid away, curled up with a torch and my personal paperwork from 1960.

It was strange how I could not look at this stuff until I was totally hidden, and no one knowing where I was. I needed to be safe!

I slowly worked through the pages...

My birth father's name was Stephen Stylianou and he was a Greek Cypriot living around the London area.

My birth mother was called Gwynne and was also living around the same area. She was Welsh and had a typical Welsh surname (that I can't disclose).

They were both about 24 when they met. They saw each other regularly for only about two months, ending it seems with the act that led to my conception in October 1959.

When my father was informed of the pregnancy by a third person, he wanted nothing to do with it.

Gwynne hid her pregnancy from her mother (her father had died when she was very young) and left her home in February when she was a few months pregnant. She went to stay in a girl's home in London somewhere and then moved to a mother and baby home near Wimbledon in mid-June. On July 9th she travelled a few miles north to the hospital in Hammersmith.

And I came out!

Hi everyone.

I was named Colin.

She stayed in the hospital for over a week and then returned to the mother and baby home near Wimbledon.

Then, on August 5th 1960, she left me there, and disappeared over the horizon.

It doesn't actually say 'disappeared over the horizon' in the paperwork though!

There were many other bits of information in the paperwork but I won't spill it all out in the book - but I will share a very special bit.

In amongst the papers was a handwritten letter from my birth mum. It wasn't actually written *to* me.

BUT, one part of it was *about* me. It was written ten months after my birth in response to being told that her son was now the the lawful son of his adopters.

It was the final correspondence from Gwynne, to the National Children Adoption Agency.

It reads:

Dear Mrs P...

Thank you very much for your letter, concerning Colin. I am very pleased that he is with such nice parents and he is getting on so well.

I am sure that he will be able to grow up like any other boy, now that he has both a legal Mother and Father. They will be able to do so much more for him than I could.

Thank you very much for helping me. I did appreciate it, although I just couldn't write to you as it made me cry to think of Colin, in fact it still does.

I am now in a good job and have made new friends and new interests.

Thank you again for your letter.

Yours Sincerely

Gwynne ......

....

So here I was, nearly 34 years later, curled up at the back of a wardrobe near Nuneaton - catching up on some old news. Funny old world isn't it?

1994 was becoming quite a year, with bits of blossom getting blown off all sorts of limbs.

A few days later Kathryn, who was on the staff at Kings Lodge said, 'Did I ever tell you the picture God gave to me for you Mark?'

I said, 'No.'

She said, 'It was of a sword and a feather and I felt God is cutting into your wound like a very sharp sword - but He will be as gentle as a feather. The work will be as delicate and precise as micro-surgery. He will carefully and skillfully get to the root of your hurt and extract it out. He is doing, and will continue to do, a perfect work.'

On a practical level, the next step after our DTS finished at the end of May was getting explored. There were discussions about us staying on at Kings Lodge after the birth of our second child in June. A YWAM vehicle workshop was needed for the Midlands area and it was something that seemed suitable for me to be involved with.

....

At the end of March the lecture phase of the school was ending and the outreach phase was soon to begin.

The speaker for the last lecture days was a guy called Johnny Buckner from Mississippi in America. He came with his wife and their four young sons. His talks were titled, 'Be a healing person in a hurting world.'

I really liked Johnny and he liked me too. He said I reminded him of his best friend back in America and also told me I have the gifts of mercy and sensitivity.

His whole approach was gentle and encouraging, which helped me to engage better with the teaching. It was my favourite part of the whole lecture phase.

By early April, we were all getting ready for the outreach phase.

The next two months were going to be spent abroad, with some of the students going to India, others to Africa and a smaller group to Poland.

Because Alex was seven months pregnant and couldn't go on an aeroplane - we were in the group going by road to Poland. It was a thousand mile long trip and would take three days to reach our destination.

We would leave the group after one month and come back to England for the birth.

On Tuesday April 5th at 5am in the morning our group got in a Ford Transit van and headed off towards Poland.

There were eight of us including Esme and our first destination was Harwich on the east coast of Essex. We then got on a ferry across the North Sea to the Hook of Holland and from there we drove east through Holland, staying the night with a family who was known by the leaders.

The next day we continued on the long trek eastwards until we reached Leipzig in the east of Germany. We stayed the night in Leipzig and in the morning we visited the 'Monument to the Battle of Nations', which was built in 1913 to commemorate Napoleon's defeat at the Battle of Leipzig a hundred years earlier.

The monument was often used as a venue by Hitler for his big rallies in the 1930's before the Second World War.

We drove east from Leipzig, passing through Dresden, and eventually reaching the Polish border. Once in Poland we still had two hundred miles left to travel before reaching our destination of Gliwice.

The journey had taken three whole days. The trip had been pretty tense as well. This was mainly due to our leader who was driving. He was a retired headmaster from the west coast of America. It is sometimes the case that people from the teaching profession can carry their ways of dealing with children into their relationships with adults.

Well, this guy was a headmaster and he liked to control things pretty tightly. His heart was in the right place but his leadership skills didn't give you much room to breath. It was becoming quite an issue, because it's good to breath now and then!

Even toilet stops were prohibited unless someone was desperate!

So it was good to get out of that van and into a different environment. Alex had done well being pregnant and cooped up in a mini-bus seat for three days. I think toilet stops were taken into consideration for Alex. Esme also really did well seeing as she was not even three years old.

Gliwice was an industrial city about fifteen miles west of Katowice.

We were there to support the local churches that had a link with YWAM and had invited us to Poland. As well as working with the local charismatic Catholic church, we also partnered with the Methodist church and the Pentecostal church.

We spoke at a variety of other venues too, including schools, prisons, town squares and private homes. We met people from all walks of life and even made some good friends. A lot of the time when we spoke to larger groups of people we needed interpreters but that was all organised beforehand.

The tension in our group continued on a daily basis and occasionally broke through the surface when things got too tight. Unfortunately it was nearly always to do with the leader's controlling issues. One woman in the group who was quite a bit older than us was really struggling with it all but she wasn't the only one who found it difficult.

I was glad that Alex and I were leaving to go back to England after a month. The others were there until June.

There were some really good times together as well though. We did such a variety of things. One day we went to Krakow, which is a beautiful city seventy miles east of Gliwice and not far from the Czech Republic border.

The main medieval market square there is one of the largest in Europe and dates back to the 13th century. Krakow definitely had more to offer as far as impressive buildings were concerned - even if I did only have Gliwice to compare it with!

We stayed the night there and travelled back to Gliwice the next day. It was a good break from the packed programme we had had for the past few weeks.

In one way, it would have been nice to stay in Poland longer because we were meeting some good friendly Christians who were really pleased to have us around, but without the freedom of our own timetable to meet up with them, it wasn't so enjoyable.

So leaving the group was not such a wrench. To be honest, it was a relief.

On May 6th, the day after our 4th wedding anniversary, Alex, me and Esme were taken to the local coach station. The team from Kings Lodge and a few of our newly-made Polish friends waved goodbye to us as we left for England. It was going to be a thirty hour coach trip!

And it got worse.

About an hour into the trip, a Polish football team got onboard. They were going all the way to London and they were getting drunk. They kept drinking through the night and got rowdier. It was very intimidating and they didn't care about disturbing their fellow English passengers, even if one was eight months pregnant and another was a little three year old girl. I had to be wise in how I responded to it all. It was a very difficult situation and it went on for many hours. Sleep was out of the question.

I tried praying but I was at a pretty low ebb after the last few months of trials. This last ordeal was about to finish me off.

Where are you God?

....

We eventually arrived back in London and from there, the three of us got on a bus to the Midlands. When we finally reached the Kings Lodge, we were emotionally and physically exhausted.

Alex and I had our outreach debrief talk with the two main leaders of the DTS and highlighted the difficulties there had been with the leadership of the team. They didn't really want to hear that sort of view of things but they heard it some more a month later when the whole team returned.

....

We never got to see the whole team again as it turned out because we ended up only staying at Kings Lodge a few more days.

....

Earlier in the book I explained to you the way I pictured the way our lives were going, as we left Torquay.

Here it is again, for reference:

Alex and I felt that leaving Torquay and going off to YWAM was like us leaving the safety of the harbour, and travelling to a big ship a few miles out to sea.

Let's call that big ship figuratively: YWAM.

Once on board - we were going to complete a discipleship training school. That ship was not going to travel anywhere as such, but would be floating out there in the ocean.

Then after five months of that school, we hoped and believed that God would reveal his mainland of calling to us (where to go next).

Basically we needed to move out into step one, and only after that was completed, would step two be made known to us.

....

We had moved out into *step one* okay but *step two* wasn't looking like I had expected it too.

Let me explain, using the same imagery, how I felt - four months later!

We had got onboard the *'big ship of YWAM'* (figuratively speaking) and soon began to feel *seasick*!

The 'discipleship training school' was *swilling* me about all over the place and as I became emotionally *unstable on my feet*, confusion also set in.

The confusion went deep and made me question why God would treat me in such a way - when I had stepped out in faith, to serve HIM.

The outreach phase in Poland had finished me off.

I was well and truly *seasick*.

I didn't want to stay on this *ship* any longer.

I wanted off.

I didn't even want to do anything for God actually.

I didn't have any desire to go to any *mainland* of calling (missionary work abroad).

I was hurt, disillusioned and angry. Angry at God.

I also couldn't face going back to the *harbour* - which was Torquay. I wasn't robust enough to face people who couldn't see why we were leaving in the first place.

But we needed somewhere to live because Alex was pregnant and due in the next few weeks!

It was then, that an idea came to me.

I phoned a couple I knew, who lived in Bath. Their names were Tim and Anna. Anna had been on the Lee Abbey community with us. She had worked in the kitchen with Alex. After leaving community she had met Tim and they got married.

Tim and me had been on the phone together back in January. He had said how exciting the news of Alex and I joining YWAM was. I had told him it was because we didn't have anywhere to live after it had finished.

He then said, 'Yes you will.'

I said, 'No we won't - we are leaving our flat in Torquay.'

He said, 'Yes but you will still have somewhere to live.'

I said, 'What do you mean??'

He said, 'You can come and live with us. If you ever get stuck, our house is here for you.'

I thanked him for his love. I knew he was being very sincere.

But I didn't think of it again.

Until that day in early May. It just dropped in my head from nowhere.

I told Alex what I had just thought.

I phoned Tim.

Tim answered the phone. I told him of our dilemma. He shouted out to Anna in the kitchen and within a few seconds they were adamant that we should come as soon as we want.

They were even excited about it.

The love. So special.

Alex wrote in her diary before this happened that because of the strong nesting instincts a mother has - it was a hard time for her because nothing was ready or settled for the new baby.

She also wrote that God was teaching her to be secure in His love and provision.

....

On May 12th we left Kings Lodge and drove south to Bath. It had been a testing few months for us. Especially me.

....

Bringing my figurative picture talk back into play - We got off the *big ship of YWAM*, and travelled across the *seawater* to the **Island** *of Bath*!

....

It was so good to be enthusiastically welcomed into Tim and Anna's house. They were the perfect people to be with. They lived on the edge of Bath in Combe Down and there was even a playpark just round the corner, where I could take Esme everyday.

I would like to tell you that I was all jolly again but I would be lying if I did. I was depressed actually.

At 4am in the morning on June 11th, Alex woke me up. She had been woken up by strong contractions. It took 20 mins to get ready and get in the car.

1 hour later - BIRTH!

Yeah we got to Bath hospital and things were happening quickly. I won't go into all the details but Praise God we were near a hospital.

At 5.19am Alex gave birth to a boy. He was 8lb 6oz.

Alex was a bit in shock because of the speed of everything but because there was a bug going around in the hospital, we drove back to Tim and Anna's within a few hours.

Now we were four.

Welcome Caleb

We named our son Caleb. We felt it was a strong name and also in the Bible, Caleb was wholehearted for God.

Numbers 14:24 New International Version (NIV)

But because my servant **Caleb has a different spirit and follows me wholeheartedly**, I will bring him into the land he went to, and his descendants will inherit it.

....

Alex has reminded me that Caleb was a very good and placid baby, waking up for feeds and then going back to sleep again. He also liked cuddles.

Having Caleb around the house was nice for Anna as well. She was grateful to learn how to look after a baby. It stood her in good stead for the future when she and Tim started a family.

While Alex rested and mainly looked after Caleb, I took Esme off for hours to the playpark most days.

In early July I picked up the project of tracing my birth parents. I started by obtaining electoral roll register information from the address where Gwynne lived with her mother and brother around 1960. The county office north of London sent me a list of all the residents of that house from 1954 - 1978. It gave me a clearer picture of things.

Continuing the search I would occasionally travel to the main Bristol library and spend a few hours looking through UK marriage records on microfiche card data. They were the local holders of microfiche records of the General Register Office for England and Wales. Microfiche data was used to store files before digital records became popular.

I needed to find out if my birth mother had got married to someone in the years after my birth, because if she had, her surname would have changed and then I would have a new lead to follow. I drew a total blank on the search at the library for a marriage record, because of Gwynne's surname being such a common one.

Back at the house in Bath, I came up with a hunch, that proved to be amazingly spot on. I phoned the register office in the town north of London where Gwynne was living with her mum before having me.

I told the lady registrar on the phone what my hunch was - that my birth mother got married within a few years of 1960 in that very town. The lady informed me that she would have a quick look if she got time that afternoon.

When I phoned her later on, she said, 'You were right, she did get married and I have the marriage certificate right here.'

I sent a cheque off in the post and within a couple of days I had a copy of the marriage certificate.

She got married in 1964 to a man that had a surname which was just about as common as her maiden name (pre-marriage surname)!!

The next step was to try and find an address for both of them and the only way of doing that was to trawl through all the birth records on microfiche at Bristol library. The information on microfiche data gave you: the name of the child, the date of the child's birth, where the birth was registered, the *surname* of the parents, and the *first* names of the father the mother (but **not** the mother's maiden name).

If I found any corresponding names that lined up with Gwynne's and her new husband, then I would have to buy a copy of the birth certificate from the the county offices where the child was born.

It would only be after getting a copy of the actual birth certificate that I would then see what the maiden name of the mother was. If it was Gwynne's maiden name, I would have found the correct couple and I would be getting closer to where Gwynne was living. If it wasn't, then I would have wasted £10 because it was some other couple with the same surname.

Do you know how many children I found who were born to a couple with that married surname and with the same maiden name as Gwynne.

I found 57 children born during the 60s, the 70s and up to the mid-80s.

There was no way I was going to write to all those different county register offices; sending a cheque to each one, to eventually get fifty seven birth certificates, and then find that although the mother had the same maiden name... not one of them had the Christian name I needed, which was... Gwynne!

The problem was the common surname Gwynne had before she was married and then the new surname she changed to after she was married - which was also common.

I felt like I had hit a dead end in my search.

Then when I got back to the house I prayed. Soon after, an idea came to me but it was scary.

But also exciting. And then scary again!

On Gwynne's marriage certificate there was the name of her husband's father and also his address!

Bearing in mind I was looking at that certificate thirty years after the marriage, so *even* if he was still alive - he would be very old and surely not living at the same address.

I knew a way to find out. I walked up the road to the red telephone kiosk and dialled directory enquiries. (Which was free back in those days!) When the operator answered, I gave them the name and address of the man on the marriage certificate. I expected them to tell me the name I had given them was not coming up on their system for that address.

BUT, they didn't and instead they gave the telephone number for him, which meant he was still alive and still at that address! Plus - I now had his phone number.

This really was ground-breaking because now I was only one phone conversation away from finding out all I needed to know.

But of course it was a big only.

It's not easy communicating how complicated this phone call was going to be.

First of all, because I am a Christian - I believe it isn't right to lie. So that narrowed my options to basically one line of conversation. And I knew that if this man deviated off that one line of conversation - I would have to hang up the phone immediately.

And once I did that, the whole possibility of getting information from this man was finished forever.

After much thought and prayer with Alex there was only one line of conversation that I could truthfully use.

Please note at this point, that when I write people's names in this part of the story - it is not their real names. I will write those names, (and addresses) in italics.

From my medical/social records I knew that Gwynne's brother *Don* knew about her having a child (me!) in 1960. So I was going to try and get his contact information from Gwynne's father in law (*Fred Taylor*).

You must bear in mind that it was very possible that Gwynne had never told her husband (*Ronald* Taylor) that she had given birth to me before she had met him.

And I was quite certain that his father, *Fred,* had no knowledge of it. So I had to be very wise in how I asked for the information I needed.

So after much nervous excitement and a final prayer with Alex, I went to the room with the phone in and phoned *Fred Taylor.*

My heart was beating hard!

He answered (and he sounded very old):

'Hello.'

'Hello is that *Fred Taylor?*

'Yes.'

'Father in law of Gwynne *Taylor?*'

'Yes.'

'I got your number from the phone directory... Gwynne's brother *Don,* knew me in the sixties and I was hoping to get back in contact with him. So I wondered if you would have his address?

'Yes I think I have it written down somewhere. Do you mind waiting?'

'No, that's fine. Thankyou.'

. . . .

Okay, so while he is getting the number(!) let me say something to you readers.

I was so excited at that point; *Fred* had not asked me any awkward questions. If he had - I would had to have hung up. I hope you understand that - just think about it!

I also want to let you know that after he gave me the address, I felt such a peace... and confidence that everything was going to be fine. And because of that peace and confidence, rather than finishing the phone call, I started asking other random questions. It was crazy. But I just knew in my spirit that it was fine to do so.

Okay, I better go I can hear *Fred* coming!

. . . .

'Hello, have you got a pen to write it down?'

'Yes, I have.'

'It is *112 Walker Road, Watling, YN9 4RF* '

' Oh, Thank you so much for that. Would you also have his phone number by any chance?'

'Yes, it is *01871 555566* '

'Thankyou... So do Gwynne and *Ronald* still live in England?'

'Oh no, they've been in Hong Kong for years now.'

'Oh right! ... Did they have any children?'

'Yes, they have two children.'

'Oh... what names did they give them?'

'*Stuart and Launa.*'

'Oh those are nice names... Thank you so much for helping me and sorry to have bothered you.'

'That's fine - If you need any more help, just phone me again.'

....

And that was the end of the phone call. I had everything I needed and he was none the wiser as to who I was.

Let me briefly explain why I asked the extra random questions. They weren't as random as you might think.

In asking whether Gwynne and *Ronald* still lived in England, I was really trying to find out if they were still married and, more importantly, if Gwynne was still alive.

The reason I asked about whether they had any children and what their names were was a bit less important. By this time I was really relaxed and next to me was the list of 57 children I had got from Bristol library birth records. I just thought - go for it, be a real clever detective!

And... there was one *Stuart* on the list, and one *Launa*! Born in different counties of England.

Now I had the phone number of Gwynne's brother *Don*. It was so exciting, amazingly exciting, and this time I wasn't even scared, because I knew Don was aware of my existence - so I wasn't stepping on any **secrets.**

After a quick prayer of Thanks with Alex to God, I got on the phone. This was going to be good. I will tell you now, that this next phone call ended up being one of the most candid and gritty of my life. It went on for about an hour. I won't include everything, but here, roughly, are some of the main bits.

'Hello.'

'Hello, is that *Don*?'

'Yes, who's that?'

'Hi, you knew me in the sixties.'

He then rattled off a name that he thought I might be, from when he was in his twenties - to which I answered No... Then there was silence for a couple of seconds, and then he said in a serious tone:

'So who are you then?'

'It's Colin.'

There was about 5 seconds of silence. Really!... Then he said in a quiet tone;

'I know exactly who you are! How did you get my number?'

'Gwynne's father in law, *Fred.* But don't worry, he hasn't got a clue who I was.'

'Well he is in his nineties, so that is probably why.'

Don, then asked me what else I knew and I told him I knew that Gwynne and *Ronald* were living in Hong Kong.

I then told him I knew the names of their children: *Stuart and Launa.*

He was impressed. So I thought I would get really clever and I told him the counties in England where they were born.

He then said, 'No they weren't - they were both born in Libya!'

Apparently Gwynne and *Ronald* had travelled around the world a bit because of *Ronald's* job.

Our conversation then continued with him asking me all about my life from the time of my adoption, through childhood years up to adulthood.

Of course I was thirty four years old at this point, so there was a lot to tell. I told him loads. *Basically everything that you readers know about me - if you have read my first book, and this book, up to this point.*

So he got a good sense of my life journey but not as detailed as in the books of course!

All the time we were chatting *Don* had to be mindful of his mother, who was at that time living in his house. She was about eighty and now lived with *Don* and his wife. She was also, of course, Gwynne's mother and it seemed that after 34 years she was still unaware that her daughter had had a baby (me) in 1960.

....

This reminds me of my favourite film, 'Secrets and Lies'. It was directed by Mike Leigh, and it is all about this subject of adoption and the complexity of relationships around it. It was released in 1996!

....

Don also said that it was also possible that Gwynne's husband *Ronald* didn't know either.

At the end of all our talking, *Don* asked me what the motive was for searching for my birth mother - what did I want at the end of it all?

It was obviously the question that needed to be asked and after a few seconds of honest thought, I told him that ideally I would like to be alone in a room with Gwynne and for her to tell me that she loves me.

As I am writing this, I'm a bit embarrassed by that answer. If I was asked the same question now, I would answer differently. I don't particularly need or want the same things that I did in my thirties. I am a lot more healed and rested in myself these days. But back then, after such an intimate conversation with Don, it was the only way to answer the question truthfully.

He then said, 'I'll let you into a little secret... Gwynne and *Ronald* are coming to England in two months' time and they will be staying with us.'

So he suggested that I write a letter to Gwynne and put it in a sealed envelope. Then put that in another envelope and post it to him. He would then secretly give my letter, in the sealed envelope, to Gwynne.

He warned me that he had no idea how she would respond but that was all he could really do to help me. It was then up to her.

He was also keen to bring in a mediator to communicate with me about the resulting consequences. So I gave him the phone number of NORCAP, who were a charity that assisted in the delicate matters of a adoptee relationships.

It had been a truly amazing conversation that tapped into some deep part of me that I had never been in contact with. It is impossible to communicate the things that were going on inside of me over those weeks of searching and digging around in my root system - culminating with that phone call to *Don.*

....

The next day I wrote a letter to Gwynne. What do you write to your birth mother, 34 years after she gave you away? Somehow I didn't struggle with writing it.

The whole search process had been empowering actually. Coming into contact with the part of me that had been buried all my life sort of woke that stunted side up. I found it brought me alive. It gave me a confidence in my deeper sub-structure.

And now I had popped my head up over the parapet. I was significant. I was a relevant reality, appearing out of the shadows, to my blood relatives.

I also enclosed in the envelope, a very recent photo of Alex, me, Esme and Caleb. It was taken in the front garden of Tim and Anna's house where we were staying and Caleb was a couple of weeks old.

This was significant as it turned out because that was how old I was when Gwynne last saw me. I suspect I looked very similar to the photo of Caleb. The timing was made to measure!

I sealed the envelope and wrote Gwynne on the outside. Then I put it in another envelope and addressed it to *Don*. Then I stuck a stamp on it and posted it off.

Over to you God.

....

Right... now for life back in Bath. Let me explain where we were at. Alex and I didn't have a clue where our life was going. We had even sunk into watching daytime TV. We knew things had got bad!

I had lost my sense of purpose in life and was still reeling from the blossom being blown off. The time in YWAM had seemed like open heart surgery.

I am obviously talking only on an emotional level. I don't want to diminish the trauma of physical heart surgery in any way and if any of you have been through that - I think you deserve a medal.

But I had felt that I had been taken apart in some way. I still felt very vulnerable and didn't want to do anything apart from exist.

I was stuck. And because I was stuck, Alex was also.

And do you know where we as a family were stuck?

You've forgotten my picture from a few pages back haven't you?!

We were stuck on the 'Island of Bath'.

I used to say to Alex that the only way that I can leave this *Island* is if God sends a message in a bottle. That bottle will have to wash up on the shore of the *Island of Bath.*

It will have to be a message that comes right out of the blue. So around the end of July, that's what we prayed for.

August 9th: a bottle turns up on the beach!

It came in the form of a letter from our friends Charlie and Dawn from St Matthias church in Torquay. Dawn was writing to tell me that my mum was dying.

Her father had died a couple of years earlier and she explained how special it had been to spend time with him in the months before he died.

Dawn felt it was important that we come back to Torquay to be around my parents at this difficult time.

So, a message had come. Alex and I couldn't ignore it. We would leave the *'Island of Bath'* and head *back to the 'harbour'* again. Torquay. It was not that I wanted to go back to the harbour again but it was blatantly obvious that we needed to.

We told Tim and Anna, who were sad we had to leave but also saw that it was God's leading. They had been such a good support for the three months we had been there.

Three days later on August 12th, the four of us got in our Hillman Avenger and headed back towards Torquay.

On the way back we stopped at Alex's parents in Plymtree, near Exeter. We ended up staying the night and informed them we were heading back to Torquay because my mum was dying.

Before we went to bed, I was with Alex on the stairs going up to our room when a picture hanging above the staircase caught my attention. I was intrigued by it because it was of an old ship with its sails up heading towards land. I pointed it out to Alex and then

I saw the title of the painting, which was written beneath the picture:

Homeward Bound

We both knew straight away that God was speaking to us. He was confirming what He had called us to do.

When we first got back to Torquay we stayed at my parents house. Mum was not well. She needed to stay in bed most days as it was more comfortable.

After about a week, a couple from St Matthias church called Rod and Trudy offered Alex and I a place to stay at their house. They had a couple of sons but they had a room which was spare. Their house was just around the corner from my parents' house and we could see their house from the spare bedroom we stayed in.

Being at Rod and Trudy's was a blessing, because trying to keep Esme and Caleb quiet in my parents' house was not easy. Mum was dying and needed quiet and rest so being just around the corner was a lot more conducive to the reality of this very difficult time.

It was good to be near and available for my parents and I am sure it helped Dad. Esme and Caleb were probably a welcome distraction from the battle he was going through.

We were finding it hard; the four of us in one bedroom, living out of suitcases. We wanted our own place to live.

It was a heavy old time. Rod and Trudy were great and a real tonic in amongst the turmoil of it all.

In mid-September, we managed to get Esme started at a play school run by a lovely woman in the church called Wendy Hastings.

The playschool was at the Brunel Manor Christian holiday and conference centre, at the edge of Torquay. Esme was three now and that playschool was a welcome addition to our weekly routine.

Mum in the meantime had been taken to the local Rowcroft Hospice for a few days - to get her pain under control.

September 19th: I received a phone call from a lady who worked for NORCAP, the charity that helped adoptee relationships. I had been fully aware that I was going to hear from them at some point because it had been two months since *Don* had told me that he was going to see Gwynne in September. By now he would have seen her and given her my letter!

The woman from NORCAP had heard from *Don.*

Which way was this thing going to go??

She was nice a woman, called Angela. Angela proceeded to tell me what *Don* had told her.

Don had secretly given my envelope to Gwynne. It had stirred up a nest of hornets. There had been a two hour drama with *Don, Ronald* and Gwynne. While all of that was going on *Don* and Gwynne's elderly mother was in the granny flat next door.

The result of this heavy drama was that *Ronald* and Gwynne wanted me to be informed that if I made any further steps toward their life - they would get solicitors involved.

I didn't get any information about the circumstances or reasons for this mandate but the message was loud and clear - Back Off.

....

I would love to have been a fly on the wall in *Don's* house that day but of course I wasn't, so the mystery surrounding it remains in the dark corner of the unknown.

So now I hope you can see the reason why I have been diligent to change names and not give any surnames. I don't need any solicitors on my back. This incident happened a long time ago, so some of those people will be dead by now. But I am sure some are still alive, especially my half-brother and sister (*Stuart and Launa*).

And if Gwynne is still alive, she will be in her eighties. So not lots of years left!

....

But of course this news, this rejection, didn't do much to help my already depressed state. It wasn't a nice time at all.

With all this blossom coming off, I was getting quite naked and there wasn't any circumstantial clothing around to wrap myself up in - because the wind was blowing from all angles.

Within days of that phone call, my mum (Pam) started deteriorating quickly. She couldn't move herself and was not able to speak very much.

Dad phoned my sister Julie in Australia, to warn her that Mum was going downhill very quickly. Julie got an air ticket for early October.

In the days that followed, Mum requested that Peter the vicar from St Matthias come round to pray with her. That church had been a real source of support for mum over the last few years of her life, especially since she was diagnosed with cancer.

On Sunday October 2nd, Alex, Caleb (nearly 4 months old) and me, went in our car to pick Julie up from Heathrow. Mum was by now extremely ill - she had been on a morphine syringe driver for nearly four days.

Julie's plane landed in the early evening. It was of course the first time she had seen Caleb, which was nice - but apart from that, the mood was heavy.

We got back to Mum and Dad's house in Torquay around 11.30pm. Dad answered the door.

Mum had died at 8pm.

The undertakers had taken her body away an hour or so before we arrived.

Julie was obviously really upset. She had travelled from the other side of the world and had missed saying goodbye to Mum by a few hours. She later went to the funeral directors chapel of rest, to see the body.

....

The next day, my Honda motorbike was stolen. It was a small detail in comparison with all the other things going on but it was another detail that blew my way.

....

Mum's funeral was at St Matthias church on October 7th.

She had told me in November the year before which hymns and readings she wanted at her funeral.

She chose three famous hymns:

1. I cannot tell why He whom angels worship.

2. There is a Redeemer.

3. Thine be the Glory, Risen, Conquering Son.

And one Bible reading:

Revelation 21:1-5   New International Version (NIV)

Then I saw 'a new heaven and a new earth,' for the first heaven and the first earth had passed away, and there was no longer any sea.

I saw the Holy City, the new Jerusalem, coming down out of heaven from God, prepared as a bride beautifully dressed for her husband.

And I heard a loud voice from the throne saying, 'Look! God's dwelling place is now among the people, and he will dwell with them. They will be his people, and God himself will be with them and be their God. 'He will wipe every tear from their eyes. There will be no more death' or mourning or crying or pain, for the old order of things has passed away.'

He who was seated on the throne said, 'I am making everything new!' Then he said, 'Write this down, for these words are trustworthy and true.'

....

Mum was only in her early sixties when she died.

We were left to grieve.

A few days after the funeral, we were offered the opportunity to live in the house that the church owned, which was usually the residence of the curate at St Matthias. It was empty because Philip (the curate) and his family had recently moved up to Yorkshire - he was going to be a vicar in a church near Leeds. So until a new curate was found for St Matthias, the house was empty.

It was only going to be a very short term solution for Alex and I because the church expected to appoint a new curate within 2 or 3 months. But it gave us some extra space and allowed us to unpack our bags at last.

By the way, before my sister Julie flew back to Australia, she was walking down a small road in Torquay one day and spotted my Honda motorbike. So we went there and reclaimed it.

Now that Mum had gone, my grief started to kick in. I had no blossom left anymore. I was avoiding as many people as I could in the streets, in case I bumped into someone I knew. I felt like I had come back in the *harbour* with no identity at all. I was just the *bare hull of a sea-going vessel.* I had been to sea, got tossed about by the waves, been flung onto the Island of Bath and then led back to Torquay in tatters. I had nothing visible to show for what we had done. Anyone looking at us now would see no purpose for such a vessel. We weren't a boat with any recognisable function.

I was still confused and angry at God.

I said to Him one day, **'OK, so you've brought us back into the harbour; Now what are you going to do with us??'**

And I heard something back from Him immediately. Not audibly. But by a very definite and distinctive thought dropping right into my head:

' I'm going to put ballast in you.'

*Ballast is material that is used to provide **stability** to a ship. It is a **heavy substance placed in the bottom of the hull**. It keeps the ship low in the water - to prevent it being top heavy. If it is not there, the ship will fall over.*

....

Since we had got back to Torquay, things had not gone smoothly. It had been one thing after another getting poured into our lives. Not nice stuff, just circumstantial heaviness.

By December, things were getting difficult for me. There were builders coming in to the house each day to make improvements before the next curate and his family arrived. There was no peace and quiet to grieve properly.

I went to the doctor. I was in a mess. I was depressed. Alex had suggested I go and see the doctor. He listened to my story from the previous year and at the end of it he offered me anti-depressants. I wasn't expecting that - It hadn't even crossed my mind.

I told him I would go away for a few days and see how I was when I came back. After talking with Alex I decided to go and see my friend Johannes who was on the community at Lee Abbey. I used to work with him on the garden team six years earlier. He had also left community the year after I left but had recently gone back to do another year on the gardening team.

Johannes was Dutch and he was a gentle lanky giant. It was good to spend time with him and relax in the familiar and peaceful surroundings of Lee Abbey. After a few days of relaxing, talking, and crying, I started to feel better. I returned to Torquay with a bit more hope.

The church decided to hold the builders off from coming in to work on the house, until the New Year, which was music to my ears.

The church leadership suggested I do some voluntary work while I had nothing to do. I don't think they totally understood I was grieving and struggling with life.

The house had a garage attached to it and I told them that the only thing that I wanted to do for therapy was totally strip my motorbike down, and rebuild it. When the builders were around, it wasn't possible to use the garage. Now they were gone I had the garage to myself.

It was a Godsend, it really was. It might be hard for everyone to understand, but there was nothing else on planet earth that I wanted and needed to do at that time in my life. It was my grieving therapy.

I had bought that Honda 250cc Motorsport in early 1986, soon after I got back from Turkey. It was now over twenty years old and the engine needed a rebuild. I had lent it to someone when I was away with YWAM and it was not really looked after well, plus it had been stolen recently, so I wanted to bring it back into good condition.

Mechanics was my trade. It was what I knew. I was going to get stuck in to what I knew.

I tidied up the garage before I started doing anything. Then when I was happy it was all clean and organised - I slowly started taking the whole bike to bits, shelving all the parts neatly.

I found the top compression piston ring was broken into ten bits. All the bits were still in the piston ring groove. So it was definitely good that I was stripping the engine down. So satisfying!

At the end of the month, on New Years Eve, my old biker friend Dan came to see me. It was good to see him and his wife Kate. While Alex talked with Kate in the house, Dan and me talked out in the garage about the past year and all the things that had gone on. We also chatted about my stripped down bike and about his time out in North East Uganda in the late eighties when he was fixing Honda trial motorbikes, similar to mine, for Leprosy Mission.

Spending time with Dan was a good tonic for me at the end of a hard year.

1995

Sunday January 1st

Living at the curates house was useful for going to church - it was a five minute walk to St Matthias.

The sermon on this first morning of the year focused on a covenant prayer that is used in the Methodist tradition. St Matthias church is Anglican but all things are equal! All the denominations have something useful to say and this covenant prayer hit the mark with me that day.

A covenant with God

I am no longer my own but yours.

Put me to what you will,

rank me with whom you will;

put me to doing,

put me to suffering;

let me be employed for you,

or laid aside for you,

exalted for you,

or brought low for you;

let me be full,

let me be empty,

let me have all things,

let me have nothing:

I freely and wholeheartedly yield all things

to your pleasure and disposal.

And now, glorious and blessed God,

Father, Son and Holy Spirit,

you are mine and I am yours. So be it.

And the covenant now made on earth, let it be ratified in heaven.'

....

The part that really spoke to me was;

put me to doing,

put me to suffering;

let me be employed for you,

or laid aside for you.

I did feel that I was being laid aside but hearing that prayer made me feel ok about it. My identity would be no less in God's eyes. He was the orchestrator of the season Alex and I were in.

That Sunday was a real new start. Something lifted off me. I had hope.

In December I had been right on the edge and felt like I was going to go under, but as January unfolded - I sensed the ballast had stopped being poured into us.

Maybe now the ship was down in the water to the correct level. 1995 was the year that the ballast was going to settle and find its place deep down inside of us.

It was a time to bring stability to our family. Back in the harbour.

Alex and I would often take Esme and Caleb down to see my dad. They cheered his days up as the year progressed. He was struggling with life now Mum was gone. They had been married for over forty years.

The Honda rebuild was going really well and by the end of January I had it totally finished, which was good because we had to move out of the curate's house. The new assistant vicar and his family were due to arrive in February.

We moved into a rented three-bedroomed terraced house in the Upton area of Torquay. It was owned by a woman we knew at St Matthias.

And what a blessing it was to us. We had been living in very temporary places for just over a year up until this point.

We could at last settle and find which way round we were!

It was in a quiet side road and even had a shed to put my bike in, a parking place for our car and a little grass lawn at the back for the children to play in.

Around this time I was going along to a weekly meeting in Paignton called 'Times of Refreshing', which was led by a woman called Barbara. Barbara attended St Matthias church and had recently gone to Toronto, Canada, where there had been what some Christians were calling an outpouring of the Holy Spirit. It was a contentious issue with Christians all around the world but it had started in a small warehouse at the edge of Toronto airport in a church called 'Vineyard.' Many people seemed to be getting deeply touched by God and that included a large number who were travelling from around the globe.

Alex and I had heard about this outpouring in Toronto about a year before. It had started around the time we first joined YWAM.

Well, Barbara had just got back from visiting the Vineyard church in Toronto and she was very touched by God out there, so had started these 'Times of Refreshing' meetings in Paignton.

I was going along to them because I definitely needed a time of refreshing! It was at one of these meetings I heard a chap called Steve Hutch speaking, who had also just got back from Toronto.

He spoke about a picture he felt God had given him about a small starving baby curled up in a bundle, next to a river. *He felt the child was him.*

And as that baby drank from the river it got healthy and well.

He shared how he had gone out to Toronto after he had been given the picture. He believed that God was telling him that the river in the picture equated to the flow of the Holy Spirit out in Toronto. So he went to Toronto, to drink from the river of the Holy Spirit. He was deeply restored in his inner being. It was inspiring to hear how God had touched him.

Like I said earlier, there was, and still is, a lot of conflicting opinions about what was happening at that church in Toronto. But amongst it all, many people around the world were having their lives deeply touched, which was giving them a new vigour to go out and serve God with more love in their hearts for people.

Anyway Steve was one of them and hearing how God had touched him made me hungry for an intimate experience with God.

Some would say that we shouldn't be looking for experiences but I believe God enjoys us knowing Him in an experiential way sometimes. Of course, there are other times when life is tough and in those winter seasons the knowledge of His goodness is dependent on faith alone.

I was starting to believe that God was leading me to go to the church in Toronto. In a lot of ways I had no desire whatsoever to travel to another country at this time because we had just settled after having a very difficult year - and I wanted to hide in the safety of the harbour.

But in spite of my acute sense of vulnerability during this period, I was also in need of an intimate connection with God in my inner man.

A few clues had come my way that got me to step out and buy an air ticket. I also booked ten days accommodation at a nearby motel to the church out there.

In early February Alex drove me to the Torquay coach station and I started my journey. I felt like a vulnerable little boy as the coach pulled away from the coach station, with Alex and Esme waving to me. Caleb was there too but he was a bit too small to know about waving!

When I eventually reached Heathrow and got on the plane, I realised how vulnerable I really was. As the plane took off, I started to cry like a little boy. I was definitely out of my comfort zone.

I won't spend too long describing all the things that went on when I was in Toronto but I will mention a few.

The weather was so cold that you couldn't go for a walk for more than just a few minutes.

The first evening I walked in the large church amongst hundreds of people and listened to the speaker - I didn't like it. I stayed away for days after that and just watched TV in my motel room, thinking I had made a big mistake coming to Toronto. Finally a German girl staying at the motel encouraged me to give the church one more go, which I did. From that point on I was liberated to receive all God wanted for me out there.

I gave some testimony on the stage to what God was doing in my life and how I had struggled on my first visit to the church.

I had some very deep prayer ministry that helped tears of disappointment, confusion and grief to start coming out from inside of me.

Travelled with a few people to see Niagara falls. Lots of ice around - that added to the drama of the views.

Got excited about what God was going to do in my life and in the lives of many who had visited the church and were continuing to do so. We had been deeply touched by the very tangible presence of God. It was indeed much needed refreshment.

When I got back to Torquay a couple of weeks later, Alex said, 'You're different!'

And I was.

....

Another support for me around this time was a group called 'Western Approaches'. It was started up around the time my mum died. It was a two year course, run by the Bishop of Exeter's wife. We used to meet in a room next to the Cathedral on a fortnightly basis and there were about ten people in the group. We used to sit in a circle and basically wait until somebody wanted to talk about themselves and what was going on in their life. There was an agenda of vulnerability that pervaded the evening but that was a good thing, because it developed an atmosphere of respect for each other and gave people room to just be themselves. I was able to be transparent about coming in contact with the fragility of my life - due to the various circumstances that had arisen over the previous twelve months.

Over the two years 'Western Approaches' ran, our small group slowly began to trust each other and I personally enjoyed our times together.

In June, Alex and I, did the same as we had done with Esme when she was younger and had a special dedication at St Matthias for Caleb. There was a slot in the service where we as a church gave thanks to God for the life of our son and we committed his life over to God - for Him to lead Caleb in the plans and purposes He had for him.

I must also just mention something else that occurred this month up at a church in Cullompton near Exeter. St Andrews church were holding weekly Saturday evening meetings where they would ask the Holy Spirit to come and have His way. It was similar to the times of refreshing that were continuing to happen out in Toronto. They were our sort of *tribe* really! I was at one of these evenings and a chap from that church called David, who I had met once in Nottingham a few years back, started praying for me and he got a picture from God. He said, 'Mark, you are like an old galleon ship with its sails full in the wind. An ornate and beautiful ship, like the ones that sailed across the Oceans to find new lands.'

The following week my attention was grabbed by a photo and an article on the front page of our local Torquay newspaper - it was entitled, 'In full sail for Torbay.' The colour photo was of an old galleon ship with its sails up and the article was informing the public that on Tuesday, a full size working replica of Sir Francis Drake's 'Golden Hind' ship had come alongside Torquay harbour for a month long stay. It was travelling around the world as an educational vessel and was open for the public to come and walk around.

The following Saturday evening we were back at the weekly Cullompton meeting at St Andrews church, and I saw David again. He said to me, 'Hey Mark, did you see on the TV about the ship that has come into Torquay? Because it made me think of you and the word I gave you last Saturday!'

I told him that I had seen it in the paper and that it also reminded me of his picture. I planned to visit the ship as it was in Torquay for a whole month.

A few days later I made my way down to the harbour in Torquay to visit the ship. Apart from the crew guide chap, no one else was there. I was pretty excited actually because I had a strong sense that God was going to speak to me somehow! When I walked onboard the guide asked me what I would like to know about the ship. I noticed that there was a cross on the main mast, so I asked him why that was there and he told me that Francis Drake was a devout protestant. He then asked me what else I would like to know about the ship, to which I suggested that he decide what to tell me about it.

I wanted to leave the discussion open - to see where God would lead it.

Get ready!

The guide then said, 'What do you know about ballast?'

I thought to myself - here we go!

I told him that I knew what ballast was.

He then proceeded to tell me that in 1577 when the 'Golden Hind' left England to sail the seas, it had ballast of *pig iron and rock.*

On its long voyage at sea, it did battle with a Spanish galleon and won. The galleon had been full of treasure, so the bounty was then transferred to the Golden Hind. But in order to make room for it all - the ballast of *pig iron and rock* was chucked into the sea.

In 1580 the Golden Hind returned to Plymouth, England. It had left England with ballast of Pig iron and rock and it had returned with ballast of gold and silver.

....

I have since found out that the treasure it returned with would be worth the equivalent of £480 million these days.

I believe that God was telling me on board the Golden Hind replica that the ballast He had deposited in my life may not look pretty but it needs to be in the hull. If it isn't - the ship will rock about too much and will not survive the rougher seas.

The recent maiden voyage to YWAM last year proved that!

But once the ship is properly prepared for sea (By Him) it will be sent out - and the reward will be great.

It was exciting to have God speak so clearly.

....

I told the new assistant vicar Andy about what God had been saying through the Golden Hind replica visit. He was encouraged and also felt that the Golden Hind with its sails fully available for the wind was a picture for the way he hoped St Matthias was going - in making itself as a church open to God's Holy Spirit. A few days later he was preaching at church and in his message he talked about the Christian life being a pilgrimage. That we are not supposed be settlers. Pilgrims are open to moving on, settlers don't want to move on. It made me think of the Golden Hind, with its sails up and being blown forward by the wind.

But it also reminded me of **another** Golden Hind replica ship that is permanently moored in Brixham harbour, which is five miles across the bay from Torquay harbour.

It's true! There was another full size Golden Hind replica ship in nearby Brixham harbour - being visited by thousands of tourists every year.

It is firmly fixed to the harbour floor by steel and could never sail. It's been there for years. *It is a settler - with no intention of moving.*

I know... that there are times to settle but Andy was saying that we should always be alive and *ready* to put our sails up when God is wanting to move us on. Ships are made for the sea - not the harbour.

There is a choice in the Christian life: *to be pilgrim or a settler.*

....

Andy and his wife Ann were an encouraging support for me and Alex in those few years they were at our church. They were on the same page as us spiritually. Andy was also someone I could go to if I was really struggling in life about something. He made sense of things for me on numerous occasions.

Over that summer Alex and I drove up north for a couple of weeks. We went and visited an old Lee Abbey community friend called Ruth who was living in Chester. Her husband ran a church and they were holding a conference that we wanted to attend. Our family stayed with them for a few days and then drove further north to see yet another Lee Abbey community friend called Julian who lived just on the edge of Newcastle. While we stayed with him, we visited a large church on a council estate in Sunderland. This particular church was well known for allowing the Holy Spirit to move in its meetings. There were lots of people there from the immediate area that would have normally not attended church. But they were attracted by the freedom and joy in the people they saw who came out of the place. It was a special evening with people crying, laughing, dancing, lying on the floor and listening to other people's stories of how they had been set free from all sorts of rubbish in their lives!

From Newcastle we explored part of Hadrian's wall on the border of Scotland and visited various sites on the North East coast of Britain, including the Holy Island of Lindisfarne.

It was good to get away from Torquay for a while and spread our wings in some unfamiliar parts of the country. We sent postcards to my dad from places we visited, being aware that he was still in the middle of his grief.

Later in the year, soon after the first year anniversary of Mum's death, he also started struggling with his health.

Around November Alex and I went to a healing retreat at Weycroft Hall near Axminster in East Devon. We were still not hunky-dory in our marriage and Alex often struggled with the lack of emotional connection between us. We both had some counselling and deep prayer ministry that helped us on our way for a bit. It has been an ongoing issue in our lives, with God slowly and carefully getting nearer and nearer to the root of our insecurities. It was me who had more walls up concerning emotional attachment though.

I might just mention, to help lighten things up, that while we were there a guy called Mike rushed up to me. He had been trying to find me for years apparently. He told me he was hitchhiking one evening on the north coast of Devon about eight years earlier and I had been living at Lee Abbey at the time. As he was talking to me, I suddenly remembered him and the incident on Countisbury Hill near Lynmouth. He reminded me that I had told him how I had become a Christian in Turkey. He also had been searching for what life was all about and I had prayed for him that evening in the car. Apparently that time with me had sown a seed in his heart about God and, sometime after, he asked Jesus to be Lord of his life.

He was really pleased to see me at Weycroft Hall. He had always wondered where I was in the world. Then he went on and told me that after he became a Christian he had helped a good friend of his called Chris to become a Christian. Ten months after that, Chris had died in a motorbike accident.

Mike then informed me that Chris's mum was in the building there at Weycroft Hall. He went and got her and introduced her to me. Well she was so pleased to meet me because she had heard about me from Mike in the past. Suffice to say, she was very grateful for how my life had indirectly helped her son become a Christian before he died.

So, God can use us in many mysterious ways - the consequences thereof we may never know!

Amen.

1996

Early in the year I had started working for a local garage that was owned by someone that I went to college with many years earlier. It was a Volkswagen specialist, and I worked for a couple of days a week in the parts dept - delivering parts to various garages in the South Devon area.

Sometimes I was in the storage area, filing where parts were shelved.

By the springtime, working in the garage had started to get me down. The attitude of a few people there was not wonderful and it was quite a lonely experience. I was still fragile because of the grief of my mother's death, and also Dad was not well either.

These verses helped me around this time:

Isaiah 51:7-9   Amplified Bible (AMP)

'Listen to Me, you who know righteousness,

The people in whose heart is My law *and* instruction;

Do not fear the reproach *and* taunting of man,

Nor be distressed at their reviling.

'For the moth will eat them like a garment,

And the worm will eat them like wool.

But My righteousness *and* justice will exist forever,

And My salvation to all generations.'

In July I left the garage and went to work for PGH motorcycles, which was owned by my friend Paul.

You may remember I mentioned him earlier in the book, when as a new Christian I used to visit him and his workers, telling them about God. So he definitely knew I was a Christian!

I also used to work for him as a mechanic briefly before I went to Australia in 1982. In those days I was a long-haired dirty biker.

....

July 9th was my birthday, and my dad sent me a special birthday card which contained the words:

`Thank you Mark, for your support during my illness. For three months I was at a very low ebb and your family (and that includes Caleb!!) gave me a purpose to look to the future.'

Dad really liked Esme and Caleb and even though Caleb was only two years old he used to make Dad laugh. Although Dad had recovered from how he had been feeling, he was not well. It materialised that he was in the later stages of prostate cancer.

At the end of July, the two year 'Western Approaches' course in Exeter came to an end. It had been therapeutic support since my mum had died and in some strange way I felt another bereavement now the course had finished.

Because of the things happening around me, I was still feeling extra fragile and this state of affairs didn't compliment my wellbeing at work. Again, with this job, people's attitudes hit me harder than they normally would have. There were three other guys in the workshop who were quite proficient at their job and I felt pretty de-skilled. I had been out of the trade for a while now, so was not accustomed with working on the new bikes that were on the scene these days.

People in workplaces often subtly parade their strengths to those around them in order to boost their own self-worth, and having such a laddish mentality in the workshop was not so enjoyable for me.

I ended up doing menial tasks around the place, which compounded the sense of vulnerability I was already going through. It was quite a lonely experience.

It got to the point where I was getting depressed and I went and saw Andy, the assistant minister at our church. He spent an hour or so with me and put a few things into perspective. He recognised that there were some hard things happening in my life apart from work and encouraged me to persevere. He reaffirmed that my security needed to be in God and not in the things the world looks to for security. He of course said a lot more things, but I won't spill it all out here. However, amongst other things he felt these verses were for me at that time:

1 Peter 1:3-9   New Living Translation (NLT)

3 All praise to God, the Father of our Lord Jesus Christ. It is by his great mercy that we have been born again, because God raised Jesus Christ from the dead. Now we live with great expectation, **4** and we have a priceless inheritance—an inheritance that is kept in heaven for you, pure and undefiled, beyond the reach of change and decay. **5** And through your faith, God is protecting you by his power until you receive this salvation, which is ready to be revealed on the last day for all to see.

6 So be truly glad. There is wonderful joy ahead, even though you must endure many trials for a little while. **7** These trials will show that your faith is genuine. It is being tested as fire tests and purifies gold—though your faith is far more precious than mere gold. So when your faith remains strong through many trials, it will bring you much praise and glory and honor on the day when Jesus Christ is revealed to the whole world.

8 You love him even though you have never seen him. Though you do not see him now, you trust him; and you rejoice with a glorious, inexpressible joy. **9** The reward for trusting him will be the salvation of your souls.

....

The next day I felt so much better. Just having someone listen, understand and care really helps.

The following week at work Paul, my boss, gave me a set of new cotton overalls. They were from an oil company called 'Rock Oil' and they were really stylish. We used Rock Oil in the workshop and they were a one off pair of overalls that Paul had been given.

I was so chuffed to get them, not only because they looked good and I needed some proper overalls, but because of the words: 'Rock Oil.'

I knew they were a secret message from God to me.

Psalm 40 : 1 - 2   New International Version (NIV)

1 I waited patiently for the Lord;

he turned to me and heard my cry.

2 He lifted me out of the slimy pit,

out of the mud and mire;

he set my feet **on a rock**

and gave me a firm place to stand.

These were key verses He gave me after I got back from Turkey in 1985. I had gone travelling to find out if 'I' was a rock. I had ended up sinking and finding out I wasn't a rock. But God had told me that 'He' was the only rock that would stay firm.

He was now reminding me of that truth again.

Also the 'Rock Oil' emblem on the overalls signified something else to me: Oil is used in the Bible to represent the Holy Spirit.

When I got home that day I looked in the overalls to see where they were made! Guess where?

Izmir in Turkey.

Izmir was the City where the Holy Spirit flowed into me for the first time and turned my turmoil into peace. You may remember the incident near the end of my first book (*Torquay.. to the End of the World*).

So, I hope you are getting a picture of the wonderful ways in which God speaks, without using audible words. He's so amazing.

In August I joined the chaplaincy team at Torbay Hospital. The hospital chaplain had encouraged me to help the team on certain Sundays to take the bread and wine around the wards to patients who had requested to receive communion. It was a privilege to visit people in the wards and give them communion. Often there would be an opportunity to listen to their story and pray for them. It really was an honour.

Another honour was being asked by Andy Edmunds, the assistant vicar at our church to lead an Alpha Course. Alex and I ran a homegroup in our house one evening a week, and Andy wanted Alex, me and our homegroup to organise and run the next 3-month Alpha Course that the church was planning to launch in September.

The Alpha Course introduces the Christian faith in an easy and hopefully understandable way. It is held once a week and each session includes having a big meal all together, watching a presentation talk, then splitting into small groups to discuss the talk.

Well, our group were up for it and quite excited about it also, because Alpha Courses often bring in people who have not got a faith and certainly don't go to church.

By early September I was again getting really down at work. One day I went to see my old biker friend Gordon who worked at a local tyre fitting garage because that morning I had gone to see his mum in hospital.

I explained to Gordon that things were getting me down in the motorbike workshop where I was working. I was very honest and told him that people's attitudes were quite disrespectful and it hurt.

I was quite broken really and he was angry that I had to endure that type of atmosphere. Eventually he said, 'Mark you don't belong in a commercial garage - your mechanical skills are more appreciated by friends who need help. It's not doing you any good in there; it's demoralising and degrading to your character.'

I actually nearly choked with emotion as this person who knew me so well, showed such love and concern towards me.

My dear friend Gordon.

In the days that followed, I felt that God wanted me to persevere for a while longer at the motorbike garage. I started praying for the mechanics and also for Paul my boss.

It wasn't long before things started to shift a bit.

Esme after a school day with Caleb, on my Honda Motorsport

Esme was now five years old and it was that time in life to start going to school. There were only fourteen children in her class when she started, which probably helped the experience be a little less intense. She got on well and enjoyed the new experience of school life. The school was not far from the house we were living in, so Alex or I would usually walk with her - unless it was pouring down with rain. I still have fond memories of taking her to school in her little blue uniform and picking her up again in the afternoon.

....

Dad, somehow, found a little lease of life around this time. He had volunteered to be the church magazine editor. No one else was coming forward so Dad said that he would do it - but for one year only! It was good to see him involved with something although unfortunately it didn't last for long.

Meanwhile, back at my job in the bike garage, things were starting to shift. I had asked my church homegroup to pray for the guys in the workshop and also for my boss Paul.

Everyone at work knew I was a Christian and the odd comment would invariably be thrown my way to see how I would react. It was often tedious but it went with the territory.

Then one day, one of the mechanics started opening up to me about his life. He told me that he had been in a church youth group when he was younger but his parents had divorced, which disrupted his life. However, he said his mother was still an active Christian and went to a Pentecostal church. It was good to hear someone at work being real for once and gave me a bit of hope for the place.

Another shift at work came when I felt God wanted me to invite my boss Paul to the launch of the Alpha Course at our church.

It wasn't something I rushed into because I knew from experience that Paul wasn't really interested in the Christian faith. He was a successful businessman and already had most material things that people chase after.

I had become a Christian over ten years before and had kept in contact with Paul throughout that time. God was often brought up in conversation in our times together but that was as far as it went. Although Paul was sometimes curious about the Christian life, he most certainly didn't want to become a Christian himself.

So, like I said: I didn't rush into inviting him along to Alpha when God started to pop the idea into my head one afternoon.

Instead I said to God, 'I will only invite him to Alpha if, when I leave work at the end of the day, Paul calls me into his office to ask me how the day has been.'

Normally I just say 'bye' and Paul says 'bye.'

Well, at the end of the day, Paul, shouted out before I left work, 'How has the day been Mark?'

When I went in his office, I told him that I needed to ask him a question. When I asked him to come to Alpha, he laughed and asked me to give him one good reason why he would want to do that. I told him I would not be able to give him a good enough convincing reason. We continued the conversation and he eventually said, 'I will come to the first launch evening only - to keep you quiet.' He also told me that his wife Karen was that very afternoon at a funeral of a friend, who was a committed Christian.

The following day at work, Paul told me that when Karen was at the funeral, she had been been really touched by the sense of family at the church - in the way they loved and supported each other.

A couple of days later, the Alpha Course began. Our homegroup had been fasting and praying that people's lives would be touched.

There was a total of thirty people there on that first night and Paul did indeed turn up. He brought with him one of the young salesmen from the bike showroom. The evening went really well and the small group time after the meal and presentation was filled with all sorts of questions and opinions. There were three small groups of ten people in each and the one with Paul in was the hottest!

He actually got on with quite a few of the people in our church and was a lot more serious and mature than the guy from the showroom who had tagged along with him.

He didn't come to the following week's Alpha but did come along to a few more before it ended in December.

One evening at the end of November a famous Christian speaker from London called Steve Chalke was speaking at the local Princess Theatre, down near the harbour. Alex and I decided to invite the Alpha group to come and hear the talk, which many did - including Paul... and his wife Karen. The theatre was nearly full and people were totally engaged with what Steve Chalke was saying.

Around November time also, an opportunity came up to work three days a week at my church. It was a paid position to be a pastoral host person for the church centre, which was attached to the main church building. It entailed being around the busy church centre to welcome people who passed through during the week. It would mean leaving my part time job at PGH motorcycles in December but it was more in my heart to work for the church.

I had been spending the last week or so working at Paul and Karen's house near Teignmouth. On my last day of working for Paul, I was actually at their home mowing the lawn. When I had finished I sat down with both of them and we chatted about God. Paul said that he must be changing, because he had gone back into a Post Office earlier in the week when he noticed they had given him too much change. He said he would never have done that before - he would have kept it.

They both told me that they had been impressed with the recent Steve Chalke evening at the Princess Theatre. The talk he gave made them realise that when someone becomes a Christian it is not all easy going but God is there to help the person. Karen commented, it reminded her of the famous, *Footprints in the sand* poem, that was on their bedroom wall.

Then Paul said, 'Ohh, that's made me feel all tingly.'

God was on their case, and in a few pages time, I will tell you how things unfolded, as the months went on!

....

On Friday 29th November; three days after I finished my job working for Paul - I was due to go to a funeral at our church. A lady called Margaret had died after years of bravery fighting cancer in her body. She had become a good friend of my parents. Before my mum died of cancer, she had found Margaret to be a real companion in the struggle.

On the morning of the funeral, my dad had a doctor's appointment. Just before I left my flat to go to Margaret's funeral, Dad phoned me with the news from his appointment: the cancer had spread in his body. The doctor had prescribed morphine tablets and told him to prepare for Rowcroft Hospice.

Half an hour later I was at Margaret's funeral. In that service, emotion was brimming near the surface in me. It was surreal to be at this funeral thinking, and also somehow knowing, that I would be at my own dad's funeral in the not too distant future. It was a heavy ordeal but I did feel that God was very close to me and that He was going to support me.

My brother Robert phoned me in the early evening and said he was going to drive down to Torquay with his wife, Cherry, so that we could all talk about Dad's situation. Robert and Cherry had got married the year before and had bought a house about a hundred miles away, in Christchurch, Dorset.

They arrived in Torquay later that night and stayed at Dad's house.

Alex had gone away with the children for the weekend to see some old friends of hers at her parents' house.

On the Saturday, Robert and I chatted and he proposed the idea of taking Dad to their house in Christchurch. Robert and Cherry's house had a suitable spare room for Dad and, unlike Alex and me, they didn't have a family to take care of.

Dad now had bone cancer and the morphine wasn't killing much of the pain. He could hardly walk, and Robert's proposal seemed sensible. Robert would put in place all the care requirements to make sure Dad's last days would be comfortable.

Dad wasn't someone who wanted to spend his last days in a hospice.

Later that day Cherry drove their car back to Christchurch to get things ready that end and Robert planned to take Dad the following day in Dad's own Ford Fiesta. On the Sunday morning we helped get a few things together for Dad, all of us knowing that these were his final days and that he would never step into that house again. He was perfectly aware of this fact himself. It was a morbid affair.

Robert drove Dad off in the little blue Fiesta. It was to be Dad's last few minutes in Torquay. It had been his home for twenty years.

After they left, I felt very alone. I wrote in my journal later that day:

I'm really sad and hurting and crying. There is a weight of loss in my chest. I feel alone in my grief. I know God is with me and in control - but it still hurts. So many memories of Dad through many years. I know I'm going to miss him when he goes. I haven't really known grief like this before. I know that it is something I just have to go through.

I need all the love and care on offer Lord.

I love you Lord and I'm really glad you're around to hold me in your everlasting arms. Help me to involve you fully in my grief and not shut you out. I want to learn through this - how not to be an 'island.' Lord it's so tempting for me to feel this pain in a bubble - alone.

Lord I invite you right now into the depths of my heart - my innermost being. Teach me Lord how not to sink into myself, but instead; sink into you.

In no way do I want to deny any grief. I need to feel. Lord release my grief and release my joy - the joy you have given me.

I haven't looked back through my journals for many years and have forgotten a lot of this stuff but writing this book has forced me back into them again.

After writing that last section, I wrote that God led me to these verses in the Bible almost straight afterwards:

Isaiah 43:1b - 2   New International Version (NIV)

'Do not fear, for I have redeemed you;

   I have summoned you by name; you are mine.

 When you pass through the waters,

   I will be with you;

and when you pass through the rivers,

they will not sweep over you.

When you walk through the fire,

you will not be burned;

the flames will not set you ablaze.'

Psalm 94:17-19 New International Version (NIV)

Unless the Lord had given me help,

I would soon have dwelt in the silence of death.

When I said, 'My foot is slipping,'

your unfailing love, Lord, supported me.

When anxiety was great within me,

your consolation brought me **joy.**

....

The next morning, which was Monday December 2nd, I phoned Dad's doctor in Torquay to tell him that we had taken Dad to Dorset over the weekend. When I spoke to the doctor, he told me that Dad's cancer was running rampant in his bones and that he needed urgent medical attention. He was a nice doctor and seemed to really care.

Robert phoned later in the day to tell me that he had registered Dad with a doctor in Christchurch and the medical attention was all being put in place.

My new job at the church had now started but there was no undue pressure because of that. In fact, it provided a little distraction from the heaviness in my life. In reality it was like taking a Rennie tablet for a broken leg.

On the Tuesday, after Esme had finished school, Alex and I travelled to Christchurch with Esme and Caleb.

On the Wednesday, I spent some time with Dad. He was not looking good. I asked him if he had peace with God and he replied, 'Not really.'

I spoke to him about Jesus paying the price for our sin on the cross, so that we would have reconciliation and peace with God. He started to drift off to sleep because of the morphine tablets. I woke him up and said, 'Dad - do you believe and trust in Jesus Christ?' He looked into my eyes with all the attention he could muster and said, 'Yes I do.' I then told him, that was all he needed to do.

On the Thursday morning I went into Dad's room and showed him a bookmark I had found in Mum's Bible. The bookmark had a cross on it, and the words: **Jesus said, 'My peace I give to you.'**

I then read him some verses from the Bible:

2 Corinthians 6:2   New International Version (NIV)

For he says,

> 'In the time of my favour I heard you,

> and in the day of salvation I helped you.

> I tell you, now is the time of God's favour, now is the day of salvation.'

John 14:1-3 New International Version (NIV)

Jesus said:

'Do not let your hearts be troubled. You believe in God; believe also in me. My Father's house has many rooms; if that were not so, would I have told you that I am going there to prepare a place for you? And if I go and prepare a place for you, I will come back and take you to be with me that you also may be where I am.'

Then I asked him if he would like Alex and I to pray for him, and he said, he would.

I went and got Alex and we prayed that the Holy Spirit would draw Dad close to Jesus and prepare his heart to be with the Lord. We prayed that God would take Dad to be with Him in heaven at just the right minute on just the right day. And for comfort here and now, until that day.

Dad was coherent and grateful after the prayer.

I also took the opportunity to thank Dad for bringing me up through my childhood. And then I said, 'In case I don't get the chance to say it again - I want to say that I love you.'

He looked at me when I said it and responded, 'You too.'

As I left the room, I put my hand on Dad's shoulder and said, 'Bless you Dad.'

As I was walking out the door, he said twice the words, 'Thank you Mark.'

He was at peace.

As I am writing, I have just remembered something God did for me in the year leading up to this point.

Me and Dad had never really hugged. I had mentioned this to Alex. When Dad was first getting ill and I used to spend some time with him in his house, I used to leave, but really wanted to hug him. Yet I was too scared, he might reject my approach. Alex suggested I ask God to help it start happening. Even thinking about the scenario when I prayed for it made me shudder. But Alex and I did pray for the walls to come down so that I would be able to do it.

A week or so later - I did it, and Dad was fine. From then on, it became the norm. Thanks Lord.

Later that day I pushed Caleb in his pushchair to Christchurch Priory and, because it started to rain, we went inside. An organ recital happened to be going on. When the rain began to ease, I pushed him to the nearby Christchurch Harbour and the sun appeared from behind the clouds and a massive rainbow appeared over the Priory. When I saw it, I wished Dad could have been there too and seen the beauty of it.

Then I realised that very soon, in the flash of an eye, Dad was going to be transported from sickness and death into the full richness of beauty.

What I was seeing didn't compare.

Beauty Beyond Compare.

It put a smile on my face, thinking of Dad's surprise - that was coming soon.

....

When Robert came back from his work later that day, Alex, me and the kids travelled back to Torquay.

In three days' time, my sister Julie was due to arrive in England from Australia. She needed to see Dad before he died.

On Sunday December 8th, Julie landed at Heathrow and travelled straight to Robert's house where she was going to stay.

Dad was now on a morphine syringe driver. He was often asleep and not too lucid when he was awake but he recognised Julie when she went in his room and it was good that they could spend some precious time together. Julie needed that, after what had happened when she travelled back to see Mum two years earlier.

On the morning of Tuesday December 10th, I was at work at the church centre, and the phone in the office rang. It was Alex. She told me that Julie had just phoned our house and told Alex that Dad was very near to dying.

I left work and went home to get our car. Alex stayed in Torquay with Caleb because Esme was at school. I drove to Dorset but on the way I felt led to stop in Newton Abbot and go to 'Choice Words', the local Christian bookshop. Dad really liked Psalm 23 in the Bible, and I wanted to buy a CD that had the Psalm being sung on it.

I found a CD called Gloria, which was a Cambridge Choir singing alongside an orchestra; conducted by John Rutter. Track six was entitled 'The Lord is my Shepherd.' The words the choir were singing on that track were all the words from Psalm 23.

Perfect.

I somehow knew that if Dad was still alive when I reached Christchurch; I needed to play that track to him.

I arrived at 3pm. He was alive.

I found a CD player and played the track in his room. It was the first time I had heard it.

You will find out later why I needed to buy that CD and play it to Dad.

Julie was of course staying in the house now and Robert and Cherry were hosting us. The atmosphere was heavy. Death was in the air.

In the evening a lady called Shirley arrived to look after Dad through the night. She was a nurse who worked for the Marie Curie charity that provides care and support for those with terminal illnesses and their families. She was a lovely lady and it turned out she was a Christian who attended a church nearby.

Dad died that night at 11.40pm in the night. He was 69 years old.

Shirley took it all in her stride and it was so good to have her around. The doctor arrived about midnight to confirm Dad was dead and soon after, the undertakers were phoned.

Shirley and the doctor went home.

Before the undertakers arrived, I took the opportunity to get out of the house and go for a walk on my own.

I walked to the quay at nearby Mudeford. It was very quiet. I was transfixed with the weight of the situation in my life. I had brought with me a sealed letter, that Dad had given me one year earlier. He had told me not to open it until after he died. It was written by him to me, Julie and Robert.

I won't go into all that it said but basically it was telling us that because he was infertile and unable to give Mum children of her own, it had hounded him all his life. He believed that it was God's punishment on his life.

....

I had always been under the impression that it was Mum who was unable to have children, but apparently not.

Well that was a huge secret to come out of the woodwork. I read the letter and sensed the shame and burden that Dad had carried all his life, and thought to myself: what a flaming mess people get into.

I was actually cross with him for believing such rubbish and allowing his life to be tormented in such a way.

It went some way to explaining the arguments they occasionally had at night when we were very young. The arguments were not that common, but there was a tension around that sometimes erupted into full blown arguments. There was never any physical abuse between them but hearing them shout at each other when we were in bed was very scary for Julie and I. Those incidents would often include Dad throwing some form of crockery to the floor, or banging a fist hard on a table.

When I got back to Robert and Cherry's house I gave Julie the letter to read. She ended up in tears and wanted to talk. As she talked, Robert went away to read the letter. He came back and needed to talk but I told Robert to wait a bit, because Julie was all distraught. That led to Robert feeling rejected and *it all kicked off*.

The three of us were already covered by the weight of Dad's death and now this letter had caused a hornet's nest to bust open!

Cherry was in the wings of all this and probably would have enjoyed some of that morphine if it was still about!

Joking aside, we got through it. At 3.30am in the middle of the night, I got the four of us to join hands and I led a prayer asking God to help us in our grief, and to use this season to bring us more into a knowledge of His love for us.

We were all emotionally exhausted. After getting a few hours sleep and having some breakfast, I made my way back to Torquay.

The undertakers would transfer Dad's body to Devon later that week.

Robert also drove Dad's blue Ford Fiesta to Torquay and left it outside the front of our house, because Dad had said that he wanted me and Alex to have it.

The funeral was seven days after Dad died.

The day before the funeral, Alex phoned my work and told me that she had broken down in our Hillman Avenger. The whole driver's side rear suspension had broken off the rear chassis. It was totally crippled at the side of the road. My mate Pete who was still a local AA patrolman picked it up the next day with his spec lift (spectacle lift) van and towed it to the back of our house. There was no way it was going to be fit to drive in the near future.

I mention all this to give you an idea of God's care for us. If our car had broken down like that any earlier, it would have been very upsetting because we needed it to visit Dad when he was in Dorset. He ended up being there for only ten days, but we needed our car to do the few trips we did.

Now that it had broken down, there was a pristine Ford Fiesta at the front of our house to use. It was all ours. We really felt that God was holding us safe in His hand at this very difficult time in our lives.

The funeral was held at our church in Torquay on December 17th.

There were two hymns:

Dear Lord and Father of mankind, and, *Thine be the glory, risen conquering Son.*

And there were two Bible readings:

Psalm 23   New International Version (NIV)

1 The Lord is my shepherd, I lack nothing.

2 He makes me lie down in green pastures,

he leads me beside quiet waters,

3 he refreshes my soul.

He guides me along the right paths

for his name's sake.

4 Even though I walk

through the darkest valley,

I will fear no evil,

for you are with me;

your rod and your staff,

they comfort me.

5 You prepare a table before me

in the presence of my enemies.

You anoint my head with oil;

my cup overflows.

6 Surely your goodness and love will follow me

all the days of my life,

and I will dwell in the house of the Lord

forever.

....

Revelation 21:1-7 New International Version (NIV)

Then I saw 'a new heaven and a new earth,' for the first heaven and the first earth had passed away, and there was no longer any sea. I saw the Holy City, the new Jerusalem, coming down out of heaven from God, prepared as a bride beautifully dressed for her husband.

And I heard a loud voice from the throne saying, 'Look! God's dwelling place is now among the people, and he will dwell with them. They will be his people, and God himself will be with them and be their God. 'He will wipe every tear from their eyes. There will be no more death' or mourning or crying or pain, for the old order of things has passed away.'

He who was seated on the throne said, 'I am making everything new!' Then he said, 'Write this down, for these words are trustworthy and true.'

He said to me: 'It is done. I am the Alpha and the Omega, the Beginning and the End. To the thirsty I will give water without cost from the spring of the water of life. Those who are victorious will inherit all this, and I will be their God and they will be my children.'

....

I received a letter near the end of December from our friend Roy who had left St Matthias a couple of years earlier. We had kept in contact with each other, and Roy, being of a similar age to Dad, had also struck up a friendship with my dad. Here is an extract from the letter:

Your father went downhill so rapidly at the end, that his death was quite a shock for all of us. I had many happy chats and prayers with him over the months when his health was poor, and I was always encouraged by his solid faith. He was a man of wide experience and he could talk on many subjects. He is now with your dear mother in the presence of the Lord - What a comfort!

1997

Because I lived in Torquay, the task of slowly working through all my parents' belongings was up to me. Julie had gone back to Australia and Robert was back in Dorset. They had taken the important things they wanted from the house. Now the onerous task of sorting through the rest was in my hands.

It was a very cold January and on the third day of the New Year I drove to my parents' old house, which now was empty of humans. As I unlocked the front door of that little terraced house I felt empty and, as I walked in, I felt the emptiness of the house, now Dad wasn't around.

The freezing cold temperature didn't really help the occasion either. The place indeed felt very cold and barren.

As I walked into the sitting room where Dad often spent his time I was confronted with a sight that I could have done without!

Water was gently streaming down from the ceiling onto the contents of the room. I quickly ran upstairs and could hear water flowing from the loft. I fetched a ladder and climbed into the dark dank loft space. I then saw the problem. It was an old house, so there was a water tank in the loft that supplied water to the taps in the bathroom. The ballcock valve had stuck open, which normally wouldn't cause too much of a problem because the excess water would escape through the overflow pipe that protruded through the wall, to the outside of the house.

But, because of the freezing temperatures, the end of the overflow pipe had totally frozen causing the water to spill over the edge of the metal tank and go right down through the house!

I immediately went and turned the water off at the mains. As I surveyed the water damage in the rooms concerned, I struggled to stay in the house - it was hard enough being there anyway, without this depressing drama adding to my woes. I spent a few minutes moving various bits of paperwork and furniture to drier places, then I left. I would have to come back another day, my emotional stamina was totally spent.

As I drove away from the house, I cried out to God. With the minute faith I had at that time, I asked Him to somehow bring good out of this upsetting predicament.

At the end of the road, the thought of house insurance popped into my head.

A couple of days later, I found that Dad had insurance, and the company sent an assessor round to survey the damage and give a compensation quote. I told them I would do the work that was needed to redecorate the house. They agreed to give us a couple of thousand pounds and leave me to do the work however I wanted.

The house ended up drying out and in the spring I just painted the damaged areas with some white paint I found in the basement. The couple of bits of furniture that had got wet were old and I would have thrown them away anyway.

So, the money the insurance company gave us totally covered the cost of what we had paid for Dad's funeral the month before.

....

I want to mention at this point that the year of 1997 was very heavy for me. I really struggled with grief. I remember going into shops and not being able to count out the correct coins to give to the cashier. I would just give them all the coins and let them take what they needed, and I wasn't embarrassed - because I didn't care.

I was beyond counting and I was beyond caring.

So I was often in a mess.

The emotion would get so pent up in me that it needed to come out. And there was only one way to get in contact with the deep emotional loss.

It was to listen to track six (The Lord is my Shepherd) on the 'Gloria' CD, by John Rutter. The CD that I had bought on my way up to see Dad on that last day he lived. The track that I had played in his room a few hours before he died.

As soon as the track reached the 13 seconds point, I would just burst into tears. I didn't like to listen to it, because I knew it was going to get me in contact with my pain - but I had to go and listen to it when my life was getting too heavy.

And always, after listening to that track, I would feel relief. I could breathe deeper. I would feel so much lighter.

God had given me an instrument to pop the bubble of my aloneness.

I was free again. For a few days!

My new job at the church was now taking shape, usually I was at the centre befriending people. Often, they wanted to chat while I made them a cup of coffee, usually ending in a time of prayer. I was also sent out to see people who specifically requested a home visit. They were usually struggling with bad health or loneliness. It was an honour to be trusted with their vulnerability.

Another part of the job I was given to do later in the year was being a tour guide for an Acapella Choir from Canada who were touring around England. I guided them around South Devon and took them to places like Buckland Abbey near the moors and to other famous landmarks, including some locations that were used in films like 'Sense and Sensibility'. The choir was mainly made up of people in their twenties, with a couple of older teachers. I had a great time guiding the the coach driver around and speaking into the coach's microphone to everyone in the back when we passed a place of interest. I was a bit of a clown as well - so they were especially fortunate to have me as their tour guide!

I was also the new church magazine editor. Dad had taken this on a few months before he died, so I decided to complete his original commitment to the church, of doing it for one year. It allowed me to bring a more spiritual content to the pages, which I felt it needed.

In February I took Paul (my old boss at PGH motorcycles) and his wife Karen to an Alpha Course in Teignmouth. Paul had missed quite a few of the Alpha talks in our church the previous year, so he wanted to do another one. The one that started in Teignmouth was perfect for them - being a lot nearer to where they lived.

After completing that course and going to a few other Christian meetings, they both gave their lives to God and became Christians.

That was over twenty years ago and they are both as committed as ever. Paul has been a real evangelist in his shop and in the biker world beyond the walls of PGH motorcycles. Karen has also been sharing her faith to many that she meets through her cattery business and of course beyond the walls of the cattery.

In 2018, Paul sold his bike business and now spends a lot of his time working for the church.

....

In the late spring we found out that Andy, the assistant vicar, was getting prepared to move on with his family to another parish elsewhere in England. Their three year term at St Matthias was coming to an end and they were starting to have some interviews in various parts of the country. Alex and I always knew they would probably not stay in Torquay but when this became more apparent, we started to realise that the charismatic influence they had brought into our church was probably not going to remain. We had often struggled with the laborious nature of much that went on in the Church of England but we had been encouraged to stick with it when Andy and Ann came along. They were not embarrassed to openly speak about things of the Holy Spirit and were more interested in people moving on with God than just `pew filling' and social events.

They were on the same page as us. We and a few others were going to miss them a great deal.

....

In June, I started to go and see a local Christian Counsellor called Eileen. She was the wife of a local vicar and had been recommended to me by Dawn, who was the friend who had written the *'message in a bottle'* to us a couple of years earlier, when we were living in Bath. Dawn suggested I go and see Eileen because she had really helped her when she had lost her dad.

I had been struggling, so Dawn's advice was, yet again, very timely.

I only saw Eileen a few times but they were very special.

I remember her asking me about some good memories of my dad. One memory was when he used to play football with me on the lawn at our house in Horley when I was around ten or eleven years old.

That really got me crying.

Another time when I was at Eileen's, I read out Dad's letter that I had opened just after he died.

Eileen and me both agreed that it was sad.

We began to realise that my parents had their own personal issues in life. And as a result of my rejection issues from my birth parents, I had learnt early in life to **fit in,** to whatever and whoever.

I grew up, not being able to express myself fully. I was not free emotionally.

There was a part of me that was stunted.

That part was Colin. The enthusiastic, expressive, emotional - *Welsh/Greek* Cypriot **Colin.**

Eileen felt that I could write a letter to that ignored and neglected part of me that I had left behind in my life.

This is a part of the letter I wrote:

Dear Colin,

I am writing in recognition that you have been left behind by me. It's time for you to be affirmed little one, yes little Welsh/Greek Cypriot one, loved and created by our God and Father.

You have been squashed. You have been squashed after daring to move out of the womb of death threats. You are a brave little warrior and it is time for you to receive honour oh little free spirited one. God your Father has loved you from the beginning of time and has never forgotten you - not for one millionth of a second.

And, to my detriment, I have been forced to hide you in my cellar. I'm so sorry little Colin - it seemed the only way for me to gain a glimpse of acceptance. You were not wanted by other people so I left you behind, while I went in search of love.

But I realise now - you are so important to me.

*Because you **are** me.*

I've so longed and longed for my emptiness to be replaced with life.

God has filled me but I've leaked. I believe the hole that God's Spirit has leaked from can only be filled by you Colin. I need you in my life like no other person has needed you.

Colin come out of the cellar and dance your beautiful dance for everyone to see and I will not be ashamed to dance every step you dance, oh beautiful one.

So pure and innocent. And our Lord Jesus will dance with us and show us how to dance the perfect will of God.

I don't want to remain separate any longer. Come let's be healed by God.

We might have to be known as Mark - but don't feel any loss of identity in that. It seems like we are made to be Mark.

Let's go for it - Welsh/Greek Cypriot/English Mark!

I want to know you more, so that I can be the warrior God made me to be.

....

Well I expect that was a bit weird for some of you but hopefully, for others, it will mean something.

During the course of the year I had continued to slowly sort through and empty dad's house. It was slow because it was hard to know what to do with everything. People seem to gather a lot of stuff in a lifetime! And of course, much of it held memories for me which made it even harder. By the summer I had given a lot of things away to people but, as is often the case, people have enough of their *own stuff*.

My friend Duncan who had his own second-hand bookshop in Torquay came round and got some books and most of the rest I took to various charity shops. Charity shops were a very useful place to unload many items from around the house.

Dad had left me the car like I mentioned earlier but he stipulated in his will that I should also be given the TV and video player. There was probably a smile on his face when he did that because he knew I didn't like televisions, and certainly didn't want one in my home. I gave them away to a friend. Sorry Dad!

My old biker friend Gordon came round one day with his large tyre company pickup wagon. We loaded it right up with all sorts of unwanted furniture and other unusable items. He and another old friend called Dave drove it to the council tip for them to sort through and dump.

I had slowly and sensitively gone through everything in the house. Many things in the house went to good homes, often to people who personally knew my parents. It was a privilege that I was only working part-time and could spend lots of hours there working through everything. It was so therapeutic in helping me grieve properly. I would often just sit on the floor in the corner of one of the rooms and cry. There was no one around to disturb me. I had the house all to myself.

....

In July, things came to a head concerning our church attendance at St Matthias. I had first started going there twelve years earlier and I had many fond memories of my involvement there. It had also been a wonderful church for my parents to venture into, after years of not going anywhere - they had found much support there.

But Alex and I had reached the point where we couldn't stay there any longer.

We felt the tide was going out and the opportunity for the church to put its sails up to the Holy Spirit and leave the harbour was ending. It was content to be like the Golden Hind replica that was moored permanently in Brixham harbour.

We felt that if we stayed, we too, would spiritually become mired in that same mentality.

We did not belong in that mentality.

In our daily reading notes we were getting confirmation from God that we were on the right track. The theme of making the decision kept coming at us from all angles in various things we read:

Many Christians, and far too many churches try and blow their own human breath into the sails - no wonder the boat doesn't go anywhere! So stop blowing your own breath into the sails of your life, or your church. The Spirit of God in Hebrew is ruach, meaning 'wind'. Ask for a fresh wind to fill the sails. Without the Holy Spirit we will go nowhere.

Today God is calling you to a decision. How long will you waver between two options? If the Lord is God, follow Him.

You will never arrive if you don't set out. And you may have to go it alone!

It will make you take down the walls of your tradition and cry out like David did in the Bible, 'So panteth my soul after Thee, O Lord.' (Psalm 42: 1)

You don't need to know where you're going, you just have to know you're following God!

You have gone round this mountain long enough. (Deuteronomy 2: 3)

God has promised you favour but sometimes He has to change your address to get it to you.

At work one morning I knew I had to make the big decision. I arranged to speak to Peter the vicar. Over the years, we had got to know each other quite well. He had been there right at the beginning of my Christian walk, when I first got back from Turkey. But I knew that I needed to move on. I had been there long enough. Peter tried to reason with me, but I was very sure of my convictions.

I made sure that I completed the church magazine 'year commitment' that Dad had hoped to complete, and at the end of July, Alex and I finally left the church.

We didn't know what was next but that was over to God. We had done our bit.

In August, Esme, who was nearly six, had a very clear dream about Jesus:

He picked her up and took her to heaven. They sat down and had a meal together - all the time Jesus was cuddling her. Then He brought her back to earth and they went for a walk by a fountain, while Esme played with His hair.

Then for a second time, He took her to heaven and she saw Granny and Grandpa looking at flowers. They both looked happy.

Well, it really touched me also, because my mum and dad were there in it. Esme drew a coloured picture of what she had seen.

....

At the end of August, Princess Di died in a car crash in Paris. Most of England seemed to be in some type of shock and grief. It was a very strange time for a few days and I was intrigued to see what effect it was having on the nation. Alex and I took the kids up onto Dartmoor on the day of the funeral to get away from all the media frenzy. It was so refreshing to be up on the moors on our own. We hardly saw anyone, because most of the nation were sitting in front of their televisions!

The day before the funeral, Mother Teresa died, but her passing away was hardly noticed.

Ten years earlier, Alex had gone to help in Mother Teresa's 'Home for the destitute and dying', in Calcutta (known also as Kolkata since 2001), for a few months with a couple of her friends, Ali and Suzanne.

One of our many visits to Dartmoor together

....

In September, Caleb who was now three, started going to playschool for a few hours during the week. This gave Alex and I a few hours without either Esme or Caleb, which was a new experience for the both of us.

It was also in September that Alex's parents Bernard and Isabella celebrated their Fiftieth wedding anniversary, which brought together the Wisdom family and immediately connected family. There were twenty of us in all and we all met up for the weekend at Middle Clyst, which was the big house Bernard and Bella lived in on the edge of Plymtree, near Exeter.

On the Sunday morning, I drove into Exeter and checked out a Vineyard church that I had heard about. There were lots of young people there from the local University and also a few friends of ours from Torquay too. It was a good service. The sermon was on deliverance from demons and spirits - so there was no holding back there!

At the end of September we heard that Andy and Ann, the assistant ministers at our old church, St Matthias, had found a new job and were moving on. They were going to move to Derbyshire where Andy was going to be the vicar for a church in Ripley.

In October, the house that belonged to my parents was nearly ready to go on the market. A couple of friends were helping me to paint the last few places that needed a touch of paint. I had tidied up the small rear garden and that was now looking nice. So it was nearly the end of an era, that was sad, but also in some ways exciting.

Having my parents die when I was *fairly* young (mid thirties), seemed to be bringing me into an arena of invisible maturity that I had not known before in my life. It's maybe strange to read this but I had been thrust into a form of adulthood that I think someone cannot really fully appreciate until their parents are not around anymore.

Don't get me wrong - I was still in the grips of grief at this point, which continued for most of the following year to come; but there was a slight breeze of liberation in the air also.

In November, Alex started nursing two days a week at a Nursing home in Torquay. Also during the month we went on a marriage weekend near Totnes. There were a few other couples there as well and we were all there to assess where our marriages were at, and how to improve them. The food was amazing, as was all the hospitality but it was probably all a little too intense for my liking. Having a public/private x-ray machine exploring how I was doing as a husband didn't sit comfortably with me.

Soon after that weekend, I went away for a week on my own to attend a bereavement conference at Lee Abbey. Dr Marie Bew, who was leading the week, was a medical practitioner and also a Spiritual Director (whatever that is, but it sounds good).

She was good, and as it was coming up to a year since Dad had died it gave me some good insight into understanding the nature of the bereavement journey.

In December, I finally put my parents' house on the market.

1998

The first part of the year, I was grieving deeply over the loss of my dad. The fact that his house was soon to go helped trigger it but also I was reading his journal that he wrote when he was a merchant seaman. I had reached the part where he was on his first sea voyage from Glasgow in Scotland to Bombay (now Mumbai) in India. It was in early 1944 during the Second World War, and he was still sixteen. Reading through the pages helped me get more in contact with my loss of the dad that I was even now finding out more about.

Got a phone call from Paul, my old boss. He phoned me up to tell me he had got back from a weekend conference in Sidmouth and that he had been baptised in the Holy Spirit, and had got the gift of speaking in tongues.

He had been crying, laughing and shaking. He was basically very happy. I had seen Paul a couple of months earlier when we had gone out for a drink together. He had told me then with tears in his eyes that he loved Jesus.

This was a new man!

2 Corinthians 5:17 (NIV)

Therefore, if anyone is in Christ, he is a new creation : the old has gone, the new has come!

....

In this first month of the new year I read two books about the life of Gladys Aylward; 'The Small Woman', and 'The London Sparrow'.

She was a famous missionary to China, who died in 1970. She is definitely one of my 'heroes of the faith'.

She wrote in the front of her Bible: *The eagle that soars in the upper air, does not worry itself, how it is to cross rivers.*

I love that quote.

By February we were, as a family, often driving up to Exeter on a Sunday morning and attending the Vineyard Church. After the service we usually drove to Alex's parents in Plymtree and had lunch with them. So although Exeter is about twenty miles from Torquay, it worked out well, because we could make a full day of it.

In late March, my parents' old house sold. The money was split three ways between Julie, Robert and me.

Alex and I felt we wanted to give ten percent of the money we received to various ministries we were keen to support.

After we had done that, we put the rest in our bank account. The amount we had was about ten thousand pounds and at that time we were receiving some housing benefit to help us pay our monthly rent. That benefit then came to an end, when we declared that we had some savings in our bank account.

Over the next twelve months, most of the savings were gone.

But selling the house was definitely the end of an important chapter in our life.

In April, I started working as a self-employed gardener for a few days a week. I arranged my workload to suit Alex's part time work at the nursing home. When she was working, I looked after affairs at home; getting Esme to school and back, looking after Caleb, cleaning, shopping and cooking. And when I was gardening, Alex was at home doing those jobs. It worked out well.

The spring had arrived and it was good to be out gardening at various locations during the week.

Around this time, I had also started going to a homegroup at a house in Kingskerswell, which was nearby. Sue, whose house it was, used to go to St Matthias when we were there but had since left, for much the same reasons as us. It was a good group, with some people even coming from Exeter to attend. As the weeks went on, we got a babysitter for Esme and Caleb, so that Alex could come to the group too.

It was more our sort of tribe. We never knew what was going to happen when we all got together. It was very informal but very God-centred also.

In May, my friend Duncan asked me to help him out occasionally with his business. He owned 'Duncan's Bookshop', which was a second-hand bookshop in the town centre. He offered me some part-time work, running the shop whenever he was away from Torquay. He was also a Christian and was not far off retirement age. We had known each other for over ten years and I had often hung out with him in the shop when I got some spare time.

In the summer I got knocked off my motorbike by a car. I was taken to the hospital in an ambulance and was quite shaken up. I had to have a few stitches in both legs and I had bruises and grazes in different parts of my body.

When the car hit me, I seemed to be thrown up in the air in slow motion, almost like my body was separate from my spirit for a second or two. Then I landed on the tarmac road and lay there on my back.

I have often heard other people talk of a similar slow-motion experience when they have had an accident.

Anyway - that aside, let me tell you what had been going on an hour before that car hit me.

I had been riding my old Honda Motorsport 250cc around the countryside over near Teignmouth and I had been thinking about how I felt I was in an emotional fog. Life had become quite lackadaisical and I didn't seem to be in touch with the sharp focus of real life.

I prayed to God.

I said, *'God, bring me into contact with reality. Make something clear and definite happen. Wake me up - whatever it takes, wake me up to the reality of life.'*

Just over an hour later I was lying flat on my back in the road.

The day after the accident I was lying in my bed at home and I asked God to lead me to the right book to read, while I was recovering and resting.

I was led to a book on my shelf called 'Suffering' by Alister McGrath.

That seemed suitable!

I had not read it before, but it was the right book.

Here is what I was confronted with (I have highlighted a few words):

Page 4

*Truth is found upon the **road**. It might even be said that only when a man descends from the balcony that he was looking from to the road, whether of his own free will, or because he has been pitched from it by providential circumstances, does he begin to know what **reality** is.*

Page 29

We are called by God, to find our Rest in Him.

We do not want to admit our own mortality. Suffering strips away our illusions of immortality. It causes anxiety to rear its ugly, yet revealing head. It batters down the gates of the citadel of illusions. It confronts us with the harsh facts of life, And it makes us ask those hard questions which have the power to erode false-hood and propel us away from the false security and transient rewards of the world, towards our loving God.

Suffering, though tragic, is not pointless. It is the pin which bursts the balloon of our delusions, and opens the way to an urgent and passionate wrestling with the reality of death and the question of what lies beyond.

....

In my journal from that year I wrote that, after the accident, I felt closer to God and in no way blamed Him for it, but believed He allowed it, to give me a new depth of understanding of my pilgrimage with Him.

He had also protected me. The doctor on duty at the hospital told me I was very lucky. My back was fine, I had no broken bones, I had no head or facial injuries and I had no permanent damage to my body, I would just have some discomfort for two weeks!

I seem to remember my Honda got broken in a few places though.

My main physical injury was on my inside left ankle where something had lacerated my skin. the doctor cleaned my wounds out and sewed me up. Don't forget that 'inside left ankle' - it's going to turn up again in a few months' time!

....

From September, Caleb was attending playschool for two and a half full days a week. He was now four years old and in January would move to the Primary School that Esme was in.

As the Autumn season took over from Summer, we started to explore cycle paths around Devon. It was something we continued to do as a family in the years to follow. Caleb had learnt to ride his bike when he was only three and Esme, being not so keen, slowly got the hang of it when we started doing these trips around Devon.

For our first bike adventure, we drove all the way to North Devon and cycled some of the 'Tarka Trail.' It follows the route of an old disused railway line for over thirty miles from Braunton, on the North Coast, to a small village called Meeth, passing through such places as Barnstaple, Instow, Bideford and Great Torrington.

We parked the car at the old Meeth railway station and cycled north to the site of Petrockstow railway station. Esme fell off a few times but, with persuasion from me, reluctantly got back on again and kept going. Caleb was more at home with the whole idea. The whole trip was about six miles in all, so they both did really well.

The following week I went up to North Devon on my own and spent a few days exploring the whole Tarka Trail. I loved cycling it's route, which mainly followed the beautiful waterways of the River Taw and the River Torridge. As I cycled alongside the Torridge Estuary at Instow I even got sight of the Island of Lundy, twenty miles out to sea.

I so enjoyed those couple of days exploring on my own in such a beautiful part of England.

At the end of October, we as a family ventured to West Devon and cycled some of the Plym Valley Cycle Trail from Clearbrook, on the edge of Dartmoor, to the nearby Bickleigh Viaduct. Again, it was about a six mile round trip but this time involved more inclines. Esme enjoyed this trip more than the first. She didn't fall off and we went through a long tunnel. So that helped the enjoyment.

In November, Alex joined the nursing bank staff teams at Torbay Hospital and Rowcroft Hospice. Being on the bank staff gave the freedom to choose when and where she worked, as she could decline or accept any shifts that were offered - depending on how she felt.

The last part of the year involved me being dressed up as a nine foot high, silver sprayed star.

The Vineyard Church in Exeter were doing a snazzy Nativity drama in the middle of Exeter shopping centre, just before Christmas. My part was being the star over Bethlehem.

So if you can't be the star of the show - just be the star over Bethlehem!

On New Years Eve, the Vineyard Church had a disco party in Exmouth. It was so much fun to just enjoy that sort of dancing with the crew from the church. I remember well my favourite track of the night: Blue Monday by New Order.

I was able to be myself with that one!

1999

Three fairly significant things happened within the first week of this last year of the century;

1. Our son Caleb started Primary school. Esme also had been waiting for this day. She and Caleb enjoyed playing with each other in the school break times.

2. At the homegroup in Kingskerswell, they prayed for me in this new season, now that both our children were at school full time. One of the ladies called Clare, prayed that God would give me something to **run** with, so that I could run and keep running.

A month later - God gave me that something!

3. Number three involves that 'inside left ankle!'

I was in the bath and I noticed that the ankle injury from my bike accident in August was slightly swollen. It had obviously been irritated when I had danced the night away a few days earlier at the New Year's Eve party. I had noticed it seemed to be taking longer than normal to heal and feel right. My reasoning had been that a good strong dance would help it along. In the bath I felt the lump around the injury and was shocked when what seemed like a splinter of bone pricked my finger slightly. What on earth was going on in there.

I went straight to my doctor in Torquay and got an appointment the same day. He also could feel it, so he got me to lay on the stiff bed in his surgery and came to the conclusion that something was under the skin that shouldn't be there. He gave me a local anaesthetic, and set too with his scalpel knife.

Whatever it was, it was bigger than we thought, and it didn't want to come out easily.

But in the end, it did.

It was about the size of a small fingernail and also pretty thick. It was a lump of front headlight glass from a Ford Escort car.

In the accident it had pierced my skin and deeply lodged into my body. It had not been seen by the hospital when they had put five stitches in, to seal the wound. I felt so good after it was removed. My ankle would heal properly now.

Better out than in!

I'm glad I danced hard on New Year's Eve, or else I suspect my body would have let it hide away forever.

....

The Vineyard Church was planning on taking a group of people from the church to India for three weeks in March and Alex felt God was wanting her to go. So we paid the deposit and Alex booked three weeks holiday leave from her work.

In early February, I was sitting reading the 'Cross Rhythms' Christian Music magazine and something in an article by a DJ (disc jockey) jumped out at me. He mentioned that vari-speed CD players were now being made, which gave DJ's a choice of playing CD's if they wanted too whereas before the only choice was to use vinyl.

As I read this, I sensed God quickening my spirit. There was something relevant in this information for me. I had no idea there were CD players that could alter the speed/tempo of beats. *This speed adjustment enables a DJ to match the beats of two tracks he is trying mix together so that the beats correspond with each other.*

I started to get excited and believed that God was giving me something to **run** with.

The following weekend we went as a family to stay the weekend at Alex's parents' house, near Exeter. We invited two friends from the Vineyard Church, called Marion and Arens, to come and stay there too. During the weekend I told them that I felt God was leading me towards being a DJ. They both felt that it was indeed God's calling on my life and encouraged me to *Go for it* - to step out in faith and start looking for equipment. They pointed out that God would stop me if it wasn't from Him.

I got more excited about the reality of it all.

We started to pray together that God would lead me clearly in the way forward. Just as we were praying, a dramatic hailstorm erupted outside and then it stopped suddenly and the sun came out.

Marion felt God was saying that the *New Season* in my life was going to happen as quick as the change of weather outside had.

She said, 'It's now happened - the New season has started - it's begun - **it's now**!'

She also saw in her mind's eye an old beehive and believed God was saying that, like the bee's prepare the honey in the hidden place (out of sight - inside the hive), God had been preparing me over the last few years. The honey was about to come out of my life to refresh others and set them free.

The next day, back in Torquay, I bought a free ads newspaper, so that I could look in the music section and see if there was any DJ gear for sale.

Please remember, this was in the days before big internet sales and marketing!

Guess what I found in that newspaper?

The following Saturday there was going to be a DJ equipment clearance sale in Brixham.

I went along to the event. It was a very small affair in an old barn workshop on the edge of Brixham. It was some guy called Dave who apparently had been a DJ for many years and was now packing it up and selling his old gear. He needed more space in his workshop because he was going to be a local retail agent for new DJ equipment in the South Devon area.

He was going to make flight cases for some of their equipment and also display some of their new products in his workshop.

I had arrived as soon as the clearance sale started. There wasn't really a lot of stuff there. There were some vinyl decks and some lights but the key things I saw were two big old loudspeakers and an old 'Malcolm Hill' 800 watt amplifier. Dave told me that they were reliable and solid pieces of kit. He had been using them since the seventies and they had never let him down. He had built the speakers himself and told me that 'Hill Amplifiers' were among the best amplifiers around.

I knew nothing about all this type of sound equipment.

He told me I could have the amp and the speakers for £500 - special deal!

It was scary for me because I didn't have a clue really but I just trusted the timing of it all and stepped out in faith. I gave him £500.

Straight after I paid him, a guy walked in, saw the amp and wanted to buy it. Dave told him that I had just bought it. The guy told me it was a really good amp and that he personally would have paid more for it, if I hadn't beaten him to it.

So that was reassuring - I hadn't been ripped off.

I asked Dave if he knew where I could buy good CD decks for DJ'ing.

He told me to come to the launch of his new DJ store on February 28th, when there were going to be new CD players and mixers on show.

Amazing really, when I look back. The timing was ridiculous, because there was no such shop for miles around, back then.

This was a lot of money for me to pay out. It was not my nature to do such rash things. I wasn't even a DJ. I had hardly any suitable music CD's, no decks, no mixer, no expertise, no past knowledge, no potential gigs and no venues!

But I had stepped out. In faith.

I wanted to take the good Christian music that I had been hearing over the years on radio stations like 'Cross Rhythms' and play it at church events. I wanted to get it out there and heard.

I bought the amp and speakers in Brixham on February 15th. I now had two weeks to do some research on CD decks and mixers before the new DJ equipment store opened at the end the of the month.

In the few days between me being with Marion and Arens and now buying the amp and speakers, I had spotted something in the current edition of the 'Cross Rhythms' magazine. Once a year they produced a comprehensive 'music directory', which catalogued the various Christian music related businesses and ministries in the UK. Within it was a section for DJ's. It was an A4 sized directory and a very useful resource for finding out who did what in the Christian music world.

Of course, the internet does all that now but believe me - it was a lot different back then.

What I noticed on the day that I picked up the magazine was that February 14th was the final date for registering any new company or ministry into the next yearly edition of the 'Music Resource Directory'. At that point, I hadn't even bought the amp and speakers - I hadn't got anything, so it seemed stupid to register as a DJ.

But... it also seemed like an opportunity not to miss.

Before I jumped into registering, I needed to find a DJ name for myself!

I reasoned that having a name that began with the letter 'A' would be good, then I would be at the beginning of the list of DJ names in the directory. That got me to thinking about being called AA man! - for obvious reasons. So I then started looking in my Bible concordance book for good words that began with the letter A. The two words that stood out to me were Absolute and Abandon.

So then I looked in a dictionary to fully look into what those two words meant.

Absolute :   *complete, perfect, not limited, pure*

Abandon :   freedom from inhibition

DJ Absolute Abandon.

Great stuff - now I was rolling! It also got me to thinking about David in the Bible, when he danced with abandon.

2 Samuel 6:14 New International Version (NIV)

Wearing a linen ephod, David was **dancing before the Lord with all his might,**

2 Samuel 6:14 Complete Jewish Bible (CJB)

Then David danced and spun around with **abandon** before *Adonai*, wearing a linen ritual vest.

I sent off my DJ name, along with my address and phone number to the 'Cross Rhythms' office, before the cut-off date of February 14th. The new edition of the 'Music Directory' was due to be published in the spring and in its pages was going to be DJ Absolute Abandon.

....

On the subject of new publications, here is another example of perfect timing. I was walking around a local newsagent and on the shelf I saw a glossy magazine called 'DJ EQ'. It was issue 1 and, because it was a launch edition, it had a whole feature on all the available CD decks and mixers that were on the market. It had a photo of each model, with specifications and comments alongside each one. It was a perfect resource for researching what was out there and what would be suitable equipment for me.

After spending hours sifting through all the different makes and models, I liked the new CDN-34 anti-shock twin CD decks, produced by a company called Numark and I also liked the pro quality Numark DM1385X mixer.

There were so many choices, but I felt the Numark stuff seemed right for me, even the name Numark seemed an appropriate play on words for me! But I needed confirmation, because there were other companies that were producing good equipment too.

It was going to cost me about £1500 to buy those items, and for me that was scary. Up until that point in my life the most I had ever paid for anything was about three or four hundred pounds for things like a motorbike, an air ticket, or a car.

This was big bucks for me, plus I had already paid out £500 one week earlier for the amp and speakers.

A few days later I was at our church minister's house in Torquay having a meal with him and his family. His name was Keith, and after the meal he asked me if there was anything he could pray for, in my life. I asked him to pray that I would be guided to the right make of DJ equipment, because in a few days time I was going to have to make a decision on how to spend a lot of money.

We prayed together that God would show me very clearly which brand of CD decks and mixer I should buy.

After the prayer time, I went to the loo. When I was in the bathroom, right there in front of me was a bottle of shampoo and in big bold letters was the name 'Numark'.

I ran out to show Keith, and explained that this was the brand name of the main items of equipment I was thinking to buy.

I had my confirmation!

On February 28th I drove over to Brixham for the opening launch of Dave's new shop. When I arrived, there were two posh-looking chaps in suits there. They were the business representatives (reps) for one of the makes of equipment that Dave was going to be selling in his shop. They were the reps for Numark!

They and Dave did me a launch deal. I could have the Numark decks and mixer for £1360. As part of the offer, Dave would also custom build an aluminium flight case to mount it all in.

I also managed to persuade them to give me a free set of headphones.

The flight case and the gear would be ready to pick up in ten days time. I left a deposit and I was another step nearer to being a DJ.

....

In early March Alex was getting ready to leave England, to go to India with the Exeter Vineyard Church.

To help Esme and Caleb get a handle on how long their mum was going to be away for, we made an India trip advent calendar for them with eighteen little card doors. We hid some pictures behind each door, which we had cut out from an Indian holiday brochure.

They were allowed to open one door a day and get a sweet. The final door would indicate the day Alex would return home.

On March 10th, Alex left Torquay to meet up with a team in London. Then they flew from Heathrow to India.

I was full time house husband. Soon after Alex left, my DJ equipment was ready to pick up, so I went and collected it and shelled out the money. It was the tail end of the money we had received from the sale of Dad's house.

I got home and placed the large set up onto a table in the corner of our bedroom and connected the various phono leads to the correct positions. Then all I needed to do was work out how to use it all!

I needed to get some good CD's too. Soon after that day, I was listening to Cross Rhythms radio and a phone in competition came on. The prize was 15 CD's of contemporary Christian music. I phoned in and was live on air. I had to answer three general knowledge questions. I answered two but didn't know the answer to the third. However, in our house that morning was an engineer who had just arrived to fix the microwave and he knew the answer.

I won the 15 CD's.

Also I sent letters to the main Christian music labels, informing them that I was a DJ, requesting that they supply me with complimentary CD's. It was a slow response at the beginning but as the months went on, and after a few phone calls, they started supplying me with the dance and hip hop CD's I requested.

Another encouraging thing that happened just before Alex went to India was, we found out that a new church that had recently started up in Torquay had just found out that they could rent 'Claires Nightclub' out for one Sunday evening a month.

The church was called the 'Kings Arms' and two of our friends had been going there. It had literally started a few months earlier and was part of the New Frontiers organisation, which planted churches all around the country. 'Kings Arms' had their church services in a big community centre on a nearby council estate.

Sat with some of my new DJ gear.
The big speakers and amp are elsewhere

There were only about twenty people going there at that point but they were a young energetic lot and had a lot of vision, hence they had approached the biggest nightclub in the area to hopefully start putting on club nights.

While Alex was in India, I took the kids along to their Sunday service at the community centre. I recognised a few faces but some were new to the area. The leader was called Martin and he had come to Torquay about a year earlier to get things in place before starting the church. A few of them had been meeting in his house each week before the church officially started. We both remembered that we had spoken to each other on the phone when he first moved to Torquay. He had been given my number at the time by someone who knew me and they had suggested to him that Alex and I would be ideal people for coming on board with the 'Kings Arms.' He had invited us to their weekly meetings at his house at the time but we were already going to Exeter Vineyard Church.

It was good to meet him face to face at last. The kids and I had a good morning there. I told him Alex was in India and I also told him I was getting things together to be a DJ.

I had spoken to Alex once or twice on the phone and she was with a team of about ten people from England travelling around the north of India, quite close to Nepal. They were helping lead 'Worship and Prayer conferences' in places like Delhi, which is India's capital territory, and Dehradun, 150 miles further north, towards the border with Tibet. She was mainly part of the prayer team at the conferences.

Esme and Caleb were missing her, especially Caleb, because he was still only four years old but I was able to buoy him up if he got too sad.

I enjoyed spinning the plates to keep the show on the road back at home; getting them up in the morning, transporting them to school and back, cooking meals and settling them into bed at night. And of course that advent calendar we made was doing a great job in helping them get a time perspective about Alex's absence.

When she did come back, Caleb was quite needful of her. It had been a bit too long for him probably.

Alex came back revitalised in her faith and we caught up on all the things that had gone on while we were apart.

Once Alex was back in England, we decided to go to the 'Kings Arms' together and see if God was leading us to go church there rather than travel to Exeter every Sunday. The problem we were finding at the Vineyard Church was that we were not building any real relationships, because most of the people came from Exeter and beyond. We had wondered if God may have been leading us to live over that way but, in the end, there had been no strong indication to do so.

For the eighteen months we were there, it had been a breath of fresh air, especially after being in a traditional church before that.

In April, we started attending 'Kings Arms' and it wasn't long before I was asked by the leadership if I would consider being the resident DJ at the 'Immerse' night club events at 'Claire's Nightclub'.

The launch of 'Immerse' was to be June 27th, so I only had a few weeks to get myself ready.

This was obviously real confirmation of my DJ calling and it was so exciting.

In May, I put on a free gig for the community members at Brunel Manor, in Torquay. Brunel Manor is similar to Lee Abbey, but not as big. I went with my good friend Ben and he helped me set up my gear in the big conference room. It was the first time I had really tried out the speakers and the 800 watt amp. The evening went well and the speakers really kicked out a solid sound.

Also around this time, I got some business cards printed out and wrote to all the major churches in the area, informing them that I was available for any events they might want to put on. I can't remember actually ever getting any replies from that letter, which was a bit disheartening. But over the years they slowly woke up to the fact that I was a useful resource for them and I did many gigs for youth events, parties and even a couple of weddings. I never really liked doing weddings though because people always wanted the cheesy pop songs and that wasn't my style one bit. I wasn't that sort of DJ!

Other things that happened this month were our ninth wedding anniversary and Caleb asking Jesus to come into his life. He was nearly five years old and it was what he wanted to do. Amen.

Jesus likes that sort of prayer:

Matthew 18:2 - 4 Good News Translation (GNT)

So Jesus called a child to come and stand in front of them, and said, 'I assure you that unless you change and become like children, you will never enter the Kingdom of heaven. The greatest in the Kingdom of heaven is the one who humbles himself and becomes like this child.

....

The first 'Immerse' event at Claire's Nightclub was in June and again, my friend Ben, even though he wasn't in the 'Kings Arms' Church, came with me to help set up the gear and offer moral support.

A guy in the church called Daniel had designed a really good flyer for the Immerse events planned for that year and hundreds had been distributed around the town and beyond. It was free entry and, even though it was to run on Sunday nights, we all hoped that many would turn up. Claires Nightclub was a well-known venue in the South West, and a lot of the famous commercial `named' DJ's were regular guests there, so it was a popular place.

The doors were due to open at 8pm and at around 7.15pm a few of the main 'Kings Arms' crew who were organising the event turned up. We prayed together that God's Holy Spirit would come and make a difference in the place. It was a venue where, like most nightclubs in the land, people often participated in activities not generally conducive to the lifestyle we had now chosen to live. But, when we prayed, we really felt the presence of God turn up tangibly and it wasn't just us who felt it, as we were later to find out.

This new ground-breaking venture in Torquay was exciting and I felt privileged to be on board in the early days of its birth.

A Drum and Bass DJ had travelled down from Cardiff to do the first warm up set and then I went on at around 8.30pm. When I started, there was an encouraging cheer from the local people who knew me and as I brought in my first track of music, I shouted over the microphone, 'This is Claire's Nightclub, for Heaven's sake!', obviously putting an emphasis on the word Heaven, which brought a good response from the *crowd*.

This was my first real gig and I had a long way to go before I could beat match tracks together properly but people just enjoyed dancing together with each other and God. There was a pure vibe going on, and people appreciated it.

Later in the evening, the other DJ from Cardiff did another set and I got on the dance floor and joined in the fun. When I came off the dance floor, one of the owners of the club came and chatted to me. She felt the place was getting cleansed by us lot being there and told me that when she first walked in the bar, the skin on her whole body went all tingly.

Then as she was telling me this, she exclaimed, 'Oh, it's happening again, as I'm talking!' I told her that it was the Holy Spirit she was sensing in the place. Then we talked about God.

I went back to my decks after the chat and did the final set before we finished at 11pm.

The night had been a success. Apparently 130 people had been checked through the door during the evening - so we were encouraged.

As we were packing stuff away, one of the barmen told us it was the best night he had ever known at Claire's.

I had so many compliments during the night and in the days that followed. In my journal I recorded that I didn't think I'd ever experienced so much affirmation before from so many people.

During the summer, the Immerse gigs at Claire's Nightclub continued, up to 150 people came along some months. In July, I went to Leeds for a two week residential radio presenter course, with on air training.

It had been recommended to me earlier in the year and I had wondered whether I may be getting led into that type of career, alongside my DJ'ing.

I got a certificate at the end of it but to be honest, it didn't push my buttons.

In August, our family went camping for a week with the church to a big event near Coventry called 'Stoneleigh Bible Week.' To be honest again, I didn't really enjoy it. It was all very tight for my liking, even the onsite cafes were closed when the teaching was on. I was used to the 'Cross Rhythms' Festival, where you could just hang out and go to a variety of events whenever you felt like it... and that included hanging out at a cafe tent! The other bummer was that the only **total** eclipse of the sun in England in my lifetime was on the Wednesday but totality could only be seen in Cornwall and South Devon - Yes, including Torquay.

And there I was, in Warwickshire!

Yeah, we got to see the eclipse, but it didn't go dark, because it was only a partial eclipse in that part of England.

One of my regrets in life; not being in Torquay on August 11th 1999.

Other DJ opportunities had cropped up since I started in June, including a few slots in a pub in East Devon, for a church who were running a monthly youth event called 'Kingsize'. Another DJ there called Tom, who I met at Immerse, had asked me to be a guest DJ alongside him for a few months.

At my gigs I would sometimes mix in with the music Bible verses and lines from sermons that I had put onto Mini Discs. The Mini Disc player was on the third channel of my mixer and having those words alongside the beats worked well. When I got the volumes matching well they actually seemed like lyrics within the music.

Also, during the summer, I had met a guy called Hughie Lawrence at a concert in Bristol by a group called 'Dawkins and Dawkins'. Hughie was a Christian radio presenter for UCB radio in Stoke and he encouraged me to come up to the studios and stay with him for a couple of nights, which I did. It was good to get to know each other and a couple of weeks after staying with him, he phoned me up and said, 'Hey Mark, I've got a gig for you, up in Bradford.'

After the phone call, I realised that God was opening doors and it reminded me of Marion's words at the beginning of the year when we were praying about me setting up as a DJ. She had seen in her mind's eye: *an old beehive, and believed God was saying, that like the bee's prepare the honey in the hidden place (out of sight - inside the hive), God had been preparing me over the last few years. The honey was about to come out of my life to refresh others, and set them free.*

Things were now starting to open up, and it confirmed to me that God was opening up the hive and bringing the honey out from my life.

Just as I was thinking that, I looked up and saw the photo on our calendar. I had not even noticed it before. It was a load of bees in amongst a honeycomb and subtly written across the picture in white letters was the word: honey.

In October, I drove with my gear up to the Abundant Life Centre in Bradford, which is a huge church that seats about 800 people. I was introduced to a guy called Gus, who really looked after me well and put me up at his place for two nights. I must mention that he took me to an Indian restaurant, where I drank maybe the most lovely drink I have ever tasted in my life. It was some kind of cold mango yogurt drink that came directly from India and was a speciality in that restaurant. So beautiful.

Roll on Heaven.

The gig was for students on the Saturday night and I played in the big carpeted arena. I had by this time bought an old optokinetic projector, so I was able to project this big moving circular image of oil patterns on the far wall. It looked really good plus, Alex had made a big cotton banner with coloured cotton letters across it that spelt: *Enjoy God with Absolute Abandon.*

I didn't have to play for that long because the event earlier had overrun, but it was a good experience for me. I met a guy who came from a big church in Leeds who wanted my business card because they were going to hold an event in the Hilton Hotel and they needed a DJ that played good gospel dance music. The Abundant Life Centre gave me a good love gift of money and the whole weekend really affirmed what I was doing.

I got back to Torquay and someone phoned me and wanted to book me for a gig in a skate park in Plymouth and that led on to being booked for monthly gigs in a Plymouth church basement. So word was getting around, which was really encouraging.

....

Now for something on a totally different level.

On November 2nd, Alex's Dad Bernard died suddenly.

He was travelling alone on a train from Devon to London and was found unconscious in his seat at Paddington Station. He never recovered consciousness and died in Paddington Hospital later that day. He had had a brain haemorrhage.

This was obviously a huge shock for all the family because it came out of nowhere. Bernard had just been going up to London to attend a pensioner's lunch. Alex and her siblings rallied round Bella at her home in Plymtree and, after ten days, the funeral was held in Plymtree Church. The place was packed because Bernard was not only very popular in the village but there were also many other people who came from all over the country.

My dad had died three years earlier and I had just about got over the loss of my parents, but now here was grief crossing the threshold of our house again. This time Alex was the one being hit hard.

....

In December, Alex and I drove up to Leeds together while someone in Torquay looked after the children. I was to do a pre-arranged gig at the Hilton Hotel, for a church. The Pastor was from Africa and looked after us well, putting us up in a nearby hotel. Before we left to come back to Devon, he invited us round to his house and we chatted for an hour or so over breakfast. He encouraged me to buy a computer and set up a website for myself.

Just before Christmas I was in the 'Choice Words' Christian Bookshop in Paignton buying some presents for people and I bumped into Pam, the boss. Normally she worked in the other shop, which was in Newton Abbot but it was one of the rare times I saw her in the Paignton shop. I casually asked her if there were any part-time jobs coming up in either of the shops and she told me that funnily enough a job vacancy was coming up soon because someone was leaving. She gave me a job description form and, that evening, I posted her my CV.

Only that very morning I had desperately asked God to find me a job, because our bank account funds were pretty low and Alex was no longer working at the Nursing Home in Torquay.

She had actually felt led by God to hand in her notice there in early October. She finished working at Mount Tryon at the end of that month. *One week later her dad died!*

God knows us so well, and cares.

2000

The Twentieth Century had ended. It had been a memorable century; mostly because of the half I didn't live in. This time round, I was going to live in the first half.

....

In early January I attended an interview for the job at 'Choice Words' Bookshop. I met up with Pam and her husband Roy, who told me the job entailed working on Mondays, Tuesdays and Wednesdays, plus one Saturday a month. We chatted about my past experience not being connected with the retail trade but it didn't seem too much of a problem, which was good, although my occasional shifts at 'Duncan's Bookshop' in Torquay did count in my favour.

After the interview they told me that I was one of three possible candidates that they were thinking could be right for the job.

Over to you Lord. But by the way - I would like this job!

....

About ten days later two letters arrived in the post that ended up being very connected, in the grand scheme of God's plans. They were letters that brought very good news.

The first one arrived on January 21st. It was a letter from Alex's mum. She wanted to equally divide some early inheritance money to Alex and her siblings. The money would be available in the next month or so.

This was quite a surprise and the amount Bella was hoping to give to Alex was enough to put a good deposit on a house.

It wasn't that we were looking to get a mortgage, because the idea of getting tied down for loads of years didn't appeal to us really. Yet there was no other real alternative other than spend it all on rent for the next few years. We would pray about it. God would lead us into His perfect plan for our future. He was definitely up to something though, 'cos the ground was starting to shift around a bit!

The second letter arrived on January 22nd. It was from Pam at 'Choice Words'. I had been given the job! To start on Monday January 31st.

Come on. This new century was starting well.

A few days later, we bought a computer and a friend in the 'Kings Arms' helped me set things up for my DJ business. He also designed me a more 'street cred' business card.

My email address was dj@godmusic.co.uk

and my website was www.godmusic.co.uk

The 'godmusic' name is not operating anymore but it was pretty unique at the time.

On the last day of the month, I rode six miles on my Honda motorbike, to the Newton Abbot branch of 'Choice Words' Bookshop and started my new job!

In February, our rent went up and almost on the same day we received the early inheritance money from Alex's mum. So, without further ado,

we visited local estate agents to see what was on the market in our price range. In our price range meant the low end of the market, which was about £50,000. After about a week of trying, we just about gave up looking, because there was a total lack of houses at the bottom end of the market. We walked into nearly every estate agent in Torquay and it was the same everywhere.

In the end, we did give up. God was obviously not leading us to buy a house!

Around this time Alex started volunteering to do some shifts in the 'Straight Street Kiosk' in Torquay. It was an initiative started up by our friend Charlie, the carpenter, who I had worked for ten years earlier.

He had got permission from the Torbay Council to set up a temporary canvas kiosk in the town centre, for people to stop at and enquire about the Christian Faith. It was put up by Charlie at the beginning of each day and taken down again in the afternoon. It was manned by a rota of volunteers who represented many of the different churches in the area. Its purpose was not to advertise the different churches but to make available a better understanding of who Jesus was and is.

The name 'Straight Street' was the name of a street in Damascus that is mentioned in the Bible (Acts chapter 9).

Near the end of February, I got a phone call from an estate agent in Torquay, asking me if we were still interested in a house. I told her that we had sort of given up on the idea but asked her what she had. She told me that a terraced house had **just** come up in the very road we were living on. We were number nineteen, so I asked her what number house in our road was up for sale - she said number eighteen.

Crazy.

I looked across the road and said, 'Well they haven't got a *For Sale* sign up!'

She then went on to tell me that the owners only wanted low key advertising for some reason. I was literally the first person the estate agents phoned about it. The house was selling for about the price we were looking for. I told her not to tell anyone else and that I would phone her first thing the next day.

Immediately after that phone call, I looked out the window and saw the lady who owned the house sweeping her front path. I was in an excited and mischievous mood because somehow, I knew God was in this thing.

So I casually walked across the road to number eighteen. Now at this point you must bear in mind the relationship this couple had with people in the road; they definitely kept themselves to themselves and would not generally enter into any conversations.

So when she saw me approaching her, it was probably already a threat but, like I said, I was feeling confident and mischievous!

I said, 'Hi, you're making a good job of sweeping your path, it makes me think you're trying to sell your house!'

She stopped her sweeping, looked up at me and said indignantly, 'How do you know that?'

I started laughing and explained that I had just had a phone call from the estate agent they were registered with because we were on their list of wanting a house in the area. She then relaxed a bit and I asked her if it would be alright if Alex and I came round in the evening to look at the house, because it may suit us well. She told me she would ask her husband when he got home.

Alex and I had moved to that road five years earlier, so we knew the neighbourhood quite well and Esme and Caleb had a few friends they played with in the adjacent houses. So it made a lot of sense, plus there would be no removal costs!

Alex and I spoke about it when she got back to the house. We were both excited about the prospect that God was brewing something up. Our only regret was that it would only have one toilet, like the house we were living in. Now there was four of us, we had always liked the idea of having two toilets but we could let go of that luxury!

In the evening, the husband of the couple at number eighteen knocked at our door and told us that we could come and look at their house.

They had a family and a dog but we manoeuvred around all of that and quickly had a look around. The guy led us out to the back garden through the ramshackle conservatory that was just about holding and I pointed to a couple of doors that were to one side of the covered area, asking what they were for. He told me they were little utility rooms, one had a washing machine in and the other had a toilet. I got all excited and said 'a toilet!' He was surprised at my excitement but showed me inside the small room and, sure enough, under loads of junk there was a toilet. He told me that it was in working order but they didn't ever use it.

Love it. God was on the move. Don't you just feel it? We did!

Then there was even more. The rear garden had a totally different feel to the house we were living in because there were no other houses behind this one and the view was looking in a southerly direction to a small wood on a hill. Up until that point Alex and I had no idea that the houses opposite from where we were living had such a great view from their back gardens. The actual house itself was in need of much cleaning and decoration (I am being generous with my description there)!

But, Alex and I could sense lot of potential and we particularly liked the feel at the back of the house because of the extra privacy and views.

We discussed the price there and then. I offered him £3000 less than he was asking and he was fine. We shook on it, and over the next few days the ball was rolling along well.

We had been to see a building society and, because of our substantial deposit and my new job, on top of Alex's bank nursing, they approved the mortgage. And, to make matters even more amazing, our monthly mortgage payments were going to be quite a bit less than the rent we had been giving to our landlord.

In March, I did a few more gigs around the county, including one at Lee Abbey, for a 20's and 30's weekend. I had done a gig there before Christmas which had gone well and that had prompted them to ask me back.

The job at the bookshop was also going well and it actually complimented my DJ calling too. As the months went on, the various customers that came in found out I was a DJ and, subsequently, word got around on the grapevine.

On April 16th we got the keys for our new house - number eighteen!

We didn't move in until one week later because it wasn't that habitable once it was all empty. Over the week, various friends came and helped clean the place up. The carpets were in a bad state. We had to remove them all and dump them. We just had bare floorboards, which ended up being a feature in our house. I had to rip out all the ceiling light fittings in every single room. None of the lights had been working!

Wallpaper was hanging off the walls, which made it easier to pull off. We quickly paint-rollered the walls with funky Mediterranean colours, just to clean the place up. Nothing fancy, just a light coat. A proper job would have to wait. The garden revealed that a dog used it a lot! All the windows were totally rotten, and the associated leaks had damaged the plaster walls that were around them...

I could go on, but you get the idea. It transpired that there had been some financial difficulties in the past.

On April 22nd, we walked over the road from number nineteen with the last of our belongings and slept the night at number eighteen. Our new home was where we would now live. Thank you Lord.

The following weekend Alex's family scattered Bernard's ashes from a boat into the sea near Falmouth, in Cornwall. Going to Cornwall in the spring for a long weekend has become a regular event for Alex's family over the years, due to that commemorative act back in 2000. We usually all camp at a campsite near St Agnes.

In late May, my back was giving me trouble and I was physically run down from trying to get the house in order. There were so many things to do and by the time June came around, I had developed flu and was not in a good way. Alex was also really struggling with the loss of her dad and it was hitting her hard. We were in a right state!

Caleb's sixth birthday was coming up on June 11th, so when that weekend arrived I took Caleb to Lee Abbey for a couple of nights. It gave Alex a bit of a break and even though Esme was still around, she had reached the age where she could occupy herself.

I took Caleb's presents with me, so that I could give them to him on the Sunday morning. We had a nice quiet room above the chapel that overlooked the north lawn and it was a birthday that Caleb still remembers well. On the Sunday afternoon, after lunch, we drove back to Torquay together.

On the Monday morning I went to work in the Newton Abbot bookshop and I was physically delicate due to my back still not feeling strong.

Hey readers, I just want to pop out of the book for a minute.

I am still in the empty house in West Wales (Nov 2018), I got up this morning and looked out the front window and there was a huge rainbow slowly forming in front of me. The colours came crystal clear, and there it was, arching over the Irish Sea. Thanks God. This coastal village is pretty remote, so I couldn't say to anyone else 'Wow - look at that rainbow !' So I will tell you lot instead. I haven't got a smart phone - so no photos. Right, I will just drink my hot lemon and ginger drink and then I will jump back into 'June 2000', and start writing for the day. Back in 5 minutes!

Right, where was I? Ah yes, in the bookshop.

By the afternoon, my lower back muscles were really tightening up and at around 3pm, I leant over to put some books on a low shelf and my back went into intense spasm. There was a lady customer right next to me as I fell slowly to the floor and she just kept looking at the book she was looking at, as if nothing had happened.

That's the British way I suppose!

Anyway, I explained to her that my back was giving me a problem and she just carried on doing what she was doing. I couldn't move even a tiny bit without intense pain but if I stayed perfectly still I was in no pain at all. I was totally stuck, lying on my back on the floor of the shop. She found the book she wanted and hoped that I would serve her but I explained I couldn't. I then asked her to please help me, by walking across the road, to the Doctor's Surgery and getting someone to come and see me. She wasn't that keen but she did it. After she was gone, another customer came in called Graham, who was a Baptist Minister from Hele, in Torquay and he was really nice to me. He used the shop phone and called Pam and Roy, who owned the shop.

Within 20 minutes, the surgery had phoned for an ambulance, and Pam and Roy were around to cover for the shop. It was a very humbling experience for me, because I was lying on my back, absolutely unable to move my torso or legs. And the shopfront was made of glass, so any privacy, *was out the window*! *(Just thought of that pun).*

But seriously, it was a humiliating and embarrassing situation for me.

The ambulance arrived from Torquay and the two ambulance men were really kind and, after checking my disability, they explained that they needed to get me into the ambulance. They did their best to get me up and half carry me through the small shop but we were very restricted for space and it was so painful. It was a very slow procedure. A few people had gathered in the street to see what was going on, which is always nice when you are in pain and don't want anyone to see you!

As it happened, when we reached the Torquay Hospital, the A and E department was extremely busy for some reason or another and our ambulance was seventh in line to be unloaded. The two guys apologised but I assured them I was fine and in no pain while I just lay still. When it was finally time to move me though, it would be a whole different story, but in the end they managed to wheel me in on a gurney.

Alex arrived soon after (because Pam had phoned from the shop) and we waited for a long time until, eventually, a doctor came into my curtained off area. I could tell he was in a rush. He lifted my leg with his hands and asked me if it was hurting. As he lifted it, it was fine because I wasn't using my back muscles to lift or hold the weight but, when he let go of my leg in mid-air, I cried out in pain. When he saw my pain, he had to quickly support the weight and slowly lower my leg back down to the bed. He wasn't patient with the slow bit either. But what really annoyed me was that he then lifted the other leg and let go of it in exactly the same way. He wanted to write stuff on his report and move on to the next patient.

Anyway, what can you do?

My back slowly relaxed again after that roughshod treatment and I wanted to stay lying down there but the bed was needed. A nurse gave me a few anti-inflammatory pills and I waited a good forty-five minutes for them to kick in but they never really kicked hard because, when the staff tried to get me into a wheelchair, it was still a slow and painful process.

They wheeled me out to our car and, eventually, managed to get me sitting in the passenger seat. It was late evening and starting to rain by now. It had been a long day. Esme and Caleb were being looked after by a friend who lived in our road. Before Alex went to get them, we needed to get me into the house, which was not going to be easy. I asked Alex to get two dining room chairs from our house, then she parked in the middle of our small road, as near to our house as we could get. The next job was to get me out of the passenger seat and sitting on one of the dining room chairs in the road. After that Alex went and parked the car further up the road (because at that point there was no parking place at the front of our house). She then returned to me on the dining room chair and we very carefully slid me across onto the adjacent second dining room chair. This whole process was slow and painful. Then she moved the first chair next to me again but on the other side; the procedure gradually moving us closer to our house. In amongst the pain and difficulty, we laughed at the predicament I was in but I couldn't properly laugh because my back muscles would start to go into spasm again. I was grateful it was dark and that no neighbours could see our predicament - but I wasn't glad it was raining. It took an age to get me to the front door and then I managed to painfully slither down onto the floor in our front lobby. We shut the door. Safe in our own house. I lay there for a while to slowly let my back calm down again, while Alex went upstairs, brought a mattress down and lay it in our front room. The room was still quite bare because we had only lived there for a few weeks and everything was still in disarray. The wooden floorboards and naked walls didn't really make it a cosy rehab centre but, to be honest, I was just so grateful to lie down in a position from which I wouldn't be moved. My back could now rest. I lay in that room for a few days and if the house had caught on fire, it would have been almost impossible for me to escape. I was stuck there. I obviously had to go toilet in that room too. But not on the floor of course - I'm more sophisticated than that.

I forget when I actually went back to work but it was probably about two weeks later. However, I do remember that on my birthday, about a month later, my back was still tender and weak.

We held a party in the orchard next to Alex's mum's house in Plymtree. My DJ gear was set up on a spot near the apple trees and lots of friends from Torquay and few other places drove out to celebrate my birthday. Well it was quite a big one.

On July 9th 2000 - I was forty years old!

I like to mix my parties up a bit, so a lot of people met each other for the first time. As it got dark, some of them even got into dancing to the tunes, including me. I'm pretty sure I was the first to enjoy the tunes further than just tapping a foot but that's just the way I am!

I couldn't dance with *absolute abandon* this time though - because of my back!

Later in the month, my family received a very unexpected present from me. They were totally shocked to be honest but I'm glad I did it because it ended up blessing the four of us richly.

Remember my dad's old TV and video player? Well, the guy I gave it to three years earlier had bought a new system for himself and at about the same time, a friend of ours called Richard had privately been pestering me to get a TV for our family to watch. He told me that it was perfectly legal to not have TV licence and just watch videos on it.

In the end I submitted to the idea and went and retrieved my dad's old TV and video player from the guy who didn't need it anymore. When I reached our house, I first went inside and told Alex and the kids to go to the back of the house for a few minutes. Then I rushed back to the car and brought the TV and video player into the front room and set it up on a table in the corner. I then told them to close their eyes and come into the room. When they opened their eyes, they let out a scream. They were happy.

I cut off the aerial lead, so that we could not pick up any television channels and from that day forward we were able to watch films that we rented from the nearby video rental store. A couple of years later we were given a second-hand DVD player too. Luxury.

We used to get excited walking round the 'Picture Palace' rental shop up in Plainmoor and choosing a film together. I think the staff enjoyed our friendly family coming in and cheering the place up.

I'm glad Richard persuaded me to change my mind.

And my dad got his wish after all!

In August I did a few DJ gigs around the West Country. There was a Christian festival every August called 'New Wine', which was held at the Royal Bath and West Showground, near Shepton Mallet, and somehow they had got hold of my name. They wanted me to do a few gigs at a couple of venues there. I was well chuffed but, when I got there, it ended up being a bit of a let down because, at one gig, my time slot overlapped with another very popular artist in the main tent, which many people went to. It was the London Community Gospel Choir, so I was definitely a sideshow compared to them. Another slot I had was in the Fringe Cafe and that was a more laid back slot, which suited me fine. But all in all they paid me well and it was an experience.

I also did a couple of outside gigs, one in a field near Launceston for a fairly big youth event on a farm. The other was the Lee Abbey Youth Camp, which was a large camp held in a field on the Lee Abbey estate, next to the beach.

I asked my friend Ben to come with me on the trip to North Devon.

You may remember me mentioning him earlier in the book when he helped me set up my gear for that first Immerse gig in Claire's Nightclub.

At that time he wasn't going to 'Kings Arms' Church but he started to come along soon after because he quite liked a girl called Jane who was involved with the 'Kings Arms'. After a while they started going out with each other. That was a year ago and now they were both very much involved with the church and they had also recently got engaged too.

As Ben and I travelled up to the Lee Abbey Camp gig, he told me that they were planning to get married in November. He then came out with a surprise request, by asking me to be his best man.

I was honoured.

The DJ gig went really well and I was asked back for a few years running.

The following month I did some more new gigs around South Devon for churches of different denominations. I did an open air event in Teignmouth town centre for the local Baptist Church, which also became a regular occurrence, and a couple of other events for a Methodist Church in Newton Abbot and an Anglican Church in Torquay.

I also started taking the family to events I did. Sometimes just Alex and I would go, sometimes I would take the whole family, and at other times I would just take Esme because she was nine now and enjoyed dancing. In fact, we actually rented a church hall out for Esme's ninth birthday and I took my gear along to do a disco for her. She was proud that her dad was the DJ!

By October my back had almost fully recovered from the injury in June, and what a relief it was to get back to normal health. The house was beginning to feel like home at last and it really did feel like 'our' home, because we were free to do with it as we wished.

We put our own unique stamp on the place, which did not involve the safe colour of magnolia!

We painted walls and ceilings around the house with colours like aqua, turquoise, yellow, blue, terracotta, salmon, green and orange. These were all light washed Mediterranean shades and our back room, where the woodburner was, had two walls one colour and the other two another... and the ceiling another! It looked good though, and we had plenty of people complimenting the unique atmosphere in the house. A few years later we painted the outside of the house bright poppy red. That didn't fit in with all the blander colours in our road but someone has to set an example. No one else followed suit.

Well at least I tried!

When Alex's mum Bella used to come and visit us in our new house, she would always get out into the back garden and bring some order to it all. She came with little shrubs, and planted them in strategic places that she knew would benefit from that particular position in the garden. And she dug up the plants that were not good for the garden. I think she said they were called weeds.

Bella would always arrive with a basket of produce that we would enjoy eating and drinking together for lunch or supper; special cheeses, farm ham slices, homemade pickles, good quality olives, quality nuts and crisps, chocolate, local farm cordial drinks, natural fruit juice. I really could go on but you get the idea.

In November Alex wrote the blue Ford Fiesta off that dad had given us. She went into the back of a car when she was driving to pick the kids up from school. The loss of her dad was still hitting her hard and she was still quite vulnerable in that area. Having the accident shook her up, although no one was hurt physically. We had had the car for four years and it had been a real blessing to us but do you know what - writing the car off was a blessing as it turned out!

I bought a Ford Escort diesel estate car with the insurance settlement and still had over £400 left afterwards. But, apart from that, the estate car was much more suitable for our family of four and it was a lot better than the Fiesta for carting around all the DJ equipment.

It also allowed us to go to gigs as a family, whereas before we couldn't if it was too far away because there wasn't enough room for everything and everyone in the car.

On November 21st, Ben and Jane got married. Esme was a bridesmaid and Caleb was an usher! Esme had always wanted to be a bridesmaid at somebody's wedding, so when Jane asked her, she was over the moon. I did my best man speech, which ended up being a lot of fun. People were literally 'crying' with laughter, including Ben and Jane.

At the end of the month I did my first 'Spiritulized' gig in Kingsbridge. It was a monthly event that was run by the Baptist Church, and was held at the nightclub in town called 'Fusion'. It was for young people who were of secondary school age. I had earlier been asked by a chap called Alan, who was the leader of the event at the time, if I would consider being the resident DJ. Soon after that proposition, I went before a group of decision makers and other volunteer staff for the event. They had been told that I was a Christian DJ and had a good collection of relevant style music for 'Spiritulized' but they first wanted to meet me to find out what I was like. 'Spiritulized' had become a very popular event in the area but some people in the church were concerned that it needed more of a Christian ethos to it and that the music often played there in the past was not leaning that way at all! This opinion was not shared by all those at the meeting, as some were quite happy to have the popular music from the charts being played each month.

I made it clear my music was nearly all Christian. I told them that if they had me as the DJ, I would not compromise my position and it was very probable that a lot of the kids would stop coming because of the fact that they wouldn't hear music from the pop charts.

It was up to them as a group in which direction they wanted to take 'Spiritulized.'

The vast majority of the people there were encouraged by my stance and were excited about changing the ethos of the event, but there were a few that weren't happy.

My first gig at the end of that month went fairly well but it was hard being the DJ that was saying no to their pop chart requests. There were a couple of hundred youth there and a lot seemed to be getting on with the night without noticing, but there was a `hard core crew' who were peeved that they recognised hardly any of my tunes.

My next gig there in December was well attended because it was Christmas. There were 250 kids moving around the place.

Also that month, I started my first gig at a monthly student event in Exeter that was held in an ex-nightclub under a large church near the river. It went really well and the leaders, who were truly excited by what I was bringing to the event, lined me up for future dates in the following year. It was a good set up they had going on there and I was really encouraged to be involved with it all.

The December 'Immerse' at Claires Nightclub in Torquay was also one of the best I had experienced since it had started eighteen months earlier. There were even hints that we were going to rent the place out on a weekday evening but somewhere along the line it all fell flat and it ended up being the last 'Immerse', which was really sad.

The weather was getting really cold now and our house didn't have central heating. Our source of heat was a woodburner that Ben had given me. It didn't heat the whole house but it kept that room really warm and took the chill from Esme's bedroom, which was directly above.

I am someone who loves to utilise stuff, so getting free wood from a multitude of different places over the years was really satisfying and made good use of the estate car too. I made it a mission to never pay for any wood and I was always on the lookout for it wherever I went. If the Council were cutting a tree down, or I saw a skip with off cuts in, I was on the case. Our friends would also alert us to where they had seen suitable wood and it became quite a hobby really. As a family we would go off on scavenging missions in the car to a recently spotted location.

I mean, why take the kids to Disneyland when you can take them out on wood collecting tours!

It got us out of the house and stopped us hanging around on street corners at night.

2001

My first Kingsbridge 'Spiritulized' gig of the New Year went well. The kids there seemed to have realised that I wasn't going to play the tunes they wanted; which often included lyrics about what someone wanted to do with someone else's sexy body. Sometimes songs would be released in the charts that had a particular positiveness about them, so I would purchase the CD's and play them at the event.

My second gig at the Riverside Church in Exeter also went well. This event was for people over eighteen and it drew a crew of local students.

In February, the bookshop I worked at in Newton Abbot moved premises. A team of us one Saturday moved the entire contents of the small shop which was just off the high street, into a much larger premises on Queen Street. 'Choice Words' was now very visible to throngs of shoppers that walked by its window each day. Roy and Pam re-carpeted the floors and had new floor-to-ceiling bookcases fitted around all the walls. A new serving counter was designed and made, and after a few weeks, things were slowly finding their correct place. In our shop we sold Bibles, books for adults and children, CD's, cards, gifts, posters, magazines and basically anything that churches around the area needed. We also supplied schools with a whole variety of literature that was part of their school curriculum.

I had been working there for a year now and was getting the hang of things. There was a variety of tasks each day; boxes of books and other items to unpack and price up, serving customers, answering queries, taking orders, ordering products from wholesalers around the country, arranging the shop to look presentable and appealing, preparing products for local church bookstalls and conferences, thinking up new ideas to highlight promotional deals, bagging up periodical daily Bible reading notes and Sunday School material for regular orders, taking a lunch break and being friendly to everyone.

I was really good at the last two!

Around this time, as well as moving shop location in Newton Abbot, an additional change came to my weekly geographical work location. 'Choice Words' also had another shop in Paignton and Pam asked me to work over there on Tuesdays to assist Steve, who was the manager in that shop. Working in the Paignton shop with Steve gave a bit more variety to the job and I enjoyed the mixture. There was a whole set of different customers that came into that shop, which gave Tuesdays a different flavour too.

In February, Alex and me drove to Gillingham in Kent, where I had a gig. We stayed with the organiser of the event for a couple of nights. It was really encouraging to travel further afield with the DJ'ing and it was nice to go with Alex sometimes too, when we could get cover for the children. Like a mini holiday!

It was Alex's 40th birthday in March. We went out for a meal together, then we drove Esme and Caleb to Plymtree and they stayed with Bella while I took Alex into to the Northcott Theatre in Exeter to watch a play. The next day I drove Alex to Cornwall and we found a Bed and Breakfast place in Polperro. After having a meal in the village, we stumbled across a Blues Band playing live in an old Cornish pub down the road. They were really good.

The next morning we made our way back through Cornwall towards Devon. It was around the time of the foot-and-mouth disease that was spreading throughout Britain and we were often getting diverted away from areas where affected farms had been shut down. At that particular time there were 580 farms closed up around Britain and this number rose to over 2000 as time went on, in which over six million cows and sheep were killed.

Any vehicles or walkers that were travelling near an affected farm had to drive, or walk, over a 'ground covering material' that had disinfectant in it, so as not to spread the disease to other areas.

In the Spring I enjoyed my favourite gig, it was at the Riverside Church in Exeter. They had now named the event 'Promised Land' and had moved it from the basement clubland area to the upstairs cafe, which was at the front of the building next to the road. One of the crew called Lizette had obtained some funky wall hanging drapes from a nightclub in the city and hung them around the cafe, which really set the atmosphere. Also, there was food and drinks available and people were just having a good time. I got lots of compliments during the evening concerning my style of music and people were getting right into the dance mode. It was the first gig where I used my smoke machine and it seemed to add a bit of intrigue to the proceedings.

I was so grateful to God for how the night went.

Also in the spring I bought a bunch of herbs and plants for our back garden: Fennel, French Tarragon, Black Peppermint, Old English Lavender, Lemon Thyme, Hyssop, Veronica Dianthus and a Curry plant. The garden was looking in good shape after Bella's influence.

Around late June time, we found out that Alex's mum, Bella, had been diagnosed with cancer. Alex was still grieving about the death of her father and couldn't really cope with the prospect of losing her mum too. It was a tough time.

In July we went again as a family to the 'Cross Rhythms' festival up on Dartmoor. It was still, by far, our favourite Christian event.

In August I did various gigs, including another one at the Lee Abbey youth camp on the north coast of Devon. I also did the music at a bikers event in the car park of a large pub in Torquay.

As a family we spent a couple of weeks that month driving around the country seeing and staying with friends. We first went and stayed with old family friends of Alex, called Henry and Rosemary, who owned a small farm in Corscombe in Dorset, Esme and Caleb loved running about on that. Then we travelled east to Beaconsfield in Buckinghamshire to see one our friends called Penny, who we were in the Lee Abbey community with fifteen years earlier. She now was married and had a family. While we there another friend from Lee Abbey community days came and hung out with us. It was Anna, who we had not seen since we lived in her house in Bath, 7 years earlier. When we had been living with Tim and Anna in Bath, they had had no children. Since then, they had accumulated four. That grew to six a few years later!

It was good to catch up with these dear old friends again.

We travelled from there to Oxford and spent a couple of days with our friend Charles, who was also our friend from Lee Abbey community days. Not long after seeing him in Oxford, Charles drove down to Torquay and spent a few days helping me totally rebuild the ramshackle and rotten wooden conservatory that was caving in at the back of our house.

We regularly keep in touch with Charles and have crossed paths many times over the years, even beyond the shores of England.

Also in August, Bella was taken into Exeter hospital. Her health was deteriorating and she needed medical care.

In early September we drove to the hospital to see her, as did other members of the family. She was weak and tearful and it was a sombre time in many ways.

There was a newspaper in the ward with the headlines 'Planes fly into Twin Towers.' There was a lot of drama around in our lives that September.

Ten days later, Bella was released from the hospital to go and spend her last days at home. The cancer had spread and she didn't have long to live.

On the first day of October, Bella died.

Alex and all her siblings had all been attending Isabella's bedside when she was dying.

Soon after the funeral, a week later, Alex said to me that she now understood what I had said to her soon after my dad had died; that it hits deeper after the second parent has died.

She told me that she felt like the 'covering' was gone - now that both her parents were not around.

Two hours after she told me that, she received a card from a good friend of hers called Alison, who she had done her nursing training with many years before. Alison had written out a prayer/poem inside the card. It was entitled 'The Shield' and it spoke about our Father God being a 'covering' for us.

Come on!

....

Alex now had another couple years of going through the journey of loss, bless her. All four of our parents had died within 7 years. We were going through the mill.

That Christmas; we didn't have any parents and Esme and Caleb didn't have any grandparents.

2002

I started jogging every week, sometimes on my own, sometimes with one or other of my friends - Marc or Ryan. It somehow made me feel more alive, maybe 'cos it got my heart and lungs working more than usual. It definitely helped having someone else to run with, because it was too easy to not actually do it, without the extra reason of commitment to the other person. After the run though, it was always worth it.

During the spring Alex and her siblings went to Cornwall and scattered Isabella's ashes into the sea, like they had done with Bernard's.

I had a gig that weekend so was unable to go.

More new gig opportunities kept arising, on top of my regular ones. A couple I will mention. One was an all-nighter until daylight up in Launceston (which took a couple of days to recover from), and another one a lot further away in Norwich, Norfolk. We all went as a family to that one and stayed with my Auntie Margaret and Uncle Paul for four days. Esme and Caleb spent some really good time with them on their own and loved it. One day Paul and Margaret took them to a small Dinosaur Park nearby, which they loved. Esme was ten and Caleb was nearly eight.

It was nice when my gigs could compliment our family activities, and they often did. As Esme was getting older, I would take her along with me, and it wasn't too long before Caleb started coming with me too.

School photo of Caleb and Esme in May 2002

Alex was really struggling with grief this year but occasionally we would get away together and leave the kids with friends of ours. That spring we both went up to a weekend conference in Dudley, run by a crew called 'Revival Fires'. They had a building that was originally an old court house. They were a wacky lot in some ways, but they were our sort of tribe; we liked the informality and freedom of the meetings.

Some Christian leaders tend to explain or talk - rather than allowing God's Spirit to come fully into a meeting.

I used to have a saying which addressed that tendency, it was: **don't talk - just kiss!**

The guys up at Dudley were comfortable with experiencing the **kiss** from **God's heart**.

....

As the summer began kicking in I received a very special offer from my old boss and mate Paul, from PGH motorcycles. He was now riding around with a big white cross on the back of his leather jacket. He was hanging out with some other Christians who had motorbikes and he wanted me to come on some of the rides too but realised that my old Honda Motorsport 250 was a bit small for such runs.

He wanted to give me a fairly new 600cc bike for cost price, which was a very kind gesture because it was the same sort of money that I could sell my old Honda for.

The Honda was nearly thirty years old and I had owned it for nearly seventeen, so it was ready for changing.

I took ownership of a blue Yamaha XT 600cc Enduro bike. It was in pristine condition and I loved riding it about. It had so much more power and everything worked so well on it. The sort of improvements over my old bike were: disc brakes, electric start, monoshock rear suspension, indicators, more power, comfy seat(!), and everything worked nicely.

For over twenty five years I had only used open face helmets and had an aversion to the enclosed full face ones. But Paul even somehow persuaded me to buy a new black full face helmet.

And I'm so glad he did because the days of cold wind, rain, little stones and flies in my face were at last over. Thanks Paul.

A few months later another Christian friend of mine called Matt, who owned a motorbike workshop in Totnes, sold my Honda for me. The story was complete!

Having a bigger bike meant that I would soon start taking Caleb around as a pillion passenger, which he loved.

The summer involved the usual monthly gig slots plus a few extra ones that popped up in places like Ross on Wye, Cornwall, and others that I did in rented halls locally, plus some parties in people's houses.

In July, Alex went off on her own to 'The Call', which was a big Christian event held at the Reading Football Club's Madejski Stadium. There were over 19,000 Christians in the Stadium praying for the UK.

While Alex was there, God really stamped His approval deeply in her heart and she returned home with a stronger sense of identity. She has told me over the years that 'The Call' was a very special time for her.

Esme was coming up to eleven years old and was due to start Secondary School in September the following year. If she had been a few days older, she would have started a lot earlier. Her birthday was on September 8th.

Her Primary School had warned us to start searching out which Secondary School we wanted her to go too. We had prayed about it but we prayed some more!

In August we went to an open day at a large Secondary School near to where we lived. We were shown around the place and it seemed very modern and up to date. At the end of the day, Alex and me talked about it and both felt that before we committed to registering Esme at that school, we would first go and visit a friend of ours called Paula who lived in Plymouth. Paula was a single mother who Homeschooled her two children and we had noticed over the years how good a relationship they had together as a family. The respect we saw they had for their mother we attributed to them being Homeschooled.

We had in no way felt it was what we should do but we needed to at least look into it.

In September, we went as a family to see Paula. Paula explained some of the nitty gritty details of Homeschooling, including the financial costs, the sacrifice of time and space in her life, the frustrations and difficulties but also the amazing benefits and rewards it had brought to the three of them. Her daughter had completed her first year at mainstream Secondary School but was now at home for her schooling. We asked her about the possible reduction of friends in her social life and she told us that it was better because she could now 'choose' her friends!

As the afternoon went on, Alex and I became very aware that Homeschooling would be a real sacrifice in our lives for eight years - taking into consideration, Caleb's schooling as well.

It seemed like a huge commitment and one that we weren't even sure we could manage.

But... we just knew we needed to do it. The benefits were too special to miss out on.

We made our decision there and then. With God's help we would walk this journey one day at a time.

We would start in one years time (Sep 2003) after Esme left Primary School. We also decided that we would pull Caleb out at the same time.

....

The final couple of months in 2002 were spent doing what our normal routine was: Alex doing a couple of days bank nursing at the hospital; me working in the bookshop and doing DJ gigs; collecting wood(!); going to the 'Kings Arms' Church and its associated activities; and sitting round the woodburner enjoying the fruits of our labours - heat!

In November we went up to Lee Abbey for a few nights to attend a Lee Abbey community reunion gathering. It was so much fun seeing many of our old friends from fifteen years ago. Everyone looked older, apart from me amazingly!

I'm funny aren't I? The answer is Yes.

On New Years Eve we went to a party at our good friends Steve and Jo's house in Paignton. Many people from our church were there and it was a busy old night.

A group of children including Esme and Caleb were watching a film in another section of the house. Around fifteen minutes before midnight, Alex and I went and joined the young ones because a lot of the adults had gathered around the TV in the sitting room and were watching some concert, followed by the live link to the London celebrations. We preferred the quieter room where the kids were watching the animated film 'Prince of Egypt'. We wanted to engage a bit with things of God at the end of another year and 'Prince of Egypt', although animated, is about the life of Moses in the Bible.

We could tell when midnight had struck because of the loud cheering coming from the revellers in the sitting room down the corridor.

But at exactly the same time, a very poignant moment was happening in the 'Prince of Egypt' film that we were watching with the kids.

It was where God reveals Himself to Moses in the Burning Bush.

Exodus 3:1-5   Good News Translation (GNT)

God Calls Moses

One day while Moses was taking care of the sheep and goats of his father-in-law Jethro, the priest of Midian, he led the flock across the desert and came to Sinai, the holy mountain. There the angel of the Lord appeared to him as a flame coming from the middle of a bush. Moses saw that the bush was on fire but that it was not burning up. 'This is strange,' he thought. 'Why isn't the bush burning up? I will go closer and see.'

 When the Lord saw that Moses was coming closer, he called to him from the middle of the bush and said, 'Moses! Moses!'

He answered, 'Yes, here I am.'

God said, 'Do not come any closer. Take off your sandals, because you are standing on holy ground.'

....

God later tells Moses to go back to the Israelites, who are under the harsh rule of Pharaoh in Egypt, and lead them out of captivity to the promised land. He wants Moses to tell Pharaoh to 'set the captives free'. But Moses is scared!

Exodus 3:11-14 Good News Translation (GNT)

But Moses said to God, 'I am nobody. How can I go to the king and bring the Israelites out of Egypt?'

God answered, 'I will be with you, and when you bring the people out of Egypt, you will worship me on this mountain. That will be the proof that I have sent you.'

But Moses replied, 'When I go to the Israelites and say to them, 'The God of your ancestors sent me to you, 'they will ask me, 'What is his name?' So what can I tell them?'

God said, 'I am who I am. You must tell them: 'The one who is called I Am has sent me to you.'

So this was the poignant moment in the film as the clock struck midnight at the party.

It was God declaring His Majestic Splendour.

It was a fitting end to the year and it was a fitting start to another year.

Alex and I were very pleased to be in that room at midnight.

2003

Speaking figuratively here: *God had led us back into the harbour from the island of Bath back in 1994. I had felt like a bare hull of a sea-going vessel. Soon after we had returned to Torquay I had said to God, 'What are you going to do with us now then?', and He had responded with, 'I'm going to put ballast in you.'*

It was a hard pill to swallow but of course I could see the sense of it. It now seemed that we were being kept in the harbour for even longer than we had first expected - surely the ballast was all in place by now?

God must be kitting us out to be a certain 'type' of sea-going vessel - one with a particular purpose, to carry out a unique function.

Meanwhile, the still waters of the harbour were certainly a gentle and safe place for bringing up a young family.

God would reveal to us what vessel we were in His own good time, and when He saw fit - He would launch that vessel, out into the sea of His calling upon our lives.

....

This year had started while watching a film at a New Years Eve party. Films have often been used in my life to speak something precious to me. This month was no exception to that rule. I watched for the second time 'Dances with Wolves', starring Kevin Costner.

The first time I watched it was at the cinema with Alex, when it was released in 1990. Driving home from the cinema, I had to stop the car and just weep.

I was now watching it again thirteen years later, and it affected me just the same. It gives me hope when I cry because it proves my heart isn't totally shut down and I am in contact with my emotions.

The point in the film that gets me is very near the end, when the character, *Wind in his Hair*, cries out to the character *Dances with Wolves* from the top of the ravine: '*I will always be your friend.*'

If you have seen the film you will probably know the bit I mean.

Alex is encouraged when I cry. It proves to her I am alive and well and getting freer!

When people's hearts have been hurt over the years, the tendency is to shut down the emotions; knowingly or unknowingly. I personally believe that God is the only one who can fully set us free to be who He originally made us each to be.

I have found over the years that He occasionally leads me to get some deep ministry - for instance the time I mentioned earlier in the book, when He led me up to Scargill House in Yorkshire, and took me back into the womb.

Funny old life eh!

It was for a similar reason that I was led to another such place of healing in January of that year.

This time I went to Harnhill Christian Healing Centre in Gloucestershire. The place is located at an old manor house near Cirencester and is surrounded by countryside.

Many deep things went on in my counselling sessions over the three days I was at Harnhill and, while it is impossible to translate it all on these few pages, in brief - God was impressing on me that:

I am the apple of His eye.

Deuteronomy 32:10 (NIV)

> In a desert land he found him,
>> in a barren and howling waste.
> He shielded him and cared for him;
>> he guarded him as the **apple of his eye**,

He will always look after me.

Isaiah 49:15 (NIV)

> 'Can a mother forget the baby at her breast
>> and have no compassion on the child she has borne?
> Though she may forget,
>> I will not forget you!'

Psalm 81:16 (NIV)

> 'But you would be fed with the finest of wheat;
>> with honey from the rock I would satisfy you.'

He will change my name.

From the song by D. Butler (Mercy/Vineyard publishing 1987)

I will change your name,

you shall no longer be called;

wounded, outcast, lonely or afraid.

I will change your name,

Your new name shall be;

confidence, joyfulness, overcoming one, faithfulness, friend of God,

One who seeks my face.

....

Like I mentioned earlier: the healing journey takes a while. Like a whole lifetime! But, when God is on the case - it is a journey worth travelling.

Paul says in the New Testament;

And I am certain that God, who began the good work within you, will continue his work until it is finally finished on the day when Christ Jesus returns.

Philippians 1:6 (NLT)

....

In the spring, I was struggling with my DJ'ing. I was feeling rubbish about myself. I was trying to get a regular evening slot at a nightclub down by the harbour but they had rejected my demo tape. It was around April time. I didn't feel worthy to be a DJ. One evening when I was at the peak (or should I say trough) of being depressed, I went into Esme's room to say goodnight to her. She was eleven at the time and as I was leaving her room she told me that God had told her to draw me a picture, which she then handed to me.

It was of two roads; a black one and an orange one.

At the junction of **black road** was a sign that read: *Quitting. Way to go home,* with an arrow pointing to the end of that particular road. At the end of the road was a wall that was named: *Dead End - valley of shadows and misery.*

At the junction of **orange road** was a sign that read: *Carrying on. Not giving up. The way to God's plans,* with an arrow pointing to the end of that particular road. At the end of the road was a picture of a bright sun and the words: *The plans God has for you.*

....

It was a special picture that Esme had felt God had definitely led her to draw for me. She then prayed for me that God would help me to not give up.

The next morning I told Esme that I was going to make another demo tape and try to meet up with the manager of the nightclub by the harbour.

She said that me doing another demo tape was like me walking on the orange road in her drawing!

That same day, a Bible page literally fell out of my Bible onto the floor. There were a couple of verses on that page that confirmed what Esme had been telling me. I sellotaped the page back in and went off to work. I was working in the Paignton shop that day and I showed Steve, the manager, the verses that God had highlighted to me earlier. He then suggested I look up the same verses in the Message version of the Bible, which I did, and they spoke to me even more clearly!

Hebrews 10 : 35 - 36 (MSG)

So don't throw it all away now. You were sure of yourselves then. It's *still* a sure thing! But you need to stick it out, staying with God's plan so you'll be there for the promised completion.

It won't be long now, he's on the way; he'll show up almost any minute.

But anyone who is right with me thrives on loyal trust; if he cuts and runs, I won't be very happy.

But we're not quitters who lose out. Oh, no! We'll stay with it and survive, trusting all the way.

....

So, I made another demo tape, using again the genre of 'house music' with a slight gospel edge to some of it.

In May, I got an appointment to see the manager of the club. I took the tape with me, gave it to her, and we chatted for five or ten minutes.

After the meeting, I looked out from the club balcony window that overlooked the Torquay inner harbour. At the point where the inner harbour narrowed and connected to the outer harbour there was a stainless steel footbridge reflecting light in the sun. The bridge was a new initiative to allow people to cross the channel of water where the two harbours met. It was yet to be opened to the public but as I looked at the impressive structure, I could see a small crowd of people to one side of it. It suddenly struck me that it was being officially opened that very day. I walked quickly down to the road and made my way around the side of the harbour to where the people were gathered at the end by the bridge. As I walked, I passed another small group of people waving to the local Mayor who was all dressed up in his garb. He was on a RNLI lifeboat that was alongside the harbour wall and was obviously around for the opening of the new bridge.

When I reached the new stainless steel bridge, I saw that it was already possible to walk over to the other side, so I quickly walked onto the bridge. Just as I did an alarm signal went off and lights started flashing to indicate that the bridge was about to open. I quickly ran across to the other side of the small bridge to where the harbour master was putting a piece of chain across the way to stop any more people crossing. It was obviously a special occasion and something was about to happen but I didn't even have time to think what it was. The next thing I knew, he was pushing some buttons next me that controlled the bridge lifting mechanism. The bridge started to split in the middle and each side slowly started to lift up like the Tower Bridge system in London.

It was the first day that this bridge had been operational and I was right there as it was happening. As I stood there and the footbridge started to become vertical in front of me, I had a strong sense that I was in exactly the right spot on planet earth, at exactly the right time. God had engineered that I was to be there on that bridge right then. I felt I was on Holy ground. I know it might sound funny, but I did.

It was very similar to the feeling I had in that cafe in Dunster in 1987 just before God started speaking to me through the, *'This in future',* picture on the wall.

There was the same kind of pregnancy in the atmosphere on that bridge, like God was about to say or do something significant.

Then, just as the bridge reached vertical, I felt God say 'Mark, I will open the gates for you in your life'.

I thought, Wow, that's powerful.

The bridge was actually being lifted to allow the lifeboat to exit the inner harbour.

As I watched it leave the harbour, God pointed at the lifeboat and said, **'And that's what you are!'**

Okay, I didn't see God's actual finger and I didn't hear His audible voice, but without doing either of those two things, *That's what He did!*

It's hard to explain how God speaks, because He does it in so many different ways. On the harbour bridge He did it by ambushing my mind with such a strong and poignant impression that coincided instantaneously with a concept that was not even within my imagination radar capabilities.

He was telling me that I am a lifeboat! And He has continued to confirm that fact over the years in so many ridiculous and ingenious ways; just so I don't forget it.

So now I know what sort of sea going vessel I am. I believe he has made me someone who has a gift to help people who are really struggling in life but who are also really sincere in their cry to be rescued. I can manoeuvre in close, pluck them out of the water, which is consuming them, and transport them to land. I then pass them onto someone else who will look after them more long-term while I am sent off on more missions.

Alex is also part of the lifeboat too; she is often a radar for the way forward and is an important companion on some of the lonely and scary voyages.

By the way, I never did get a DJ job in that nightclub by the harbour. But if I hadn't pushed forward with that second demo tape and subsequent meeting with the manager, I wouldn't have been down at Torquay harbour on the opening day of the Bridge.

In June, we drove our old Ford Escort diesel estate car down to the south coast of France for a family holiday. We stayed in a small mobile home about 5 miles inland from Saint-Tropez. We didn't have a boat big enough to hang out in Saint-Tropez itself. In fact, all we had to give us any credence there was the old Ford Escort but even **that** didn't seem to pull any punches with the rich people drinking champagne on their yachts.

It was the hottest June in France for fifty years! So we often hung around the camp where we were staying, watching Esme and Caleb have lots of fun in the outdoor swimming pool that had a small man-made wave machine and river in it. We all got really brown.

While we were down in the South of France, we met up with two of our good friends from our church in Torquay. They just happened to also be in that area on their holiday at the same time, which was bizarre.

Dave and Tina had become Christians a few years earlier at one of the 'Cross Rhythms' festivals we went too. They had both been heroin addicts for many many years. They were totally set free with no `cold turkey' effects when they gave their lives to God and came off the heroin. It was a miracle. Their lives totally changed and now, over twenty years later, they are still together and have important jobs helping other people who are caught up in drug addiction.

On the drive down from England, we passed by the Alps and saw their impressive snow-capped peaks. However, we decided to choose a different route back because we just wanted to get away from the hot south as soon as possible. The car had no air conditioning so we just wound all the windows down and I drove as fast as I could. Every hour we travelled north we could feel a slightly cooler temperature in the air outside. We had left the campsite at 3.30pm in the afternoon to avoid the main heat of the day and by around 8pm, the temperature in the car was more pleasant. It wasn't until around midnight that the horizon went totally dark because of being close to Midsummer's Day, and at 3.30am we arrived at Calais. It had been a real fun blast of a drive, in more ways than one.

All four us really enjoyed that holiday. It had given us all a new lease of life and we felt very much alive for weeks after.

Soon after we got back, Alex got a permanent contract at Torbay Hospital working in the Urology and Short Stay Surgical ward. She only worked there two days a week but they were guaranteed shifts, unlike the bank nursing rota she had previously been on.

Later in the summer we went on our jaunt to the 'Cross Rhythms' festival, and I was pretty busy with my DJ'ing gigs around various churches in Devon. I even had one at the local Project 58 centre, where people who were homeless or on drugs used to gather and get help.

In August, I took Esme with me to the annual Lee Abbey youth camp. The gig went really well and, the following year, Alex and I booked Esme in for the two week camp as she was by then old enough to attend. A couple of years after that, Caleb was also old enough to attend, so we would drop them both off for the fortnight.

Near the end of the summer I was interviewed by the local Herald Express newspaper, and an article was published about my DJ work in the area. It also featured a picture of me and a section about how I had become a Christian.

I used to have fun with my hair

In September, we started the Homeschooling!

The Headmaster of the Primary school had not been impressed when we had told him at the start of the year we were going to Homeschool Esme and Caleb after Esme reached Secondary School age.

Soon after that, Esme got top grades in all her Primary School SATs exams, which further led him and quite a few other people to believe that we were doing the wrong thing!

But we were undeterred and confident that we were making a good decision.

We had bought a term's worth of workbooks for all the subjects and I had built a wall mounted, hinged desk for each of their rooms. Alex taught them for the first three days of the week, while I was working in the bookshops and I taught them on the last two days of the week, while Alex was working at the hospital.

It was a daunting task we were undertaking, but slowly as the weeks went on, we all got into the routine of the system.

Meanwhile, our house had old, deteriorating asbestos tiles on the roof. They needed to be replaced and in November I got scaffolding put up at the front and back.

Alex and I had become good friends with a couple from Essex called John and Jackie. We had met them at 'Cross Rhythms' a few years earlier and had stayed in touch.

John was a roofer and soon after the scaffolding went up, John and his elderly dad (who was a roofer also) came to stay at our house for a few days and did the roof. At the time, Jackie was due to have their second child, so it was all a bit tentative timing but Josiah was born after John got back to Essex.

The whole project was stressful for me because I was fully aware that if it rained, or John had to rush back to Essex, our house would not have a lid on it!

On the first day, when John and his dad removed all the old tiles from the roof, my friend Ryan (who I jogged with once a week) came to the house to help out. He collected the old tiles as they were being removed and went to the edge of the scaffolding platform and chucked them into the big metal skip below.

I was at work while that was going on, but I was around on the day when they were nailing the new tiles on, and managed to cut out some roof rafters and fit in two big Velux Roof Windows before John and his dad had reached that level. Having those two windows in the roof brought a lot of natural light into the loft space, which facilitated a project I did a couple of years later.

John and his dad were heroes - they completed the job in the dark on the final day they were there. It was such a relief.

I kept the scaffolding up for a week longer while I fitted the plastic fascia boards and guttering to the front and back of the house. While I was up there, I fixed a wooden cross I had made to the top of the front gable end. Job complete. The house was sealed for the winter.

Me and John have remained good friends ever since and our adventures together haven't stopped!

In December, Alex and I bought four air tickets to Australia. Early in the New Year we were all going to visit my sister Julie for a month.

Also in the New Year I hoped to start a new monthly chill music social event called 'Rendezvous'. I was going to hold it in a local Christian holiday and conference centre called Brunel Manor.

2004

Now that Esme was twelve years old, I took her along with me to the monthly 'Spiritulized' gigs in Kingsbridge. The event was for Secondary School pupils so she now fitted the bill. It was brave of her really because she didn't know any of the other kids apart from about two. The two she knew were both being Homeschooled in the Kingsbridge area and their parents were the people now leading the event, so Esme soon got to know a few of the older kids. It was nice for me to have her around and the twenty mile drive back to Torquay in the late evening gave us a chance to chat about the things that had gone on.

In February, we were due to fly to Australia and just before we left I managed to just about finish the bathroom revamp in our house. I had obtained a good white bath, toilet and sink from various locations, including the local recycling centre. The old pink stuff that was in there originally was not good!

I had tiled around the bath with white tiles and a few funky aqua in amongst them, to add some visual flavour. The other walls were aqua washed `tongue-in-groove' wooden panels from the floor to waist height, and the top half above was painted white.

The floor was bare wooden floorboards and I had changed all the rotten wooden windows at the back of the house with plastic, including the bathroom window.

So, it was all about finished apart from the new electric shower that I had fitted. That was causing me some problems! It was a very good make of shower, which I had plumbed and wired in myself but it kept cutting out when it got hot.

I was pretty sure the shower was faulty, and not the wiring to it. The shower company offered a free call out guarantee to fix or replace the unit. But if the engineer deemed it was not their product at fault, I would have to pay them £50 for the call out.

The engineer who arrived was a nice chap and, after doing some checks, assured me that the shower was fine. He diagnosed that the fuse and RCD in the fuse box downstairs needed upgrading.

As the problem was not the shower unit itself, I got ready to pay out the £50 call out fee. He got his forms out and as he was filling them out he told me that, because I was a nice guy, he would just report to his company that the unit had a slight fault, which he had fixed - thus annulling the £50 call out fee I was due to pay.

This was a nice gesture but as he continued to fill out the form for his company, I began to feel very uncomfortable in my spirit.

I interrupted him and said, 'Stop, I want to pay the £50!'

He stopped and looked up at me and said, 'What do you mean?'

I told him I was a Christian and I would not feel free if I knew that I had been part of a lie. He assured me that it was fine to not pay the fee and that surely being a Christian meant being kind to animals and things like that.

He continued to try and persuade me that it was fine to avoid the cost. In the end I told him I wanted to pay the money. He became resigned to the fact that I was sure of what I wanted to do, filled out another form and then took my bank card details. I felt so liberated after I had paid the money.

He was pretty gobsmacked with my decision to be honest, which didn't really make sense to him. However, as he left our house he said, 'Well, I can say I've met a real Christian now.'

The next day, our family travelled to Heathrow Airport and boarded a plane to Melbourne, Australia. It was a long trip in which to initiate Esme and Caleb to the experience of flying but with the help of in-flight movies, they didn't complain once.

I had decided to fast from food for a couple of days because I hadn't seen Julie for over seven years and I wanted to dedicate this time in Australia to God, for Him to really move in Julie's life. Julie had lived in Australia for over twenty years and although she had enjoyed herself, she had also been knocked about. She had experienced some rough relationships and, if the truth be told, she was quite broken. But she put on a brave front because she had always been a fighter.

She had been heavily involved with outlaw biker gangs for many years and had worked in some tough jobs. These included working on fish trawlers in the Gulf of Carpentaria for two or three months at a time, without coming back to land and being the only female crew member amongst a dozen Aussie men. Then she had a job driving the huge Dump Trucks in the Northern Territory mining quarries. She even worked as a manager in a red-light district parlour house.

She had seen a fair bit of life while she had been out there!

We spent nearly a month in Australia, mainly staying at Julie's house in the bush area north of Melbourne. Julie was living with a guy called John when we were there but she wanted an end to the relationship, so it wasn't a great atmosphere. John drank a fair bit but seemed to have a nice temperament and we actually got on well with him. He took a liking to us and was intrigued about our faith, often wanting to talk about it. Caleb and him also hit it off well, which was nice for Caleb. While we were out there, I took Caleb to a large Army Tank Museum because of his long standing interest in anything to do with the Second World War.

The whole time in Australia was like a long Homeschooling education field trip for Esme and Caleb.

Alex, me and the kids also drove to New South Wales for a couple of days to climb to the summit of Mount Kosciuszko, which is the highest point in Australia. We only just made it back to our car before dark because Alex's legs started to seize up. We were out there on our own and it was good nothing went wrong really because we were very isolated. We had no phones in those days and at one point on the walk a snake crossed our path.

It was a relief to finally get back to the safety of the car before darkness prevented us from doing so. We all slept well that night.

Julie liked to take us around the various `Op' shops around her area. An `Op' shop is another name for a charity shop, and Julie, Alex and Esme particularly enjoyed hunting around for clothes.

Alex, me and the kids caught the train into Melbourne one day. We enjoyed riding around on the free trams in the city but our main reason for going into the city was to hear one of Alex and my favourite bands. They were an Australian band called 'Rivertribe', who were due to be playing that day on the street-side somewhere. Well, we found them and it was such a good time. There weren't many people gathered around, which gave me more room to dance!

The band played ethnic Australian chilled beats with electronic equipment and didgeridoos. It was such an enjoyable time, dancing around to those tunes.

In our times with Julie, the subject of God came up quite a few times. In one conversation, Jesus's words in the Gospel of John became a contentious issue (the highlighted parts being the problem):

John 15: 4 - 5   Living Bible (TLB)

4 Take care to live in me, and let me live in you. For a branch can't produce fruit when severed from the vine. **Nor can you be fruitful apart from me.**

5 'Yes, I am the Vine; you are the branches. Whoever lives in me and I in him shall produce a large crop of fruit. **For apart from me you can't do a thing.**

It was an affront to her pride and independence to suggest that nothing good could come out of her life unless it was connected to Jesus.

....

Esme, Caleb, Harley, Julie and me

One Sunday morning, Julie took me on the back of her big Harley Davidson motorbike into the city. I wanted to take her to a well-known biker church. The leader, Dr John Smith, was the founding President of the 'God's Squad Christian Motorcycle Club.' God's Squad started in the early seventies and were basically God's ambassadors to the biker fraternity in Australia. They are now an international biker club with chapters all around the world.

Julie had heard about them when she was with the outlaw gangs, so it was good to introduce Julie to John Smith and a few others there.

Soon after I had become a Christian, I had written a letter to John in Australia (even though I didn't know him), telling him about my sister being out there in a bike gang. I had asked him and the club to keep her in prayer.

I had read a couple of his books and often listened to his speaking slots on 'Cross Rhythms' radio in England too, but this was the first time I had actually met him face to face.

....

During our visit, Julie took Esme and Caleb off to see her friends up the road who owned some horses. They both got to ride them around but Caleb didn't enjoy the experience because one of the guys there was retelling the story of how he had been thrown off a horse and ended up with loads of broken bones.

The new film directed by Mel Gibson, 'The Passion of Christ', was being released in cinemas whilst we were there and John, who lived in Julie's house, wanted to go and watch it with Alex and me. He ended up being deeply touched by the film and it got him thinking more seriously about Christianity.

On the day we were leaving Australia, John asked Alex and me if we would lead him in a prayer, so that he could ask Jesus to come into his life. He said the prayer and was quite emotional afterwards.

Alex and me felt privileged to have been used by God to help John at that particular time in his life.

Our family had enjoyed being exposed to a different culture while visiting Julie in Australia and the whole experience was one that we will always remember.

....

When we got back to England, Alex and I felt so enriched by our time in the Southern Hemisphere. It had helped us get back in contact with our mutual love of travelling and adventure. God had stirred up that appetite in us again and we were excited about how His plans for us would unfold in the future. For now though, it was life as normal back in the harbour, establishing a strong family unit together.

Next to the River Dart, soon after we got back from Australia

In the spring, I launched my monthly social event at Brunel Manor. 'Rendezvous' was where people from around the area could come and relax, meet each other, drink coffee and listen to chilled beats from my DJ equipment. I used to turn the lights off and have my DJ lights and a slide projector giving different effects on the surrounding white walls, which improved the ambience of the place. I also had candles and cloth wall hangings dotted around the venue too.

The event helped people get to know each other in a non-threatening environment and it was a good place to meet people for the first time because they came from different churches. It was mainly Christians who attended but that was not always the case as it was open to anyone people wanted to invite.

In the dictionary, Rendezvous is described as a place and time of meeting, or gathering together - a place to assemble. The event helped create a new and fresh arena for that to happen in. It was often a place where people met each other for the first time and, on one occasion, two people met there and ended up getting married a year or so later!

....

In July, the big open air Christian Music event 'New Eden' was held on the big green by Torquay seafront. It had started in 2002 and was the brainchild of our friend Charlie, who I had worked for as a carpenter's labourer in the early nineties.

It had been a courageous step of faith by Charlie to have even contemplated setting up such a large event in Torquay. It ran for three days every summer and entailed much logistical juggling with the local council, health and safety issues, artists and musicians, stage hire, sound equipment, tents and marquees, catering, marketing and promotion, finances, plus a host of other things that I won't bother to spell out!

But anyway, he managed to pull it off for four consecutive years with much help from a tight team of friends and colleagues who were his vital mainstays of support.

I used to do the infill music slots between the different acts, and Paul (my old PGH motorcycle boss who became a Christian) was the MC at the front of the stage who introduced and interviewed the different artists.

Over the four years that it ran we had so many different artists perform there including Shane Lynch, Janey Lee Grace, Phats and

Small, Note For A Child, Heartstrings Black Gospel Choir from London, M.O.D, plus a rich variety of Pop Bands, Solo artists, Hip Hop artists, dancers, Rock Bands, Worship Bands, Classical Musicians and even a crew of World Champion freestyle skateboarders from America.

This particular year we brought along a friend called James, from Plymtree, who Alex had known for a long time. He was struggling with a few things in life and we had taken him to a couple of Christian festivals. He stayed at our house for a couple of days and came along to New Eden. I was quite busy doing my DJ'ing but he met a lot of our friends and listened to a lot of the stuff people were speaking and singing about on the stage during the weekend.

At our house after the event, he wanted to ask Jesus into his life. He had some addiction problems, so it had been quite a battle for him to come to this decision, but he handed over his life to God in our dining room and felt the Holy Spirit touch his life. His life wasn't all a bed of roses after that but he recognised and valued the fact that he could talk to God about his struggles. He sadly died a few years later but we are still in contact with his daughter Emma, who used to come along to festivals like 'Cross Rhythms' and 'Creation Fest' in Cornwall with us and James.

By the end of the summer we had been Homeschooling for one year, and Esme had become a teenager!

Esme at her Homeschooling desk

Here is a brief overview of some of the activities we got up to when we were Homeschooling.

Visits to places like the Hands On Science Museum in Bristol, Brixham WW2 museum, various Wildlife Centres, the Zoo, and National Trust properties.

Regular trips to Plymouth to do drama and creative writing projects with another Homeschooling family. Esme really enjoyed the creative writing projects, which included drawing pictures.

Running up and down 120 steps in the next road, for exercise and to break up study times.

Cycle trips to mix in leisure and exercise.

On the cycle path next to the River Exe

Weekly trips to a local swimming pool with a couple of other people.

Pet care sessions, that basically consisted of cleaning out and taking good care of Esme and Caleb's guinea pigs - Cocoa and Squeaky.

Alex has mentioned to me a few of her thoughts from that time.

Generally I loved it, because it fostered a real close relationship with our children and we were able to have a greater influence on them for a longer time, because people say that once a child is in Secondary School, their peers have a bigger influence on them than their parents.

Having that influence on our children helped cut out some of the unhealthy habits of the English culture, such as watching lots of TV, materialism and the supposed need to have all the latest gadgets.

People used to say to me, 'Mark, you can't protect your kids from the world all their life!'

To which I responded, 'I know that, but I am choosing to keep them in the greenhouse for an extra five years. Then they will be old enough to walk away on their own, yet their roots will have had a longer opportunity to get a grip on who they are in their own right.'

And it was interesting as the years went on, because people used to come and compliment us on the behaviour and attitude of Esme and Caleb. People would comment on how refreshing it was when children actually entered into dialogue with adults and showed a real interest in people a lot older than themselves.

But of course there was also a healthy dose of mixing with kids their age too, such as the ones in our road that they often played with after school hours, kids at our church, our friends' children and various other kids that we bumped into at different events we often went too.

Esme also went to Girl Guides every week. She had been a member of the Girl Guides since 2001 and before that she had been in the Brownies for three years.

By the end of the year a couple more gig venues had opened up for my DJ'ing work. One was in a pub in Exeter, the other was a youth event in a nightclub in Teignmouth.

It was while doing a gig in the Exeter pub that I bumped into a guy from my old AA days. He was also an AA patrolman and we hadn't seen each other for over ten years. He was keen to strike up conversation with me about God because he had been very ill in hospital and it had got him thinking about deeper things. He was really happy to see me and saw the whole incident as being some kind of message from God to him.

2005

Every January, Roy and Pam who owned the 'Choice Words' bookshops, treated all the staff and their partners to a night out in a country restaurant. It was a time to welcome in the New Year together and report back on the previous year's business. There were usually nearly twenty of us at these yearly functions and they were a lot of fun with Roy telling his jokes, then splitting us into two teams for a quiz night.

I had been working for 'Choice Words' for five years at this point, which was the longest I had ever worked at one place. The job was perfect for the season Alex and I were in at that time. It allowed me to do two days Homeschooling with the kids, and it also worked well alongside my DJ work which was in the evenings or at weekends.

It was during this year that I gradually converted our loft at home into a large bedroom. A friend called Richard got me to start the project, by pushing me to buy the long lengths of timber to build the loft floor with; 8 x 2 inch binders and the 6 x 2 inch joists. He then helped me carry them all up into the loft space. Once I had the materials on site, it sort of motivated me to get stuck in.

I managed to find time in the evenings, or when the children were getting on with their schoolwork by themselves during the day, to slowly proceed with the job. In fact, I really enjoyed the satisfaction of seeing different stages of it getting completed. Once I had all the joists fixed in place, I was able to start putting down the chipboard flooring. After that I started to build and put in place a six winder staircase from the first floor landing up into the loft space. I cut all the six kites out of one 8 x 4 foot sheet of inch thick plywood. The finished staircase was a real good piece of handiwork, if I do say so myself. Even some professional tradesmen over the years complimented me on it, because it was so strongly put together.

....

In the spring I took Caleb on a 'Dads and Lads' weekend at the Beacon Activity Centre on the North Devon coast. The purpose of the weekend was to help bond the relationship between dads and their sons.

My relationship with Caleb was good because we did a lot of things together anyway, but the opportunity came up, so we went for it.

We got involved with climbing, archery, fire starting without matches, rope assault courses, night-time woodland walks and sitting around a bonfire on the beach with the other dads and sons. We ended up having a really good time together.

Also in the spring we went as a family to the camping weekend at St Agnes in Cornwall, that Alex's family organised every year. There were about twenty of us. Esme and Caleb spent most of the daylight hours bodysurfing in the sea with some of their cousins.

When we got back to Torquay, my Yamaha XT 600 had been stolen. But... it was fine because we found it dumped in a small service lane not far from our house, and it was not really damaged.

In June we went to Spain for our holiday and while there, we celebrated Caleb's eleventh birthday. I had not been to Spain before and the part that I saw I wasn't that keen on. There were new half-built houses everywhere and the surrounding landscape was not at all interesting. However, we drove south and visited the medieval Alhambra Palace and fortress in

Granada, Andalusia. It was a five hundred mile round trip to get there and back but I am pleased we made the effort because it helped us see a nicer part of Spain. During the days' activities, we waved at a group of people picking watermelons in the fields of a farm. Then I decided to stop the car and go and help them because they looked hot and tired. The four of us got down on our haunches and proceeded to help them harvest the crop (Homeschooling field trip in Spain)! We only did it for a few minutes because we couldn't speak the language, but it cheered them up and made us all laugh together. When we left, they gave us a few of the melons, which we were not expecting.

At other times during the holiday, Esme enjoyed wearing a fancy traditional Spanish dress we bought her and Caleb enjoyed visiting a submarine floating museum in the nearby harbour.

Caleb didn't enjoy the treat we got him for his eleventh birthday. It didn't turn out like we had hoped. We took him to a lake to have a water-skiing lesson. We were all quite nervous about it, including Caleb, but we wanted him to have a special experience for his birthday. Caleb told us later that he was extra scared because he had seen a guy on the pontoon who only had one leg, and he thought the guy had lost his other leg in a water-skiing accident. So Caleb was silently carrying this fear in him before he had even started.

Anyway, the instructor gave Caleb a wetsuit to put on, and Alex, Esme and me got into the speedboat alongside. Neither the instructor with Caleb, nor the speedboat pilot with us, could speak much English!

Caleb looked nervous and we started to wonder about the whole thing but the boat started to pull away, the line went tight, then the boat accelerated but Caleb couldn't keep his legs straight because he was scared. So, as the boat pulled, Caleb just got dragged through the water face first and the boat stopped immediately. This was tried a couple more times but Caleb was not looking good. The instructor stopped the lesson and we went back to the pontoon. He was a kind guy and gave us our money back. Caleb will always remember his eleventh birthday!

We were actually so proud of him and the four of us went back to our flat after buying Caleb and us all some ice creams and whatever else Caleb wanted to eat. He was our hero.

....

Over the summer months on Wednesday evenings, hundreds of bikers take their bikes and parade them along Paignton seafront. A charity called BMAD (Bikers Make A Difference) started the annual gathering in 2003 and it has continued ever since. I used to take Caleb along on the back of my Yamaha on a lot of the Wednesday nights because it was a good opportunity to go and see some bikes together and bump into some of my old biker mates. Caleb and me would get chatting to all sorts of characters and sometimes there would be over a thousand bikes parked up over the course of an evening.

In August, Alex and I took the kids to the annual Homeschoolers Sports Day in Cornwall, which was a bit of fun. It was not a huge event and wasn't especially competitive but it gave us a chance to meet up with other families doing Homeschooling.

In September, Esme was fourteen. She left the Girl Guides and moved up to join the senior section of the Scouting organisation, which was called the Rangers.

Esme's leader in both the Girl Guides and the Rangers, was the very same lady who was the girls PE teacher at my Secondary School in Kingsteignton when I was a teenage pupil there.

Thirty years later, she is taking care of my teenage daughter in the Scouting Movement. She remembered me and especially remembered my sister Julie because she had been Julie's form teacher!

In September Alex went to Toronto in Canada for a week. She attended a conference at the same church I had visited ten years earlier.

By the end of the year I had just about finished the loft room. I had wire brushed up the brickwork on one wall at the gable end and the exposed brickwork around the chimney breasts really complemented the feel of the room. I had insulated the ceiling, wired up the lights and plugs, fitted the handrails and balustrades around the top of the staircase, finished the floor, sanded and polished up the exposed purlins... now all I had to do was paint a few things and get a carpet fitted.

On New Years Eve, I did a gig at a pub on the banks of the River Dart at Kingswear. It was owned by a Christian family and Mark, the husband, was part of the team that helped Charlie get the 'New Eden' Festival going each year.

I ended up doing a few gigs at the 'Royal Dart' pub as time went on.

2006

The carpet was fitted onto the loft room floor and down the new stairs I had made. The loft space was like another land that didn't once exist, and now it did. It was a separate space that seemed away from the rest of the house, which was now Alex's and my bedroom. I even made a solid wooden double bed and cut out three hearts into the thick headboard with my router. It was the final finishing touch to a year's project.

One of the real treats of the room was that we could lie on the bed and see the sky through the big velux windows; blue sky and clouds by day, the moon and the stars at night.

My Rendezvous event at Brunel manor was going OK but it got some encouraging input at the beginning of the year because my friend Lionel, who I was now going jogging with, came and made me a proposition. He and his sister Bonnie felt God was leading them to offer their services to help promote Rendezvous. They had both been enjoying the event and wanted to make sure it continued, so they took on board the printing and distributing of flyers and posters.

I had started to diversify my music collection around this time, which resulted in me doing gigs I once would not have been able to do. I had just about got all the appropriate quality Christian music that I could use. There was of course a lot of Christian music out there but because of my particular taste in music, most of it wasn't suitable for my type of DJ'ing.

The music I liked to play had to have a predominantly positive vibe to it and I was starting to find some really good beats from a variety of different sources.

In the Totnes area there was a DJ called Robert who was running a monthly event called 'Dance at'. He had some nice tunes he used to play and when he found out I was a DJ, he invited me to be a guest DJ at some of his events. It gave me an opportunity to spin some of the new stuff I had been buying that was a bit more eclectic and the good thing with the crew that came to 'Dance at' was that they liked to dance. That really helps a DJ enjoy what he is doing!

In the spring, Esme started a paid job at 'Choice Words' bookshop. It was only on the one Saturday a month that I was working but she was a great help and I really enjoyed having her in the shop with me.

In June, I started my most exciting DJ residency. It was in a big pub at the top of Totnes High Street called 'The Barrel House'. I had written a letter to the manager a couple of months earlier and it had resulted in them giving me a monthly paid slot there.

Totnes was quite an unconventional town and 'The Barrel House' had a definite bohemian feel to it, which I liked. I was able to really explore with different tunes there because people were not looking for commercial cheesy tunes - they preferred the more underground sound. It was a venue that I took the whole family to as well. Esme was into the Totnes vibe also because of the hippy feel it had, which sort of suited her style at the time.

At one or two of my 'Barrel House' gigs I was able to charge at the door, so Alex and the kids took the money and stamped people's hands.

The family were a great help to me there in so many ways. They helped me carry all the gear up the stairs and into the venue room, they helped me hang the various bits of arty decor up on the walls and arrange the lights and wires, they used to dance and free other people up to dance, and they helped bolster me up when things were not going well. I really would not have wanted to do some of the gigs I did over the years if they hadn't been by my side.

I was still doing my monthly gigs at 'Spiritulized' in Kingsbridge, which Caleb was now old enough to go to as well and, if Esme wasn't free to come on the night, he would sometimes bring along one of his friends from Torquay.

Another venue had also opened up at a pub in Brixham owned by a couple of our Christian friends Kev and Pam. They had been at St Matthias with us back in the days when we used to attend there.

Kev had asked me if I would do a monthly DJ slot and, after my first gig there in June, they told me that it had been the best night they had known there.

For my birthday in July we had such a buzzing house party at our place. We kitted the garden and house up with my DJ lights and Sound System, laid out food and drinks on tables. Having a bonfire helps such occasions, so that was roaring away nicely until the early hours too.

Forty people came and it was so much fun watching a variety of different people we knew, meeting each other for the first time. Alex and I have always enjoyed mixing people from different lifestyles together in one place.

Also in July I watched the old seven storey Torquay Technical College get demolished. Thirty years earlier I had been studying there and now this famous building had been removed from our landscape. The building had been in clear view from the back of our house but it slowly decreased to nothing in three weeks!

It wasn't a particularly attractive structure, but it held a lot of memories for me, especially from 1976 - 81.

In August, we went to Essex for a few days with our friends John and Jackie. You may remember that Jackie was pregnant when John came and did our roof with his dad. Well Josiah was the product of that pregnancy and he was now nearly three. His older sister Lou was around Esme's age.

Day out at Duxford (Alex was taking the photo)

One day, while the eight of us were all together, we went on a day trip to Cambridgeshire. We went to the original site of Duxford Aerodrome, which the RAF used during the Battle of Britain, and is now the Imperial War Museum, Duxford.

It is the largest aviation museum in the country, home to many military exhibits from the Second World War.

Caleb was twelve at this point and he loved searching around all the military vehicles on display. Esme and Lou were probably not so impressed with the subject matter there.

To be honest, it was good fun just all hanging out together - wherever we happened to be.

Caleb's Disneyland!

In September, Esme had her fifteenth birthday and we started our fourth year of Homeschooling. You may remember me mentioning that the headmaster of Esme and Caleb's Primary School was not impressed when we told him that we were going to start Homeschooling them. Well he now had a new job - guess what it was?

He was the County Inspector of Homeschoolers!

Funny ol' world isn't it?

He used to pay us a visit each year and because he could see we were doing a good job with Esme and Caleb, we all ended up having a good laugh together.

All things come round good in the end!

At the end of the year I had a weekly Tuesday evening DJ slot outside a church in the Totnes main street. On Tuesday evenings every December, Totnes closed its main street to traffic and the place was transformed by multitudes of stalls around the town selling, food, drink, crafts, clothes and gifts for Christmas. Also, there was live music, mime acts, dance shows, juggling, fire eating... you know the sort of stuff!

Anyway, this church had asked me to play some of my Gospel DJ sounds out by the street next to their church building. I also got my lights projected up on the stone walls beside me.

It was a really good scene actually because it helped usher people inside the cosy church building, where there was a team of Christians serving up food and drinks.

I'm telling you - there were literally thousands of people shuffling along the jam packed streets of Totnes on those Tuesday evenings.

A real festive atmosphere for Christmas, and my Gospel Music tunes fitted the bill perfectly.

Also in December (but in a Totnes Hotel down the road) I was a guest DJ at a music event called 'Big Sexie'!

I had got to know quite a few alternative type characters in the music scene around that area, so word got out about my unique taste of music beats, hence I was invited to DJ at a few house parties. This was one of those type of parties.

It was good getting in amongst the different crew of people around Totnes. Totnes has been popular for many years with those who want to explore different spiritualities. Of course, many knew I was a committed Christian and that stirred up interesting conversations with people who didn't particularly lean that way themselves!

At the end of the year, I had yet another New Years Eve gig. This time in Ashburton as a guest DJ for the 'Dance at' event run by my DJ friend Robert. We all went as a family and it was good to be together as we moved into the New Year.

The good thing about the 'Dance at' events was, like I mentioned before, **they dance**! **And,** without the use of alcohol, by the way.

2007

There were many days I was depressed, lonely, and feeling totally empty. It's not the side of life that I like to advertise but it should be known that there were quite often days and sometimes weeks of feeling totally unknown to anyone on the planet.

I never lost my faith in God - He was the only one that I could truly cry out my inner pain to. I was often praying that He would heal me deep within, from an insecurity that seemed to rule my existence.

This of course affected my marriage in a lot of ways because I was shut up inside myself. I was pretty good at impressing people outside the family but the problem with intimate relationships was that I couldn't hide properly.

Alex was often upset that I wouldn't connect emotionally, apart from the odd occasion when the vulnerable Mark would get so lonely, it had to pop out. As I am writing, I think of those water reservoirs that get so low in a drought, that hidden lost villages at the bottom are exposed for a season.

I didn't consciously stay self-sufficient - it must have been a coping mechanism that was second nature to me. I read not so long ago in a couple of very good books by Nancy Verrier on adoption, that adopted children learn very early on, the art of 'adapting' to people in order to get accepted. So in adulthood the question is: Who the heck is the **real** me? I don't even know.

I used to feel like I was buried under loads of earthquake rubble. I needed to be found but no one ever hung around long enough above ground with their 'thermal imaging equipment' to discover there was a survivor still alive, hidden away beneath the surface.

And I seemed incapable of letting out a cry. It was too dangerous to make myself known. It was all that was left of me. I couldn't afford the risk of being pushed away again.

I needed someone to actually make the effort, really not ever give up, but search me out with love and commitment.

Well, God obviously did that out in Turkey. And I have been a healing work in progress ever since. He gave me Alex, who is a very important part of that healing. She is the only human that has caught more than a few glimpses of the real me.

So on that note; hope you are liking a glimpse!

Over the years I have had a secret quote for myself. It is: `Mark - don't be scared of love, it'll get you in the end'.

I believe that God is the only Love Surgeon that knows how to get me in the end. He has been doing a clever job over the years.

Philippians 1:6   Amplified Bible (AMP)

6 I am convinced *and* confident of this very thing, that He who has begun a good work in you will [continue to] perfect *and* complete it until the day of Christ Jesus [the time of His return].

....

In the spring, we went as a church to the South West Bible weekend, which was held at Taunton Racecourse. It was a yearly event that brought together the various `Newfrontiers' churches that were in the South West of England. Our church at this time had a new leader because Martin who had started the 'Kings Arms' in Torquay had moved into a new area of ministry.

There were probably about twenty or thirty of us from Torquay camped at the racecourse that weekend, with hundreds of others from all over the West of England.

At some point over the weekend, I got hurt by someone in our church. I forget what the incident was but I went into main meeting in the large marquee feeling very vulnerable and alone.

At the end of the Praise and Worship music, one of the girls in the band took the microphone and sang a spontaneous prophetic song that God had given her right at that very moment. It seemed out of sync with the Praise music everyone had been singing, but it was obviously for someone there straight from God's heart.

That someone was me.

It reached into the core of my being and has continued to affirm me ever since. The only reason I have the words now is because I went to the girl afterwards and asked her to try and remember what she had sung because I needed her to write the words on a piece of paper for me. When I told her they had spoken to me so deeply, I just broke down in front of her. She told me that God had given her the song as she launched into it. She knew God was telling her it was very important to step out and sing it because there was one person in the crowd that needed to hear it.

These are the words that God said to me on May 27th 2007:

You were never lost, you were never out of my gaze, even though you may feel lost, you are not out of my gaze, you cannot hide from my Love.

Don't let emotion dictate your love for me or let pain pluck you from my hand, or let confusion sway your path - you're mine, I won't loosen my grip on you.

You were planned, I delight over you.

I celebrated on the day of your birth - for this is your time, come run with me.

Arise and Shine, for when you shine you display my Glory.

Hear me whisper once again, I Love you, I Love you, Rise and Shine.

....

I came out of that marquee feeling so alive and confident. They were words of truth that only the Surgeon of Love could reach me with.

At the end of the weekend a guy called Ossie, who I had never met before felt led to give me this verse from the Psalms:

Psalm 138:8   New Living Translation (NLT)

8 The Lord will work out his plans for my life—

for your faithful love, O Lord, endures forever.

....

In June, we drove to Southern France and spent two weeks in the area around the Cevennes. We had managed to find accommodation in a remote chateau on a vineyard. It also had a small swimming pool, so Esme and Caleb had lots of fun in there. Our accommodation was adjacent to a large area of short grass and we would sit outside in the evening warmth watching the bats swoop all around us. While we were staying there Esme came across a big scorpion in the cutlery drawer, which we captured in a jam jar. Later we found a few more, but not so big. There was a shallow river on the land and Caleb and I spent many hours walking through the water, exploring up and down its route and seeing where it went. At one point, we startled a large group of over thirty big buzzards resting in the riverside trees. They were not expecting any visitors in that remote section of river. They made a right racket as they all took off in different directions.

One day, the four of us drove to the Ardeche Gorge and hired some kayaks for a few hours. We only travelled a mile or so down the river but the next day we all drove there again and Caleb and me hired one for the whole day so that we could paddle down the whole main route and go beyond Le Pont d'Arc.

I am not comfortable in deep water so some of the rapids were nerve racking for me and I Praise God that we stayed upright. At one point there was a lady who was getting pulled under by a swirling eddy. She was totally trapped and it was scary to see it going on. However, one chap reached her from some nearby rocks and Caleb and me were there with our kayak to catch his kayak that was getting drawn into the downstream current. The lady was very traumatised and I'm not sure she would have survived if that guy hadn't reached her, because it was a turbulent section of river where she had been dragged to.

Near the end of the holiday, it was midsummer's day and the French enjoy that day with music and celebrations. We met a fun couple from London in the town of Ardeche that night and after drinking wine together for a couple of hours, we too revelled in the whole party atmosphere.

....

During the year we got out and about as a family, going on bike trips around various parts of Devon and Cornwall. We enjoyed a couple in particular, one was riding along an old disused railway line on the northern boundary of Dartmoor near Okehampton, the other one was a section of the River Camel Trail in Cornwall, from Wadebridge to Padstow. When we reached Padstow, which is on the west coast of the River Camel estuary, we spent a couple of hours with John and Jackie from Essex, who were in Cornwall on their family holiday.

Esme was probably the least keen on our cycling adventures but she always got into them in the end, especially if there was a cream tea somewhere along the route.

Family day out on the bikes

Earlier in the year Esme had needed to come up with an idea to get her 'Baden-Powell Challenge Award' certificate for Rangers, so I created a Treasure Hunt on Dartmoor for her and another girl in the Rangers.

I had gone up and planned it all the week before, hiding clues along the route that I had come up with. It culminated in reaching the Church House Inn at a small village called Holne, then all sleeping in sleeping bags on the floor of a 'Camping Barn' in the same village. The barn had a toilet and a woodburner, it was a bit of luxury really!

The whole adventure was a lot of fun, even though the Treasure Hunt went on a lot longer than we had expected and ended up with me having to get them back on the right route, showing them where the last clues were hidden.
Esme received her 'Baden-Powell Challenge Award' certificate!

Baden Powell challenge (the girl between Alex
and me is Esme's friend from Rangers)

In September, Esme was sixteen and was starting to enjoy dressing up in crazy colourful bits of material, even wearing fairy wings around the streets of Torquay. She also had a metal teapot on a chain as her handbag. She became known as the Kitchen Fairy.

It was a unique look that she developed for herself complete with colour braided hair. Other teenagers from the local schools wondered who this outrageous looking person was who confidently roamed around without wearing any of the fashion brands that people that age were expected to wear, in order to feel secure.

The police liked her too because she brought a fun feel into the town and was friendly to everyone. One policeman told her that she was his teenage daughter's hero - even though she had never actually met Esme in person.

Esme the kitchen fairy

Near the end of the year, my Yamaha XT 600 motorbike was stolen (again!), which was sad. Fortunately, a couple in our church called Brian and Karen lent me their son's Aprilia scooter, so at least I had something to get me to work and back on.

I actually really enjoyed the simplicity of that scooter and planned to buy a similar one for myself, which Caleb wasn't too happy about. He didn't fancy going to the BMAD Wednesday evening bike nights the following summer on the back of a little scooter - not cool!

Anyway, I had the Aprilia for a few months yet, so there was no rush, and I received a good pay-out from the insurance company for the Yamaha XT 600.

So, having my Yam nicked wasn't such a tragedy after all.

On the subject of Caleb - earlier in the year a couple of old biker mates called Tony and Clive were going to drive to Bovington Tank Museum in Dorset. They were going to spend the day there and asked me if Caleb and I would like to come along. Knowing that Caleb would love to go, I thought I would give him a surprise. So I told him we had to get up at 7am the next morning because we were going on a mystery trip. Soon after we got up, Clive and Tony turned up outside our house in Clive's camper van. I had asked them not to say where we were going so it would be a surprise for Caleb.

The Museum, which is between Weymouth and Poole, has the largest collection of tanks in the world and Caleb was so excited when we arrived and he saw the destination of our mystery trip.

The four of us wandered around it's exhibition halls learning all manner of things that day.

It was a day that could also justifiably be called, a 'Homeschooling Educational Field Trip.'

So that's what I'll call it!

2008

In January, Esme wondered about enrolling to be a student at the South Devon College in Paignton, after she finished her final Homeschooling exams in July.

When we went to the college open day, Esme was really excited about the 'Performing Arts Diploma Course', it's curriculum including such things as stage makeup, dance and costume design construction. The one year course was due to start around the time of her seventeenth birthday in September - so she applied for a place.

Early this year I started to lose my heart a bit with the DJ'ing. I had started to get a bit of tinnitus in my ears from having the headphones up loud during gigs and I was getting disillusioned at a lot of the gigs by the expectation of having to play commercial sounds that people knew. It could be quite a lonely business being a DJ because you were definitely on your own out there sometimes. I had started in 1999 and the enjoyment of it all was beginning to wear thin. But I continued through the year, and did still enjoy some of my gigs, especially the ones at 'The Barrel House', in Totnes.

Around this time I bought a motorbike to take the place of the Yamaha that was stolen a few months earlier. Caleb was pleased because it wasn't a scooter. In fact, he was very happy because it was a Harley Davidson Sportster. I wasn't planning on buying a Harley but I had asked an old biking mate who I hadn't seen for ages if he knew anyone who had a small motorbike for sale and he said I could have his Harley Sportster for £1500 if I wanted.

Well, I knew Martin's bikes were well looked after, so I went and looked at it and thought - why not?

It would be a bit of fun for a few years and Caleb would love the idea, so I bought it. I spent a couple of months turning it into a `sexy' bike, because I didn't like the lines of the Sportster.

The Harley Sportster before I modified it

Turning it into a sexy looking bike entailed removing the thin front forks and replacing them with a Wide Glide front end and a 16 inch fat front wheel and tyre, fitting short rear shocks to lower the back end, fitting an exhaust system without a balance pipe, fitting a small, round, chrome holed air filter, removing the horrible double seat and fitting a single seat (plus a pad on the rear mudguard for Caleb to sit on!), replacing the small Sportster petrol tank with a big Twin Capped Mustang style tank and changing the colour scheme to black. I did a few other things but in the end I was happy with how it all looked and the final touch was to put a Bible reference on the black petrol tank.

The stickers I had designed read: ***Acts 4 : v 12***

Which if you look up in the Bible, reads:

Acts 4:12   New Century Version (NCV)

'Jesus is the only One who can save people. No one else in the world is able to save us.'

After I did the work on it

....

Around March, I prayed for God to **wake me up** because I felt my spiritual life was just drifting along. I needed God to bring my faith alive again, it had started to feel like I was just going through the motions.

In April, Alex handed in her notice at the hospital. She had been getting very stressed at work because of the added pressure that was coming into the job. She had worked in the same ward for eight years and had seen the increase of responsibility as each year passed by. It had become too much. In March, she had been signed off by our doctor with stress and decided she could not handle going back into the source of the stress all over again.

It would free her up to focus on Homeschooling, especially as it was the last term for Esme. Alex was also leading the Kings Kids Sunday School at church, which she had been doing since 2005.

Almost immediately after finishing at the hospital, Alex started to feel better.

In late April I got a phone call from the Police. They had found my Yamaha XT 600 on some heathland near the moors. I told the police that I didn't own it anymore and my insurance company had already compensated me with a payment after the theft.

I asked the policeman what sort of condition it was in after the joyrider thief had been riding it and he told me that it looked ok and he suspected it hadn't been ridden much.

I got a bit interested and went along to the police pound to have a look. Indeed, the bike didn't look too bad, it was just a bit muddy and the ignition had been smashed up.

I decided to try and buy it back cheap from the insurance company so that I could do it up and sell it on for a profit because Yamaha XT 600's were a sought after bike.

I succeeded in getting it for a couple of hundred pounds, then Caleb and me had a great time sorting it out and polishing it up.

The bike had had an intermittent problem with starting over the last couple of years that I owned it, which ended up being fortuitous really because the joyriders must have given up trying to start it and just abandoned it. (It still had half a tank of petrol in it!) If they had managed to start it again they probably would have ridden it into the ground and terminally damaged it in the process.

I found it was not starting at all when I initially worked on it with Caleb, so they must have had the same problem on the heathland. The intermittent starting fault had become permanent! I stripped the wiring loom under the headlight area and eventually found a broken wire from the starter button to the starter motor. So satisfying.

Caleb on my Yamaha XT600

That was the end of the intermittent fault that I had known before and that broken wire had saved my Yam being driven to destruction by the thieves. Praise God.

I sold the Yamaha for nearly a £1000 a couple of months later. It was a good bike and would sell for even more these days, but it worked out really well because the extra money paid for the work I had done on the Harley.

I know that doesn't float everyone's boat but it certainly floated mine at the time!

....

In June, God started to lead me very clearly to buy an air ticket to Florida. Since April, a church out there had been experiencing a powerful move of God that had even come to the attention of the God Channel on the internet. The God Channel wasn't something that Alex or I usually watched but we had started to watch the events going on in this church every evening because it was being broadcast `live' and we believed that it was God, moving by His Holy Spirit. People who were hungry for intimacy with God were travelling from all over the world and the church had had to move the meetings to a very large tent on a disused airstrip nearby. There were now about twelve thousand people in the tent every evening.

There were many Christians we knew who did not like the guy with tattoos that was speaking at the front and didn't agree that it was a move of God. We were not so interested in the personality of the guy but we did believe it was God who was moving and bringing the people.

Anyway, I could say so much more of how God led me there and what went on when I got there. But what I will mention is that it was a direct answer to my prayer a few months earlier for God to wake me up and when I got out of my rental car on arriving in the field nearby the site, I had to get down on my knees in acknowledgement that I was on Holy Ground. The Holy Spirit was so tangible that He felt like *invisible electric honey* consuming the whole area - and that was just in the car park!

It was important that I went out there on my own because I wanted my focus to be just on my relationship with God.

Over the week I was there, He met me so deeply. I have never in my life known a time like that week. It was so personal and Holy.

There was pain too but in the end it was washed away by Love.

He also revealed the potential of what it looks like when leaders let God have His way in the midst of His people.

On the plane home one week later I knew I could not go back to the formality of normal Sunday church life activity. It had made me go to sleep. And I don't mean physically.

When I got back home, Alex could see the difference in me. God had woken me up.

I said to Alex, 'I've got to leave the church.' She knew I was very serious, but I told her not to leave *because* I was leaving, only if and when she heard directly from God herself.

I went to church on the Sunday, just to make sure I was hearing right myself. I was very aware of the tight restriction on proceedings and knew that I needed to move on. It was too dangerous not too.

I made an appointment to see the church leader during the week. We met at the Grand Hotel front garden cafe, that overlooks the seafront and the harbour. I got there first and, as I waited, I prayed that God would help me have the right words. As I was sat there, a lifeboat emerged from the outer harbour and headed out to sea. No lifeboats resided in Torquay harbour. I had not seen one there since the episode with the new bridge opening in the inner harbour - five years earlier.

I knew God was speaking to me when I saw this second lifeboat emerging from the outer harbour and going directly out into the bay.

It gave me assurance that I was doing the right thing.

The meeting wasn't that long because I didn't want to beat around the bush with what I had to say, yet I did want to be respectful by telling him face to face that I was leaving the church - rather than just sliding off into obscurity.

I had been going to the 'Kings Arms' for nearly ten years but I just knew I could go there no longer.

Alex continued to go for a couple of weeks but then she told me that she understood why I had left. She also saw the restriction and realised in her heart that she could not 'go through the motions' any longer either.

Caleb, who was fourteen at this point, continued to go because he had some good friends there, especially one called Sam who he had many adventures with.

During the summer months on Wednesday evenings, I took Caleb on the back of my newly styled Harley Davidson bike to the Paignton seafront biker gatherings. The little pad that I attached to the rear mudguard for pillion passengers wasn't that comfortable for Caleb but he preferred that to sitting on the back of some little scooter!

The event was only a couple of miles along the coast road from Torquay anyway - so it was fine.

In July, Esme finished her final Homeschooling exams and got the equivalent of ten GCSE's.

It was the end of a five year marathon and she had crossed the finishing line.

In August, Alex and I dropped Esme and Caleb off at the Lee Abbey Youth Camp for a week, then the two of us drove to South Wales and had a week's holiday together exploring the Gower Peninsula and the Pembrokeshire Coast National Park.

In September, Esme started the 'Performing Arts Diploma Course' at South Devon College. She was now seventeen.

On the last weekend of September, God spoke.

Yeah - I know... big statement.

Oh well... there it is!

The previous year a guy from New Zealand called Ian McCormack had visited Torquay to speak at a Christian conference in a local hotel. We had heard the amazing story of how God came into his life a few years earlier. In the early eighties, he had been a surfer travelling around the world and, while off the coast of Mauritius in the south west Indian Ocean he was stung by five deadly Box jellyfish, which culminated in him dying, and while his spirit was out of his body, God revealed Hell and Heaven to him. I won't go into all the details but you can find his story on the internet.

Anyway, we went to the conference in 2007 and really enjoyed his teaching.

He had actually moved to the UK that year and was in close contact with a few Christians in Torquay that we were good friends with. This contact led Ian to come for another conference at the end of September 2008.

We again went to the weekend conference, being held this time at the English Riviera Centre, locally known as the ERC. (These days it's called the Riviera International Centre!)

Ian didn't speak about his 1982 near-death experience at either of the conferences because he had already spoken about it so many times before, all over the world.

Since moving to England in 2007, he had started a church in London and his ministry was more in the area of teaching and leadership.

There were a lot of people at the conference and it was going really well. Alex and I were very excited about the things God was bringing to our attention through the teaching and the very tangible presence of the Holy Spirit in the room. At lunchtime, we both decided to walk to the nearby Torre Abbey Sands and sit by the sea. I went on ahead because Alex got tied up in a conversation. As I walked past the tennis courts and the bowling green, the sky was clear and the sun was hot on my face. It was a good day and I felt very much alive. The good weather was only a complimenting factor to this feeling - the source came from a much deeper place. In fact the 'source' was filling my deep place.

When I reached the beach, the tide was out and I took my shoes and socks off and walked across the sand into the calm water. As I stood in the sea, the water glistened and sparkled in such a bright way it caused me to squint as I looked across the bay towards Berry Head and Brixham. It was a beautiful picture in front of me and the sun caressed my body with warmth as the sea caressed my lower legs with its cool ebb and flow.

As I looked across the surface of the sea and felt its presence on my skin - God spoke to me!

I didn't hear an audible voice. I have never heard His audible voice. But like He had spoken to me when I was on that bridge and the lifeboat passed by - He spoke again in a similar fashion.

This is what He said:

You are standing in this sea water, which stretches all around the world and is in contact with many nations around the planet.

In one way, the world is all connected together by this water you are standing in and, because of that, the rest of the world doesn't feel so far away to you now. And soon, I am going to move you on from here - out into that world beyond.

As I write, I am reminded of when God spoke to me through that 'This in Future' picture hanging on the cafe wall in Dunster twenty years earlier. It was similar because, like this time, it left me both flabbergasted and excited.

About a minute later, Alex arrived on the sand at the water's edge. I told her that God had just spoken to me. I said 'God is going to move us on soon, out into other nations around the world'.

I briefly explained how God had impressed on me that many nations around the world are connected together by the water in the oceans.

She believed that God was saying stuff to us. She also felt it wasn't going to happen immediately but was excited that God was saying that He was calling us abroad.

We had suspected He would one day but I had almost given up on the idea as life in Torquay seemed to have become so embedded since we were led back in 1994, from Bath. But Alex had always strongly held onto the belief that God would move us into a travel adventure again - probably to the Third World.

As we stood on the sand, Alex told me she had seen a cafe tucked away near the bowling green that looked good and I said that I had never seen a cafe there before. She hadn't noticed it before that day either, so we decided to go there for a drink and check it out because she liked the fact that it looked quite `earthy' and not commercial.

I asked her what the name of it was and she replied, '**One World**.'

I was amazed, it tied into the concept that I heard from God when I was standing in the sea water five minutes earlier.

It was the cafe we needed to go to alright. What else was God going to say?!

I just **knew** He was on our case. So exciting.

I walked at a fast pace because I couldn't wait to see this place and get the next clue!

As I approached it, I could see the name 'One World', then as we entered the fairly empty cafe, the music being played on the sound system hit us both. God is so full on sometimes.

It was the track 'Storms in Africa' by Enya that we first heard together travelling through the barren African landscape nearly twenty years earlier. We had hardly ever heard it since.

I was flabbergasted and excited all over again!

We walked to the corner of the cafe where there were some pictures hanging on the wall. The first one that got me was... wait for it... a beautiful painting from Torquay seafront looking across to Berry Head and Brixham, with the seawater glistening and sparkling brightly in the sun. It was the same view I had been looking at when God started speaking to me a few minutes earlier.

I pointed it out to Alex, then we looked at the other pictures on the wall around it. They were of African huts and African landscapes.

God was tickling us with clues!

A few days later it was October. The news was all about the financial crisis that had hit America and it was having ramifications all around the world.

I had been reading a couple of really good books around this time:

Megashift by Jim Rutz and Azusa Street by Frank Bartleman.

Around page one hundred in Frank's book, it was speaking about living totally for God and not storing up riches on earth. He quoted from the Bible:

Matthew 6:19-21   New Century Version (NCV)

'Don't store treasures for yourselves here on earth where moths and rust will destroy them and thieves can break in and steal them. But store your treasures in heaven where they cannot be destroyed by moths or rust and where thieves cannot break in and steal them. Your heart will be where your treasure is.'

As I read those pages I knew God was calling us to devote our lives to Him. I went up the stairs in our house to tell Alex but she was asleep. Still, because I felt the urgent need to tell her, I woke her up and said, 'Alex, God wants us to use our money and **GO!**'

When I told her that it is probably Africa - she started crying.

She had always had a heart for Africa since the time she visited me there in 1989 and she had never let go of the sense that God would lead us there again one day.

At the end of the year, I did my Tuesday evening gigs outside the Totnes church again. The streets were once more packed with thousands of people walking along the main street because it was closed to traffic on Tuesday nights during December. The road was full of festive stalls again and people were buying all manner of things for Christmas.

Those DJ gigs I did in the street that December marked the end of my DJ calling. I had been DJ Absolute Abandon for nearly ten years and probably done around 300 gigs over that time. I did spin some tunes at a couple of events a few years later but that season had come to an end.

....

2009

Now there was another adventure looming, one that would be a lot bigger than any of our previous ones. By a **long way**!!

To be continued……….

....

Afterword

God's next adventures would take us 'by road vehicle' through over twenty five different countries and across **four** of the five major *'circles of latitude'* around the earth.

He didn't lead us to leave Torquay the year after He spoke to me on the beach - but it wasn't too long after that.

We had some things to do before the starting gun went off.

So, I will meet you again in the next book - which hopefully I'll try and work on when I've **fully** recovered from writing this one!

Thanks to:

Jenny, Alex and Urim for proof reading, Dave (Hoppy) for organising this publishing project for me, James for helping me sort and arrange the front and back covers, Alex for being my companion on the journey, my family and friends for encouraging me through the years to write these books, and God for knowing me inside out and leading me forever forward.

If you would like to contact me: markalex.wadie@gmail.com

42889769R00219

Printed in Poland
by Amazon Fulfillment
Poland Sp. z o.o., Wrocław